Cambridge Latin Course

Unit 3

FIFTH EDITION

CAMBRIDGE
UNIVERSITY PRESS

CAMBRIDGE
UNIVERSITY PRESS

University Printing House, Cambridge CB2 8BS, United Kingdom

One Liberty Plaza, 20th Floor, New York, NY 10006, USA

477 Williamstown Road, Port Melbourne, VIC 3207, Australia

314–321, 3rd Floor, Plot 3, Splendor Forum, Jasola District Centre, New Delhi – 110025, India

79 Anson Road, #06–04/06, Singapore 079906

Torre de los Parques, Colonia Tlacoquemécatl del Valle, Mexico City CP 03200, Mexico

Cambridge University Press is part of the University of Cambridge.

It furthers the University's mission by disseminating knowledge in the pursuit of
education, learning and research at the highest international levels of excellence.

www.cambridge.org
Information on this title: www.cambridge.org/9781107070974

The Cambridge Latin Course is an outcome of work jointly commissioned by the
Cambridge School Classics Project and the Schools Council © Schools Council
1970, 1982 (succeeded by the School Curriculum Development Committee © SCDC
Publications 1988).

© University of Cambridge School Classics Project 2001, 2015

First published 1970
Second edition 1982
Third edition 1988
Fourth edition 2001
Fifth edition 2015
20 19 18 17 16 15 14 13 12 11 10 9 8 7

Printed in Mexico by Editorial Impresora Apolo, S.A. de C.V.

Library of Congress Cataloging in Publication Data

Data available

ISBN 978-1-107-07097-4 Hardback
ISBN 978-1-107-09821-3 Hardback +6 Year Website Access
ISBN 978-1-107-09822-0 Hardback +1 Year Website Access
ISBN 978-1-107-67578-0 Paperback
ISBN 978-1-107-09824-4 Paperback +1 Year Website Access

Cover photograph: Bronze head of Sulis, Roman Baths Museum, Bath;
background, Shutterstock / Marek Novak.
Maps and plans by Robert Calow / Eikon
Illustrations by Joy Mellor, Leslie Jones, Peter Kesteven, Neil Sutton, and Lisa Jiang.

Additional resources for this publication at www.cambridge.org/9781107070974

Contents

Acknowledgments

The authors and publishers acknowledge the following sources of copyright material and are grateful for the permissions granted. While every effort has been made, it has not always been possible to identify the sources of all the material used, or to trace all copyright holders. If any omissions are brought to our notice, we will be happy to include the appropriate acknowledgments on reprinting.

pp. 1, 25, 28 *r*, 51 *t*, 74, 88, 89, 100, 101 *r*, 182, 225 *b*, 236, 237 *b*, 238, 248 *b*, 250 *r*, 258, 259, © The Trustees of The British Museum; pp. 8, 15, 16, 17 *bl*, *br*, 18 *b*, 19 *b*, *t*, 20, 21, 29, 34 *b*, 39, 40, 52 *l*, *br*, *cr*, © Roman Baths Museum, Bath; p. 18 *t*, © Society of Antiquaries of London; pp. 28 *l*, 156, © www. BibleLandPictures.com / Alamy; p. 36, © Institute of Archaeology, Oxford; pp. 37, 50 *br*, 248 *t*, © RMN-Grand Palais (musée du Louvre) / Hervé Lewandowski; pp. 49, 51 *b*, © Louvre, Paris, France / Bridgeman Images; pp. 50 *t*, 91 *t*, 116 *l*, *r*, 130, 141 *t*, © Cheshire West Museums; pp. 50 *l*, 148 *l*, 167, 175 *l*, *r*, © Photo Scala, Florence; p. 52 *t*, © DEA / A.DAGLI ORTO / Getty Images; p. 53 *b*, © National Museum of Rome. Italy / Photo © Tarker / Bridgeman Images; p. 54, © Cambridge University Museum of Archaeology and Anthropology; p. 55, © Gilles Mermet / akg-images; p. 62, © Cambridge University Collection of Aerial Photography; p. 66 *c*, © PRISMA ARCHIVO / Alamy; p. 69 *l*, © Photo Scala, Florence / Courtesy of Sovraintendenza di Roma; pp. 69 *r*, 201 *b*, CSCP; p. 70, © Photo Scala, Florence; p. 71, © akg-images / Album / Prisma; p. 82, © Independent Picture Service / Getty Images; p. 84 *b*, © DEA / G. DAGLI ORTI / Getty images; p. 84 *t*, © Independent Picture Service / Alamy; p. 85 *br*, © Jeff Morgan 12 / Alamy; p. 85 *tr*, © Mark Salter / Alamy; p. 85 *tl*, © Powered by Light/Alan Spencer / Alamy; p. 85 *bl*, © Stephen Mulcahey / Alamy; p. 86, © The Ermine Street Guard; pp. 101 *b*, 103, © National Museums of Scotland; p. 102, © John Morrison / Alamy; p. 104, © Hulton Archive / Getty Images; pp. 105, 118 *all*, 142, © Cheshire West Museums / Graham Sumner; pp. 107, 119 *t*, © Culture Coventry; p. 120, © World History Archive / Alamy; p. 121, © EE Image Library / Heritage Images / TopFoto; p. 135 *t*, © Museo Archeologico Nazionale, Naples, Italy / Photo © Zev Radovan / Bridgeman Images; p. 135 *b*, © Penguin Books; p. 136 *b*, © Museum of London Archaeology (MOLA); p. 136 *t*, © Strephon Duckering / Oxford Archaeology – Pre-Construct Archaeology; p. 137 *bl*, *br*, © MOLA Northamptonshire; p. 138 *t*, © The Ancient Art and Architecture Collection; p. 138 *c*, © Whitby Museum; p. 143, © Lautaro / Alamy; pp. 148 *r*, 196 *c*, © De Agostini Picture Library / A. Dagli Orti / Bridgeman Images; pp. 150, 163 *b*, © Dan Porges / Getty images; pp. 153, 216, © Werner Forman / Getty images; p. 159, © JeniFoto / Shutterstock; pp. 160 / 161 *t*, © frankix / iStock / Getty Images; p. 162 *t*, © Werner Forman Archive / Bridgeman Images; pp. 162 *c*, 232, © De Agostini Picture Library / G. Dagli Orti / Bridgeman Images; p. 162 *b*, Courtesy of Michelle Moran; pp. 163 *t*, 164 *b*, 165, © Bible Land Pictures / Jerusalem Photo / akg-images; p. 166, © Fitzwilliam Museum, University of Cambridge; p. 176, © De Agostini Picture Library / Getty images; p. 179 *l*, © Taylor and Francis Books; p. 179 *r*, © Photo Scala, Florence / Museo Gregoriano Profano, Vatican; p. 180, © St Albans Museums; p. 181 *tl*, © AA World Travel Library / Alamy; p. 181 *tr*, © De Agostini Picture Library / G. Nimatallah / Bridgeman Images; p. 181 *bl*, © GoodLifeStudio / iStock / Getty Images; p. 183, © Andrea Jemolo / akg-images; p. 194 *b*, © Monte Testaccio, Roma (photo) / Bridgeman Images; p. 196 *t*, © Biblioteca Apostolica Vaticana, Vatican City / Bridgeman Images; p. 196 *b*, © Photo Scala, Florence / Archaeological Museum – Aquileia; p. 198 *l*, © age fotostock / Alamy; p. 198 *r*, © Dorling Kindersley/UIG / Bridgeman Images; p. 201 *t*, © akg-images / Erich Lessing; p. 202, © Wanderlust_999 / Shutterstock; p. 203, © Manchester Museum / The John Rylands Library; p. 209, © Scott Tucker / Alamy Stock Photo; p. 217 *t*, © Perseomedusa / Alamy; p. 217 *b*, © Photo Scala, Florence / National Archaeological Museum, Naples; p. 219, © Andrew Holt / Alamy; p. 220, © Museum of London; p. 225 *t*, © De Agostini Picture Lib. / A. Dagli Orti / akg-images; p. 234 *t*, © Georgy Kuryatov / Shutterstock; p. 234 *b*, © udokant / iStock / Getty Images; p. 235, © De Agostini Picture Library / A. de Gregorio / Bridgeman Images; p. 237 *t*, © Kunsthistoriches Museum Vienna; pp. 239, 253, © Roman relief, Musée royal de Mariemont, inv. B.26 / Musée royal de Mariemont / Photo M. Lechien; pp. 239, 241, © Museo Nazionale Romano; p. 247, © Ministry of Heritage and Culture Superintendence for the Historical, Artistic and Ethno-anthropological and the Museums of Florence; p. 256, © EPX / Alamy; p. 257 *t*, © Herculaneum / Werner Forman Archive / Bridgeman Images.

All other photography by R.L. Dalladay.

The current edition of the *Cambridge Latin Course* is the result of over forty years of research, classroom testing, feedback, revision, and development. In that period millions of students, tens of thousands of teachers, hundreds of experts in the fields of Classics, history, and education, and dozens of authors have contributed to make the Course the leading approach to reading Latin that it is today.

To list everyone who has played a part in the development of the *Cambridge Latin Course* would be impossible, but we would particularly like to thank individuals and representatives from the following organizations, past and present:

British Museum
British School at Rome
Butser Ancient Farm, England
Castell Henllys, Wales
Council for British Archaeology
Department of Education and Science, London
Fishbourne Palace, England
Herculaneum Conservation Project
Her Majesty's Inspectorate of Schools
North American Cambridge Classics Project
Nuffield Foundation
Qualifications and Curriculum Authority, London
Queen Mary University of London, Department of Classics
Schools Council, London
Southern Universities Joint Board for School Examinations, England
St Matthias College of Education, Bristol
Swedish Pompeii Project
University of Bradford, Department of Classics
University of Cambridge, Faculty of Classics
University of Cambridge, Faculty of Education
University of Cambridge School Classics Project Advisory Panel
University College Cardiff, Classics Department
University College London, Centre for the History of Medicine
University College London, Department of Greek and Latin
University of Leeds, Department of Classics
University of Leeds, School of Education
University of London, Institute of Education
University of Manchester, Department of Art History and Visual Studies
University of Massachusetts at Amherst, Department of Classics
University of Nottingham, Department of Classics
University of Nottingham, School of Education
University of Oxford, Department of Education
University of Oxford, Faculty of Classics
University of Oxford, School of Archaeology
University of Wales, School of Archaeology, History and Anthropology
University of Warwick, Classics Department
Welsh Joint Education Committee

AQUAE SULIS

Stage 21

1   in oppidō Aquīs Sūlis labōrābant multī fabrī, quī thermās
maximās exstruēbant. architectus Rōmānus fabrōs
īnspiciēbat.

[handwritten annotations: town, working, craftsman, inspect]

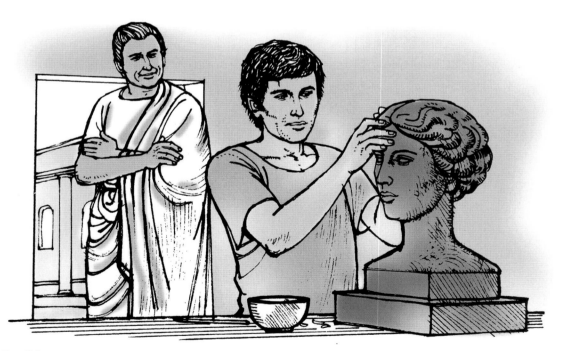

2   faber prīmus statuam deae Sūlis faciēbat.
architectus fabrum laudāvit, quod perītus erat et dīligenter
labōrābat.
faber, ab architectō laudātus, laetissimus erat.

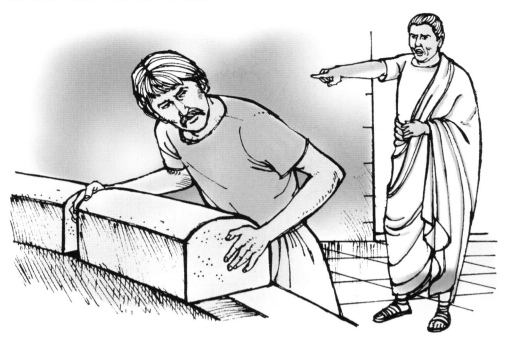

3   faber secundus mūrum circum fontem pōnēbat.
architectus fabrum incitāvit, quod fessus erat et lentē _slowly_
labōrābat.
faber, ab architectō incitātus rem graviter ferēbat. nihil tamen
dīxit, quod architectum timēbat.

4   faber tertius aquam ad balneum ē fonte sacrō portābat.
architectus fabrum vituperāvit, quod ignāvus erat et minimē
labōrābat.
faber, ab architectō vituperātus, īnsolenter respondit.

5   architectus, ubi verba īnsolentia fabrī audīvit, servōs suōs
    arcessīvit.
    servī, ab architectō arcessītī fabrum comprehendērunt et in
    balneum dēiēcērunt.

6   "linguam sordidam habēs," inquit architectus cachinnāns.
    "melius est tibi aquam sacram bibere."

fōns sacer

fōns *fountain, spring*

Quīntus apud Salvium manēbat per tōtam hiemem. saepe ad
aulam Cogidubnī ībat, ā rēge invītātus. Quīntus eī multa dē urbe
Alexandrīā nārrābat, quod rēx aliquid novī audīre semper
volēbat.

aliquid novī *something new*

ubi vēr appropinquābat, Cogidubnus in morbum gravem 5
incidit. multī medicī, ad aulam arcessītī, remedium morbī
quaesīvērunt. ingravēscēbat tamen morbus. rēx Quīntum et
Salvium dē remediō anxius cōnsuluit.

morbum: morbus *illness*
gravem: gravis *serious*

cōnsuluit: cōnsulere *consult*
cōnsilium *advice*

"mī Quīnte," inquit, "tū es vir sapiēns. volō tē mihi cōnsilium
dare. ad fontem sacrum īre dēbeō?" 10

oppidō: oppidum *town*
Aquīs Sūlis: Aquae Sūlis
   *Aquae Sulis (Roman name
   of modern Bath)*

"ubi est iste fōns?" rogāvit Quīntus.

"est in oppidō Aquīs Sūlis," inquit Cogidubnus, "multī aegrōtī,
quī ex illō fonte aquam bibērunt, posteā convaluērunt.
architectus Rōmānus, ā mē missus, thermās maximās ibi
exstrūxit. prope thermās stat templum deae Sūlis, ā meīs fabrīs 15
aedificātum. ego deam saepe honōrāvī; nunc fortasse dea mē
sānāre potest. Salvī, tū es vir magnae calliditātis; volō tē mihi
cōnsilium dare. quid facere dēbeō?"

aegrōtī: aegrōtus *invalid*
convaluērunt: convalēscere
   get better, recover
exstrūxit: exstruere *build*
deae Sūlis: dea Sūlis
   the goddess Sulis (a Celtic deity)
vir magnae calliditātis
   *a man of great shrewdness,
   cleverness*

"tū es vir magnae sapientiae," respondit ille. "melius est tibi
testāmentum facere." 20

sapientiae: sapientia *wisdom*
testāmentum *will*

Lūcius Marcius Memor

When you have read this story, answer the questions at the end.

oppidum Aquae Sūlis parvum erat, thermae maximae.
prōcūrātor thermārum erat Lūcius Marcius Memor, nōtissimus
haruspex, homō obēsus et ignāvus. quamquam iam tertia hōra
erat, Memor in cubiculō ēbrius dormiēbat. Cephalus, haruspicis
lībertus, Memorem excitāre temptābat.   5

    "domine! domine!" clāmābat.

    haruspex, graviter dormiēns, nihil respondit.

    "dominus nimium vīnī rūrsus bibit," sibi dīxit lībertus.
"domine! surge! hōra tertia est."

    Memor, ā lībertō tandem excitātus, ūnum oculum aperuit.   10

    "fer mihi plūs vīnī!" inquit. "tum abī!"

    "domine! domine! necesse est tibi surgere," inquit Cephalus.

    "cūr mē vexās, Cephale?" inquit Memor. "cūr tū rem
administrāre ipse nōn potes?"

    "rem huius modī administrāre nōn possum," respondit   15
lībertus. "sunt multī servī, multī fabrī, quī mandāta prōcūrātōris
exspectant. tē exspectat architectus ipse, vir magnae dignitātis.
tē exspectant aegrōtī. adsunt mīlitēs, ab hostibus vulnerātī.
adsunt nōnnūllī mercātōrēs, quōs arcessīvistī. tū rem ipse
administrāre dēbēs."   20

prōcūrātor *manager*	
haruspex *diviner, soothsayer*	
obēsus *fat*	
graviter *heavily, soundly*	
nimium vīnī *too much wine*	
rūrsus *again*	
fer! *bring!*	
plūs vīnī *more wine*	
huius modī *of this kind*	
mandāta: mandātum *instruction, order*	
dignitātis: dignitās *importance, prestige*	
hostibus: hostis *enemy*	

"numquam dēsinit labor," clāmāvit Memor. "quam fessus sum! cūr ad hunc populum barbarum umquam vēnī? vīta mea est dūra. nam in Britanniā ad magnōs honōrēs ascendere nōn possum. necesse est mihi virōs potentēs colere. ēheu! in hāc īnsulā sunt paucī virī potentēs, paucī clārī."

"quid vīs mē facere, Memor?" inquit lībertus.

"iubeō tē omnēs dīmittere," clāmāvit Memor. "nōlī mē iterum vexāre!"

Memor, postquam haec verba dīxit, statim obdormīvit. Cephalus, ā dominō īrātō territus, invītus exiit. in thermīs plūrimōs hominēs invēnit, vehementer clāmantēs et Memorem absentem vituperantēs. eōs omnēs Cephalus dīmīsit.

dēsinit: dēsinere *end, cease*
labor *work*
populum: populus *people*
umquam *ever*

25   **honōrēs: honor** *honor, public position*
potentēs: potēns *powerful*
colere *seek favor of, make friends with*

30   **paucī** *few*
clārī: clārus *famous, distinguished*
verba: verbum *word*
territus: terrēre *frighten*
absentem: absēns *absent*

Questions

1 **oppidum … maximae** (line 1). Why might a visitor to Aquae Sulis have been surprised on seeing the town and its baths?

2 **prōcūrātor … ignāvus** (lines 2–3). Read this sentence and look at the picture. Which two Latin adjectives describe Memor as he appears in the picture? Translate them.

3 **tertia hōra** (line 3). Was this early or late in the morning? Give a reason for your answer.

4 In line 7, the soothsayer is described as **graviter dormiēns**. Which Latin word in line 4 explains the reason for this? What does this word and the word **rūrsus** (line 8) suggest about Memor?

5 After Memor was awake, what two orders did he give to Cephalus? What did he think Cephalus should do (lines 11–14)?

6 **mandāta prōcūrātōris** (line 16). Why do you think Cephalus used these words rather than **mandāta tua**?

7 **numquam … fessus sum** (lines 21–22). What do you think Cephalus' reaction would be on hearing Memor say this? Give a reason for your answer.

8 **ad magnōs honōrēs ascendere nōn possum** (lines 23–24). What, according to Memor, is the reason for his failure?

9 In lines 27–29, how did Memor react to Cephalus' question? Make three points.

10 Which two Latin words show how Cephalus was feeling when he left Memor's bedroom?

11 What did he find when he arrived in the baths (lines 30–32)?

12 Read Cephalus' speech in lines 15–20 again. Pick out two different words or phrases which he repeats and suggest why he used each of them to try to get Memor to act.

senātor advenit

Cephalus ā thermīs rediit. cubiculum rūrsus intrāvit
Memoremque dormientem excitāvit. Memor, simulac
Cephalum vīdit, īrātus clāmāvit,

"cūr prohibēs mē dormīre? cūr mihi nōn pārēs? stultior es
quam asinus."

"sed domine," inquit Cephalus, "aliquid novī nūntiāre volō.
postquam hinc discessī, mandāta, quae mihi dedistī, effēcī. ubi
tamen aegrōtōs fabrōsque dīmittēbam, senātōrem thermīs
appropinquantem cōnspexī."

Memor, valdē vexātus,

"quis est ille senātor?" inquit. "unde vēnit? senātōrem vidēre
nōlō."

"melius est tibi hunc senātōrem vidēre," inquit Cephalus.
"nam Gāius Salvius est."

"num Gāius Salvius Līberālis?" exclāmāvit Memor. "nōn
crēdō tibi."

Cephalus tamen facile eī persuāsit, quod Salvius iam in
āream thermārum equitābat.

Memor perterritus statim clāmāvit,

"fer mihi togam! fer calceōs! ōrnāmenta mea ubi sunt? vocā
servōs! quam īnfēlīx sum! Salvius hūc venit, vir summae
auctōritātis, quem colere maximē volō."

Memor celerrimē togam calceōsque induit. Cephalus eī
ōrnāmenta trādidit, ex armāriō raptim extracta. haruspex
lībertum innocentem vituperābat, lībertus Salvium.

5 prohibēs: prohibēre *prevent*
  pārēs: pārēre *obey*
  hinc *from here*
  effēcī: efficere *carry out,
    accomplish*

10

15

20 calceōs: calceus *shoe*
  ōrnāmenta: ōrnāmentum
    badge of office
  auctōritātis: auctōritās
    authority
25 raptim *hastily, quickly*

*Memor set up a statue near the
altar of the goddess Sulis. The
statue has disappeared, but
this is the statue base with his
name on it. The altar is in the
background.*

About the language: perfect passive participles

1 In Stage 20, you met sentences like these, containing present participles:

> servī per vīllam contendērunt, dominum **quaerentēs**.
> *The slaves hurried through the house, **looking for** their master.*

> puella mātrem in hortō **sedentem** vīdit.
> *The girl saw her mother **sitting** in the garden.*

2 In Stage 21, you have met sentences like these:

> Memor, ā lībertō **excitātus**, īrātissimus erat.
> *Memor, **having been awakened** by the freedman, was very angry.*

> thermae, ā Rōmānīs **aedificātae**, maximae erant.
> *The baths, **having been built** by the Romans, were very big.*

The words in **boldface** are perfect passive participles.

[handwritten margin notes: a/ab, L>by, ablative of agent]

3 A participle is used to describe a noun. For instance, in the first example in paragraph 2, **excitātus** describes **Memor**. Participles change their endings to agree with the nouns they describe. In this way they behave like adjectives. Compare the following pair of sentences:

> *singular*   faber, ab architectō **laudātus**, rīsit.
> *The craftsman, **having been praised** by the architect, smiled.*

> *plural*   fabrī, ab architectō **laudātī**, rīsērunt.
> *The craftsmen, **having been praised** by the architect, smiled.*

[handwritten margin notes: perfect passive, 1st con, -at-, -it-]

4 Translate the following examples:

[handwritten margin notes: present active, -ns, -nt-]

  a servus, ā dominō verberātus, ex oppidō fūgit.
  b nūntiī, ā rēge arcessītī, rem terribilem nārrāvērunt.
  c ancilla, ā Quīntō laudāta, laetissima erat.
  d templum, ā fabrīs perītīs aedificātum, erat splendidum.
  e mīlitēs, ab hostibus vulnerātī, thermās vīsitāre voluērunt.
  f uxor, ā marītō vexāta, ē vīllā discessit.

In each sentence, write down the perfect passive participle and the noun which it describes. State whether each pair is singular or plural, and masculine, feminine, or neuter.

[handwritten note: ☆ Participle — verbal adjective / adjective with action]

5 Notice that the perfect passive participle can be translated in a number of ways:

architectus, ā Cogidubnō ipsō missus, thermās exstrūxit.
The architect, having been sent by Cogidubnus himself, built the baths.
Or, in more natural English:
The architect, sent by Cogidubnus himself, built the baths.

servī, ā dominō arcessītī, statim ad tablīnum festīnāvērunt.
The slaves, having been summoned by their master, hurried at once to the study.
Or, in more natural English:
When the slaves had been summoned by their master, they hurried at once to the study.
The slaves, who had been summoned by their master, hurried at once to the study.

Memor rem suscipit

I

Salvius et Memor, in hortō sōlī ambulantēs, sermōnem gravem habent.

Salvius:	Lūcī Marcī Memor, vir summae prūdentiae es. volō tē rem magnam suscipere.	**prūdentiae: prūdentia** *good sense, intelligence*
Memor:	tālem rem suscipere velim, sed occupātissimus sum. 5 exspectant mē aegrōtī et sacerdōtēs. vexant mē architectus et fabrī. sed quid vīs mē facere?	**tālem: tālis** *such* **velim** *I would like*
Salvius:	Tiberius Claudius Cogidubnus, rēx Rēgnēnsium, hūc nūper advēnit. Cogidubnus, quī in morbum gravem incidit, aquam ē fonte sacrō bibere vult. 10	
Memor:	difficile est mihi tē adiuvāre, mī senātor. Cogidubnus est vir octōgintā annōrum. difficile est deae Sūlī Cogidubnum sānāre.	**octōgintā** *eighty*
Salvius:	nōlō tē reddere Cogidubnum sānum. volō tē rem contrāriam efficere. 15	**reddere** *make* **sānum: sānus** *well, healthy* **rem contrāriam: rēs contrāria** *the opposite*
Memor:	quid dīcis? num mortem Cogidubnī cupis?	
Salvius:	ita vērō! porrō, quamquam tam occupātus es, volō tē ipsum hanc rem efficere.	**porrō** *what's more, furthermore*
Memor:	vīsne mē rēgem interficere? rem huius modī facere nōlō. Cogidubnus enim est vir clārissimus, ā populō 20 Rōmānō honōrātus.	

Salvius:	ēs vir summae callid17ātis. hanc rem efficere potes. nōn sōlum ego, sed etiam Imperātor, hoc cupit. Cogidubnus enim Rōmānōs saepe vexāvit. Imperātor mihi, nōn Cogidubnō, cōnfīdit. Imperātor tibi praemium dignum prōmittit. num praemium, ab Imperātōre prōmissum, recūsāre vīs?
Memor:	quō modō rem facere possum?
Salvius:	nescio. hoc tantum tibi dīcō: Imperātor mortem Cogidubnī exspectat.
Memor:	ō mē miserum! rem difficiliōrem numquam fēcī.
Salvius:	vīta, mī Memor, est plēna rērum difficilium.
	(exit Salvius.)

nōn sōlum … sed etiam
not only … but also

dignum: dignus *worthy, appropriate*

recūsāre *refuse*
nescio: nescīre *not know*

II

Memor:	Cephale! Cephale! (*lībertus, ā Memore vocātus, celeriter intrat. pōculum vīnī fert.*) cūr mihi vīnum offers? nōn vīnum, sed cōnsilium quaerō. iubeō tē mihi cōnsilium quam celerrimē dare. rēx Cogidubnus hūc venit, remedium morbī petēns. Imperātor, ā Cogidubnō saepe vexātus, iam mortem eius cupit. Imperātor ipse iubet mē hoc efficere. quam difficile est!
Cephalus:	minimē, facile est! pōculum venēnātum habeō, mihi ā latrōne Aegyptiō ōlim datum. venēnum, in pōculō celātum, vītam celerrimē exstinguere potest.
Memor:	cōnsilium, quod mihi prōpōnis, perīculōsum est. Cogidubnō venēnum dare timeō.
Cephalus:	nihil perīculī est. rēx, quotiēns ē balneō exiit, ad fontem deae īre solet. tum necesse est servō prope fontem deae stāre et pōculum rēgī praebēre.
Memor:	(*dēlectātus*) cōnsilium optimum est. nūllīs tamen servīs cōnfīdō. sed tibi cōnfīdō, Cephale. iubeō tē ipsum Cogidubnō pōculum praebēre.
Cephalus:	ēheu! mihi rem difficillimam impōnis.
Memor:	vīta, mī Cephale, est plēna rērum difficilium.

venēnātum: venēnātus
poisoned
datum: dare *give*
venēnum *poison*
exstinguere *extinguish, destroy*
prōpōnis: prōpōnere
propose, put forward
nihil perīculī *no danger*
quotiēns *whenever*
balneō: balneum *bath*
praebēre *offer, provide*
difficillimam: difficillimus
very difficult
impōnis: impōnere *impose*

Word patterns: adjectives and adverbs

1   Study the form and meaning of the following words: *1st, 2nd, 3rd person*

laet**us**	*happy*	laet**ē**	*happily*
perīt**us**	*skillful*	perīt**ē**	*skillfully*
stultissim**us**	*very foolish*	stultissim**ē**	*very foolishly*

2   As you already know, the words in the left-hand columns are adjectives. The words on the right are known as **adverbs**.

3   Using the pattern in paragraph 1 as a guide, complete the following table:

adjectives		*adverbs*	
cautus	*cautious*	cautē	. . . .
superbus	*proud*	. . . .	*proudly*
crūdēlissimus	*very cruel*	. . . .	. . . .

4   Divide the following words into two lists, one of adjectives and one of adverbs. Then give the meaning of each word.

   intentē, gravissimus, callidus, tacitē, ignāvus, dīligentissimus, firmē, saevissimē

5   Choose the correct Latin words to translate the words in **boldface** in the following sentences:

   a   Memor was a **very hard** master. (dūrissimus, dūrissimē)
   b   The merchant always treated his customers **honestly.** (probus, probē)
   c   The senator **very generously** promised a large donation. (līberālissimus, līberālissimē)
   d   A **cautious** (cautus, cautē) man proceeds **slowly**. (lentus, lentē)

1 Complete each sentence with the correct case of the noun. Then translate the sentence.

   a omnēs aegrōtī . . . . vīsitāre volēbant. (fōns, fontem, fontis)
   b plūrimī servī in fundō . . . . labōrābant. (dominus, dominum, dominī)
   c "fortasse . . . . morbum meum sānāre potest," inquit rēx. (dea, deam, deae)
   d . . . . Cogidubnum laudāvērunt, quod līberālis et sapiēns erat. (prīncipēs, prīncipum)
   e mercātor, postquam . . . . accēpit, ē forō discessit. (dēnāriī, dēnāriōs, dēnāriōrum)
   f senex, quī in Aegyptō diū habitāverat, magnum numerum . . . . comparāverat.
      (statuae, statuās, statuārum)

2 Translate each English sentence into Latin by selecting correctly from the pairs of Latin words.

   For example: *The messenger heard the voice of the old man.*

nūntius	vōcem	senem	audīvī
nūntium	vōcī	senis	audīvit

   Latin translation: nūntius vōcem senis audīvit.

   a *The priests showed the statue to the architect.*

sacerdōtēs	statuam	architectum	ostendit
sacerdōtibus	statuās	architectō	ostendērunt

   b *The king praised the skillful doctor.*

rēx	medicus	perītum	laudāvit
rēgēs	medicum	perītī	laudāvērunt

   c *A friend of the soldiers was visiting the temple.*

amīcus	mīlitis	templum	vīsitābat
amīcō	mīlitum	templī	vīsitāvit

   d *The shouts of the invalids had annoyed the soothsayer.*

clāmōrem	aegrōtī	haruspicem	vexāverant
clāmōrēs	aegrōtōrum	haruspicēs	vexāvērunt

   e *We handed over the master's money to the farmers.*

pecūnia	dominum	agricolās	trādidimus
pecūniam	dominī	agricolīs	trādidērunt

3 Complete each sentence with the correct word. Then translate the sentence.

   a tū ipse hanc rem administrāre . . . . (dēbeō, dēbēs, dēbet)
   b cūr mē vituperās? heri per tōtum diem . . . . (labōrāvī, labōrāvistī, labōrāvit)
   c ego, quod fontem sacrum vidēre . . . ., iter ad oppidum Aquās Sūlis fēcī.
      (cupiēbam, cupiēbās, cupiēbat)
   d lībertus, quī senātōrem . . . ., in cubiculum haruspicis ruit. (cōnspexeram,
      cōnspexerās, cōnspexerat)
   e ē lectō surrēxī, quod dormīre nōn . . . . (poteram, poterās, poterat)
   f in hāc vīllā . . . . Memor, haruspex nōtissimus. (habitō, habitās, habitat)

Aquae Sulis and its baths

The Roman town of Aquae Sulis lies beneath the modern city of Bath in the valley of the river Avon. In a small area, enclosed by a bend in the river, mineral springs of hot water emerge from underground at the rate of over a quarter of a million gallons (a million liters) a day, and at a temperature of between 104 and 121 degrees Fahrenheit (40 and 49 degrees Celsius). The water we see today fell as rain 10,000 years ago and then percolated 2 miles (3 kilometers) down into the earth before rising to the surface as hot springs. These have a low mineral content, consisting mainly of calcium, magnesium, and sodium.

Long before the Romans came, the springs were regarded as a sacred place. Since these hot springs are unique in Britain, it is not surprising that the Celts worshipped the place as the home of their goddess Sulis and believed in the goddess' power to cure their illnesses through immersion in the hot spring waters.

When the Romans arrived they were quick to recognize the importance and potential of the springs as a place of pilgrimage. They erected a set of huge public baths so that visitors could enjoy their experience of the hot springs in comfort.

The most important part of the bath complex was the sacred spring. The Romans enclosed it in a large reservoir wall of massive stone blocks, lined with lead sheets nearly one half inch (one centimeter) thick, and surrounded by a simple stone balustrade. Because of the skill of the Roman engineers, water still flows into the baths through a lead-lined channel from an opening provided in the very top of the reservoir. The hot spring with its bubbling waters overhung with clouds of steam presented an awesome and mysterious sight to the many visitors to the baths. Excavation has revealed thousands of items – coins, jewelry, and silver and pewter cups – thrown into the spring as offerings by worshippers.

The main building was a long, rectangular structure, possibly the largest and most magnificent set of baths west of Rome at this date. It contained three main plunge baths filled with a constant supply of mineral water at a pleasant temperature. The water was carried by lead pipes which still work today. The pool nearest the spring naturally contained the hottest water, whereas the furthest pool was the coolest, since the water lost much of its heat on the way to it. There was also a suite of warm and hot baths heated by a hypocaust. The bath complex at Aquae Sulis is one of the wonders of Roman Britain. The knowledge and planning of the hydraulic engineers, who were probably assigned from the army, and the skill and quality of the plumbers' work are impressive reminders of the high standards of Roman engineering.

Some people traveled long distances to Aquae Sulis, attracted by the fame of its spring and its healing powers. No doubt the heat of

The largest of the three plunge baths at Bath: it is now called the Great Bath. Notice the steam rising from the naturally hot water.

the water relieved conditions such as rheumatism and arthritis, but many people must have visited the spring in the hope of miraculous cures for all kinds of diseases. One elderly woman, Rusonia Aventina, came from Metz in eastern Gaul. Her tombstone shows that she died at Aquae Sulis at the age of fifty-eight, perhaps from the illness which she had hoped the spring would cure. Julius Vitalis was a soldier serving as armorer to the Twentieth Legion, based at Deva (Chester). His tombstone records that he had served for just nine years when he died at the age of twenty-nine; possibly his commanding officer had sent him to Aquae Sulis on sick leave.

Many visitors seeing the mysterious steaming waters would feel that they were in a holy place. They would believe that a cure for their ailments depended as much on divine favor as on the medicinal powers of the water. Therefore, a temple was constructed next to the bath buildings, with the sacred spring enclosed within the temple precinct. In front of the temple stood an altar. The temple itself was built in the Roman style with a **cella**, a porch with Corinthian columns, and a richly decorated pediment. The life-sized gilded bronze head of Sulis Minerva (see illustration, page 52) was possibly from the cult statue in the cella. The pediment of the temple was remarkable for its roundel (see illustration, page 40). The identity of the face depicted is uncertain; suggestions include Neptune (Roman god of the sea), or a sun god, or even the Gorgon, which was the emblem shown on the breastplate of Minerva. Below the roundel are Minerva's owl and helmet. By linking the name and attributes of Minerva to those of Sulis, the Romans encouraged the Britons to recognize the power of the Roman goddess of wisdom and the arts and to associate her with the Sulis they already knew.

How the Great Bath probably looked around the time of our stories, late first century AD.

A portrait of a lady with fashionable hairstyle. From her tomb at Bath.

The baths and temple about AD 100

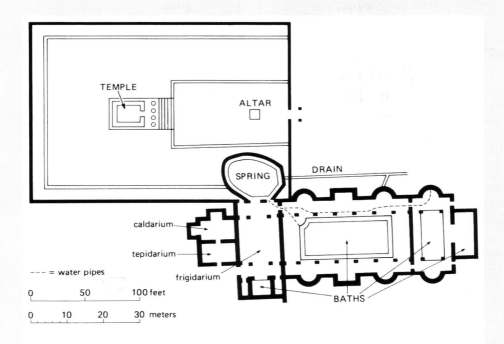

TEMPLE

ALTAR

SPRING

DRAIN

caldarium

tepidarium

frigidarium

- - - = water pipes

BATHS

0   50   100 feet

0   10   20   30 meters

Water ran from the spring to the baths through lead pipes.

In addition to the pools of natural hot water, there was a set of baths heated by a hypocaust in the Roman manner, with a caldarium, tepidarium, and frigidarium. Part of the hypocaust is seen below.

When the temple precinct was excavated, the stone base of a statue was found. The inscription records that the statue was dedicated to the goddess Sulis by a Roman official, Lucius Marcius Memor, a **haruspex**. Nothing more is known about him, but his presence attests to the reputation of the complex at Aquae Sulis, which was famous enough to bring him there. Many such officials must have contributed to the policy of romanization in this way.

At the time of our stories (*c.* AD 83), Aquae Sulis was a small but growing community. The complex of bath buildings and temple was the most impressive feature of the town. There were probably a few other public buildings, such as a basilica for the administration of law and local government, and possibly a theater, but most of the other buildings would have been houses for those who were already living there and inns for the town's many visitors. Aquae Sulis lay within tribal territory over which Cogidubnus may have had control. In our stories we imagine that he was involved in the development of the baths.

Aquae Sulis was, of course, a tourist center as well as a place of religious pilgrimage, and one can imagine the entrance to the baths crowded with souvenir stalls, much as it is today. Visitors would buy such things as good luck charms and offerings to throw into the sacred spring with a prayer for future good health. These offerings were sometimes expensive; they included beautifully carved gemstones and items of jewelry.

Reconstruction of the temple front.

A model of the temple and the courtyard.

Some of the objects people threw into the spring.

Vocabulary checklist 21

From now on, most verbs in the checklists are listed as in the Language information (i.e. perfect passive participles are usually included).

ā, ab	*from; by*
adiuvō, adiuvāre, adiūvī	*help*
annus, annī, m.	*year*
cēlō, cēlāre, cēlāvī, cēlātus	*hide*
circum	*around*
dūrus, dūra, dūrum	*harsh, hard*
efficiō, efficere, effēcī, effectus	*carry out, accomplish*
fōns, fontis, m.	*fountain, spring*
gravis, gravis, grave	*heavy, serious*
hōra, hōrae, f.	*hour*
īnfēlīx, īnfēlīx, īnfēlīx, *gen.*	
** īnfēlīcis**	*unlucky*
iubeō, iubēre, iussī, iussus	*order*
morbus, morbī, m.	*illness*
nōnnūllī, nōnnūllae, nōnnūlla	*some, several*
nūper	*recently*
oppidum, oppidī, n.	*town*
plēnus, plēna, plēnum	*full*
plūs, plūris, n.	*more*
pretium, pretiī, n.	*price*
sacer, sacra, sacrum	*sacred*
sapiēns, sapiēns, sapiēns, *gen.*	
** sapientis**	*wise*
unde	*from where*

An earring found in the spring.

DEFIXIO

Stage 22

Handwritten annotations:

thief   bath   ~~cages~~ → cautiously
                             spring

1 fūr thermās cautē intrāvit.
   fūr, thermās ingressus, ad fontem
   sacrum festīnāvit.   *hurry*

   having entered

2 fūr, prope fontem stāns,
   circumspectāvit.   *look around*
   fūr, senem cōnspicātus, post
   columnam sē cēlāvit.

3 senex, amulētum aureum tenēns, ad
   fontem prōcessit.
   senex manūs ad caelum sustulit et
   auxilium ā deā Sūle petīvit.

4 senex, deam precātus, amulētum
in fontem iniēcit et exiit.

5 fūr, quī amulētum aureum vīderat,
ad fontem revēnit.
fūr, ad fontem regressus, amulētum
in aquā quaesīvit.

6 fūr, amulētum adeptus, attonitus lēgit:

fūr amulētum dēiēcit et ē thermīs
perterritus fūgit.

Vilbia

Vilbia et Rubria, pōcula sordida lavantēs, in culīnā tabernae garriēbant. hae puellae erant fīliae Latrōnis. Latrō, quī tabernam tenēbat, erat vir magnae dīligentiae sed minimae prūdentiae. Latrō, culīnam ingressus, puellās vituperāvit.

"multa sunt pōcula sordida. iubeō vōs pōcula quam celerrimē ⁵ lavāre. labōrāte! nōlīte garrīre! loquāciōrēs estis quam psittacī."

Latrō, haec verba locūtus, exiit.

Vilbia tamen, quae pulchra et obstināta erat, patrī nōn pāruit: pōcula nōn lāvit, sed Rubriae fībulam ostendit. Rubria fībulam, quam soror tenēbat, avidē spectāvit. ¹⁰

Rubria:	quam pulchra, quam pretiōsa est haec fībula, mea Vilbia! eam īnspicere velim. quis tibi dedit? num argentea est?
Vilbia:	sānē argentea est. Modestus, mīles Rōmānus, eam mihi dedit. ¹⁵
Rubria:	quālis est hic mīles? estne homō mendāx et ignāvus, sīcut cēterī mīlitēs Rōmānī?
Vilbia:	minimē! est vir maximae virtūtis. ōlim tria mīlia hostium occīdit. nunc lēgātum ipsum custōdit.
Rubria:	Herculēs alter est! ego autem tālem fābulam saepe ex ²⁰ aliīs mīlitibus audīvī.
Vilbia:	cēterī mīlitēs mendācēs sunt, Modestus probus. simulac tabernam nostram intrāvit, eum statim amāvī. quantī erant umerī eius! quanta bracchia!
Rubria:	tibi favet fortūna, mea Vilbia. quid autem dē Bulbō ²⁵ dīcis, quem ōlim amābās? tibi perīculōsum est Bulbum contemnere, quod rēs magicās intellegit.
Vilbia:	nōlī illam pestem commemorāre! Bulbus, saepe dē mātrimōniō locūtus, nihil umquam effēcit. sed Modestus, quī fortissimus et audācissimus est, mē ³⁰ cūrāre potest. Modestus nunc est suspīrium meum.

dīligentiae: dīligentia *industry, hard work*
minimae: minimus *very little*
ingressus *having entered*
locūtus *having spoken*

fībulam: fībula *brooch*
avidē *eagerly*

quālis? *what sort of man?*

virtūtis: virtūs *courage*
tria mīlia *three thousand*
occīdit: occīdere *kill*
lēgātum: lēgātus *commander*
alter *another, a second*
autem *but*
quantī: quantus *how big*
bracchia: bracchium *arm*
Bulbō: Bulbus *Bulbus*
(His name means "onion.")
contemnere *reject, despise*
mātrimōniō: mātrimōnium *marriage*
suspīrium *heartthrob*

Modestus

Modestus et Strȳthiō ad tabernam Latrōnis ambulant. Strȳthiō, (name) *quamquam amīcus Modestī est, eum dērīdet.*

Modestus: ubi es, Strȳthiō? iubeō tē prope mē stāre.
~~order~~ ~~stand~~

Strȳthiō: adsum. hercle! quam fortūnātus sum! prope virum
summae virtūtis stō. tū enim fortior es quam Mārs
ipse. ~~the truth~~

Modestus: vērum dīcis. ōlim tria mīlia hostium occīdī.

Strȳthiō: tē omnēs puellae amant, quod tam fortis et pulcher
es. illa Vilbia, heri tē cōnspicāta, statim amāvit.
multa dē tē rogāvit. ~~having caught sight of~~

Modestus: quid dīxit?

Strȳthiō: mē avidē rogāvit, "estne Herculēs?" "minimē! est
frāter eius," respondī. tum fībulam, quam puella alia
tibi dederat, Vilbiae trādidī. "Modestus, vir benignus
et nōbilis," inquam, "tibi hanc fībulam grātīs dat." ~~I said~~ ~~free~~
Vilbia, fībulam adepta, mihi respondit, "quam ~~having~~
pulcher Modestus est! quam līberālis! velim cum eō
colloquium habēre." ~~talk~~

Modestus: ēheu! nōnne molestae sunt puellae? mihi difficile est
puellās vītāre. nimis pulcher sum. ~~too~~

Strȳthiō: ecce! ad tabernam Latrōnis advēnimus. fortasse inest ~~be inside~~
Vilbia, quae tē tamquam deum adōrat. ~~like~~
(tabernam intrant.)

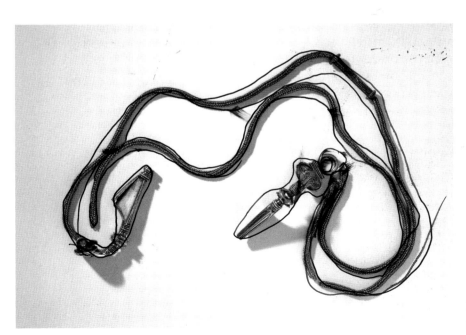

Two silver brooches joined by a chain.

About the language 1: perfect active participles

1   In Stage 21, you met sentences containing perfect passive participles:

   rēx, ā Rōmānīs **honōrātus**, semper fidēlis manēbat.
   *The king, **having been honored** by the Romans, always remained loyal.*

   puellae, ā patre **vituperātae**, nōn respondērunt.
   *The girls, **having been blamed** by their father, did not reply.*

2   In Stage 22, you have met another kind of perfect participle. Study the way it is translated in the following examples:

   Vilbia, culīnam **ingressa**, sorōrī fībulam ostendit.
   *Vilbia, **having entered** the kitchen, showed the brooch to her sister.*

   senex, deam **precātus**, abiit.
   *The old man, **having prayed** to the goddess, went away.*

   The words in **boldface** are perfect active participles. Like other participles they change their endings to agree with the nouns they describe. Compare the following pair of sentences:

   singular   puer, mīlitēs **cōnspicātus**, valdē timēbat.
   plural   puerī, mīlitēs **cōnspicātī**, valdē timēbant.

3   Translate the following examples:

   a   Modestus, tabernam ingressus, Vilbiam cōnspexit.
   b   Vilbia, multa verba locūta, tandem tacuit.
   c   mercātōrēs, pecūniam adeptī, ad nāvēs contendērunt.
   d   fēmina, deam Sūlem precāta, amulētum in fontem iniēcit.
   e   ancillae, ānulum cōnspicātae, eum īnspicere volēbant.

   In each sentence, pick out the perfect active participle and the noun which it describes. State whether each pair is singular or plural.

4   Only a small group of verbs have a perfect active participle; they do not have a perfect passive participle.

amor omnia vincit

amor *love*	
omnia *all, everything*	

scaena prīma

Bulbus et amīcus in tabernā Latrōnis sunt. vīnum bibunt āleamque lūdunt. Bulbus amīcō multam pecūniam dēbet.

scaena *scene*

āleam … lūdunt *are playing dice*

Gutta: (*amīcus Bulbī*) quam īnfēlīx es! nōn sōlum puellam, sed etiam pecūniam āmīsistī.

Gutta *Gutta (His name means "drop" or "droplet.")*

Bulbus: pecūniam nōn cūrō, sed Vilbiam meam āmittere nōlō.   5

Gutta: quō modō eam retinēre potes? mīles Rōmānus, vir summae virtūtis, eam petit. heus! Venerem iactāvī caupō! iubeō tē plūs vīnī ferre.

Venerem: Venus *Venus (highest throw at dice)*
iactāvī: iactāre *throw*

Bulbus: mīles, quī eam dēcēpit, homō mendāx ignāvusque est. Vilbia, ab eō dēcepta, nunc mē contemnit. eam saepe monuī, "nōlī mīlitibus crēdere, praesertim Rōmānīs." Vilbia tamen, hunc Modestum cōnspicāta, statim eum amāvit.   10

praesertim *especially*

Gutta: puellīs nōn tūtum est per viās huius oppidī īre. tanta est arrogantia hōrum mīlitum. hercle! tū etiam īnfēlīcior es. canem iterum iactāvistī. alium dēnārium mihi dēbēs.   15

arrogantia *arrogance, excessive pride*
canem: canis *dog (lowest throw at dice)*

ōdī *I hate*

Bulbus: dēnārium libenter trādō, nōn puellam. ōdī istum mīlitem. Modestus tamen puellam retinēre nōn potest, quod auxilium ā deā petīvī. deam precātus, tabulam in fontem sacrum iniēcī. dīra imprecātiō, in tabulā scrīpta, iam in fonte deae iacet. (*intrant Modestus et Strӯthiō, quōs Bulbus nōn videt.*) mortem Modestī laetus exspectō.   20   25

precātus *having prayed to*
tabulam: tabula *tablet, writing tablet*
imprecātiō *curse*
scrīpta: scrībere *write*

Gutta: hercle! īnfēlīcissimus es. ecce! nōbīs appropinquat ipse Modestus. necesse est mihi quam celerrimē exīre.
(*exit currēns.*)

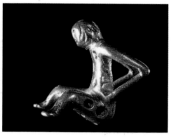

The Romans were very fond of games involving dice, both the kind we are used to (far left), and more novel varieties like the little man (left), who can fall six ways up; here he scores 2. The larger of the cubic dice has a hollow in it, possibly for loading the dice.

scaena secunda

Modestus īrātus Bulbum vituperat, quod verba eius audīvit.

Modestus: quid dīcēbās, homuncule? mortem meam exspectās?
asine! tū, quod mīlitem Rōmānum vituperāvistī, in
magnō perīculō es. Strȳthiō! tē iubeō hanc pestem
verberāre. tum ē tabernā ēice!

exanimatis – unconscious

5   **ēice: ēicere** *throw out*

*Strȳthiō invītus Bulbum verberāre incipit. Bulbus, fortiter sē
dēfendēns, vīnum in caput Strȳthiōnis fundit. Modestus Bulbum,
simulac tergum vertit, ferōciter pulsat.* Bulbus exanimatus prōcumbit, ~~*unconsciously*~~ *falls down*
*Vilbia, quae clāmōrēs audīvit, intrat. ingressa, Bulbum humī
iacentem videt et Modestum mollīre incipit.*

incipit: incipere *begin*
fundit: fundere *pour*
tergum *back*
humī *on the ground*
10   **mollīre** *soothe*

Vilbia: dēsine, mī Modeste. iste Bulbus, ā tē verberātus,
iterum mē vexāre nōn potest. tū es leō, iste rīdiculus
mūs. volō tē clēmentem esse et Bulbō parcere.
placetne tibi?

clēmentem: clēmēns *merciful*
parcere *spare*

Modestus: mihi placet. victōribus decōrum est victīs parcere. tē,
nōn istum, quaerō.

15   **victīs: victī** *the conquered*

Vilbia: ō Modeste, cūr mē ex omnibus puellīs ēlēgistī? quam
laeta sum!

Modestus: necesse est nōbīs in locō sēcrētō noctū convenīre.

sēcrētō: sēcrētus *secret*

Vilbia: id facere nōn audeō. pater mē sōlam exīre nōn vult.
ubi est hic locus?

20   **noctū** *by night*

Modestus: prope fontem deae Sūlis. nōnne tibi persuādēre
possum? *order*

Vilbia: mihi difficile est iussa patris neglegere, sed tibi
resistere nōn possum.

iussa: iussum *order, instruction*
25   **neglegere** *ignore, disregard*

Modestus: dā mihi ōsculum.

Vilbia: ēheu! ō suspīrium meum! mihi necesse est ad
culīnam redīre, tibi noctem exspectāre.

*exeunt. Bulbus, quī magnam partem huius colloquiī audīvit, surgit.
quam celerrimē ēgressus, Guttam petit, cui cōnsilium callidum
prōpōnit.*

30   **ēgressus** *having gone out*
cui *to whom (dative of* **quī***)*

scaena tertia

per silentium noctis thermās intrant Bulbus et Gutta. prope fontem ^{through} ^{enter}
sacrum sē cēlant. Bulbus Guttae stolam et pallium, quod sēcum tulit,
ostendit.

Clothes put on

Bulbus:	Gutta, volō tē haec vestīmenta induere. volō tē
	persōnam Vilbiae agere. nōbīs necesse est dēcipere
	Modestum, quem brevī exspectō.
Gutta:	vah! virō nōn decōrum est stolam gerere. praetereā
	barbam habeō.
Bulbus:	id minimī mōmentī est, quod in tenebrīs sumus.
	nōnne tibi persuādēre possum? ecce! decem
	dēnāriōs tibi dō, nunc tacē! indue stolam
	palliumque! stā prope fontem deae! ubi Modestus
	fontī appropinquat, dīc eī verba suāvissima!

Gutta, postquam stolam invītus induit, prope fontem stat. Modestus,
sōlus thermās ingressus, fontī appropinquat.

5

10

15

pallium *cloak*

induere - put on
sta/stat - stand

vestīmenta *clothes*

persōnam Vilbiae agere
play the part of Vilbia

brevī *in a short time*

vah! *ugh!*

praetereā *besides*

mōmentī: mōmentum
importance

tenebrīs: tenebrae *darkness*

The sacred spring as it is today.

Modestus:	Vilbia, mea Vilbia! Modestus, fortissimus mīlitum, adest.
Gutta:	ō dēliciae meae! venī ad mē.
Modestus:	quam rauca est vōx tua! num lacrimās, quod tardus adveniō?
Gutta:	ita vērō! tam sollicita eram.
Modestus:	lacrimās tuās siccāre possum. (*Modestus ad Guttam advenit.*) dī immortālēs! Vilbia! barbam habēs? quid tibi accidit? ō!

20

siccāre *dry*

tum Bulbus Modestum in fontem dēicit. Vilbia, thermās ingressa, ubi clāmōrēs audīvit, prope iānuam perterrita manet.

25

Modestus:	pereō! pereō! parce! parce!
Bulbus:	furcifer! Vilbiam meam, quam valdē amō, auferre audēs? nunc mihi facile est tē interficere.
Modestus:	nōlī mē interficere. Vilbiam tibi reddō. eam ā tē auferre nōlō. Vilbiam nōn amō.

auferre *take away, steal*

30

Vilbia, simulatque haec audīvit, īrāta fontī appropinquat. Modestum vituperāre incipit.

Vilbia:	mē nōn amās? ō hominem ignāvum! ego ipsa tē interficere velim.
Bulbus:	mea Vilbia, victōribus decōrum est victīs parcere.
Vilbia:	mī Bulbe, dēliciae meae, miserrima sum! longē errāvī.
Bulbus:	nōlī lacrimāre! ego tē cūrāre possum.
Vilbia:	ō Bulbe! ō suspīrium meum!

35

longē errāvī: longē errāre *make a big mistake*

40

Bulbus et Vilbia domum redeunt. Gutta stolam palliumque exuit. dēnāriōs laetē numerat. Modestus ē fonte sē extrahit et madidus abit.

exuit: exuere *take off*

About the language 2: more about the genitive

1 In Unit 2 you met examples of the genitive case like these:

> marītus **Galatēae** erat Aristō.
> *The husband **of Galatea** was Aristo.*

> prō templō **Caesaris** stat āra.
> *In front of the temple **of Caesar** stands an altar.*

2 In Stage 21 you have met another use of the genitive. Study the following examples:

satis pecūniae	*enough money*, literally, *enough of money*
nimium vīnī	*too much wine*
plūs sanguinis	*more blood*
multum cibī	*much food*

Each phrase is made up of two words:

a A word like **plūs** or **nimium** indicating an amount or quantity.
b A noun in the genitive case.

3 Further examples:

a nimium pecūniae   **c** plūs labōris
b nihil perīculī   **d** multum aquae

4 In Stage 22 you met examples like these:

> homō ingeniī prāvī   fēmina magnae dignitātis
> *a man of evil character*   *a woman of great prestige*

In both examples, a noun (**homō**, **fēmina**) is described by another noun and an adjective both in the genitive case. Such phrases can be translated in different ways. For example:

> puella magnae prūdentiae   vir summae virtūtis
> *a girl of great sense*   *a man of the utmost courage*
> Or, in more natural English: Or, in more natural English:
> *a very sensible girl*   *a very courageous man*

5 Further examples:

a homō minimae prūdentiae   **d** fābula huius modī
b iuvenis vīgintī annōrum   **e** puella maximae calliditātis
c fēmina magnae sapientiae   **f** vir ingeniī optimī

Word patterns: more adjectives and adverbs

1 In Stage 21 you met the following pattern:

adjectives		*adverbs*	
laetus	*happy*	laetē	*happily*
perītus	*skillful*	perītē	*skillfully*

2 Study another common pattern of adjectives and adverbs:

adjectives		*adverbs*	
brevis	*short*	brevi**ter**	*shortly*
ferōx	*fierce*	ferōci**ter**	*fiercely*

3 Using this pattern as a guide, complete the following table:

suāvis	*sweet*	suāviter	. . . .
neglegēns	. . . .	neglegenter	*carelessly*
audāx	. . . .	audācter	. . . .

4 Divide the following words into two lists, one of adjectives and one of adverbs. Then give the meaning of each word:

> fortis, fidēliter, īnsolēns, fortiter, sapienter, īnsolenter, fidēlis, sapiēns.

5 Choose the correct Latin word to translate the word in **boldface** in the following sentences:

- **a** Quintus was a **sensible** young man. (prūdēns, prūdenter)
- **b** Salvius rode **quickly** into the courtyard. (celer, celeriter)
- **c** The soldier was **happy** because the goddess had cured him. (laetus, laetē)
- **d** Vilbia worked **diligently** only when her father was watching. (dīligēns, dīligenter)
- **e** Salvius sometimes acted **very cruelly** to his slaves. (crūdēlissimus, crūdēlissimē)

Practicing the language

1 Complete each sentence with the correct form of the noun. Then translate the sentence.

    a Modestus per viās . . . . ambulābat, puellām quaerēns. (oppidī, oppidō)

    b Gutta, vir benignus, auxilium . . . . saepe dabat. (amīcī, amīcō)

    c Rubria, quae in tabernā labōrābat, ... vīnum obtulit. (iuvenis, iuvenī)

    d prope vīllam . . . ., turba ingēns conveniēbat. (haruspicis, haruspicī)

    e tabernārius . . . . multās rēs pretiōsās ostendit. (ancillārum, ancillīs)

    f clāmōrēs . . . . architectum vexāvērunt. (fabrōrum, fabrīs)

    g centuriō gladiōs hastāsque . . . . īnspicere coepit. (mīlitum, mīlitibus)

    h caupō vīnum pessimum . . . . offerēbat. (hospitum, hospitibus)

2 Complete each sentence with the correct form of the adjective. Then translate the sentence.

    a subitō ancilla . . . . in ātrium irrūpit. (perterrita, perterritae)

    b rēx, postquam hoc audīvit, fabrōs . . . . dīmīsit. (fessum, fessōs)

    c senātor quī aderat iuvenēs . . . . laudāvit. (callidum, callidōs)

    d omnēs cīvēs nāvem . . . . spectābant. (sacram, sacrās)

    e ubi in magnō perīculō eram, amīcus . . . . mē servāvit. (fidēlis, fidēlēs)

    f "in illā īnsulā," inquit senex, "habitant multī virī . . . ." (ferōx, ferōcēs)

    g fēmina . . . ., quae in vīllā manēbat, fūrem superāvit. (fortis, fortem, fortēs)

    h cīvēs in viīs oppidī . . . . mīlitēs vidēre solēbant. (multus, multī, multōs)

Magic, curses, and superstitions

Many thousands of offerings have been recovered from the spring at Aquae Sulis. Some of the finds indicate that there were people anxious to use the powers of the gods for unpleasant purposes, believing it was possible to "dedicate" an enemy to the gods of the underworld.

When Roman religious sites are excavated, archaeologists sometimes find small sheets of lead or pewter inscribed with curses. These are known as **dēfīxiōnēs**, or curse tablets, which call for the punishment of an enemy. Over three hundred have been found in Britain alone.

The method of putting a curse on someone followed a general formula. The name of the offender, if known, was written on a tablet, with details of the crime. The offender was then dedicated to a god, who was called on to punish the offender, usually in a very unpleasant way. If the offender was unknown, the tablet would provide a list of suspects. The completed tablet was rolled or folded up and then fastened to a tomb with a long nail or thrown into a well or spring.

About ninety curse tablets were found in the sacred spring at Aquae Sulis. One such defixio reads:

> **Docilianus, son of Brucerus, to the most holy goddess Sulis. I curse him who has stolen my hooded cloak, whether man or woman, whether slave or free, that ... the goddess Sulis inflict death upon ... and not allow him sleep or children now or in the future, until he has brought my hooded cloak to the temple of her divinity.**

The first side of Docilianus' curse.

On another tablet a woman dedicates her stolen ring to the god Mars:

> **Basilia gives to the temple of Mars her silver ring, that so long as someone, slave or free, keeps silent or knows anything about it, he may be accursed in his blood and eyes and every limb, or even have all his intestines entirely eaten away, if he has stolen the ring or been an accomplice.**

A jealous lover may have written one of the most famous tablets of Aquae Sulis, a tablet that inspired the stories about Vilbia and Modestus in this Stage:

> **May he who has stolen Vilbia from me dissolve like water. May she who has devoured her be struck dumb, whether it be Velvinna or Exsupereus or Verianus ...**
> (here follows a list of six other suspects).

The Vilbia curse.

The Vilbia curse, like many others, was written backwards to increase the mystery of the process. Magical and apparently meaningless words like **bescu**, **berebescu**, **bazagra** were sometimes added to increase the effect, rather like the use of "abracadabra" in spells. Sometimes we find a figure roughly drawn on the tablet, as in the illustration on the right. It depicts a bearded demon, carrying an urn and a torch, which were symbols of death. The boat in which he stands may represent the boat of Charon, the ferryman of the underworld, who took the souls of the dead across the river Styx.

The wording of the curse can be very simple, just "I dedicate" followed by the intended victim's name. But sometimes it can be ferociously eloquent, as in the following example:

> **May burning fever seize all her limbs, kill her soul and her heart. O gods of the underworld, break and smash her bones, choke her, let her body be twisted and shattered – phrix, phrox.**

It may seem strange that religion should be used to bring harm to people in this very direct and spiteful way, but the Romans tended to see their gods as possible allies in the struggles of life. When they wished to injure an enemy, they thought it natural and proper to seek the gods' powerful help.

Some Romans also considered it natural that the gods might give **ōmina** (omens or warnings) of impending danger and that proper action could avert a misfortune. It was safer to stay at home after stumbling on the threshold, hearing the hooting of an owl, or having a bad dream. Many people would take care to marry only on certain days and in certain months, to cross the threshold with the right foot, and to wear an amulet to ward off the evil eye. Carefully observing the signs sent by the gods and taking appropriate precautions could turn aside some of the perils of life.

Vocabulary checklist 22

adeptus, adepta, adeptum	*having received, having obtained*
amor, amōris, m.	*love*
caelum, caelī, n.	*sky*
dēcipiō, dēcipere, dēcēpī, dēceptus	*deceive, trick*
ēligō, ēligere, ēlēgī, ēlēctus	*choose*
fundō, fundere, fūdī, fūsus	*pour*
hostis, hostis, m.	*enemy*
iactō, iactāre, iactāvī, iactātus	*throw*
incipiō, incipere, incēpī, inceptus	*begin*
ingressus, ingressa, ingressum	*having entered*
lacrima, lacrimae, f.	*tear*
minimus, minima, minimum	*very little, least*
moneō, monēre, monuī, monitus	*warn, advise*
nox, noctis, f.	*night*
parcō, parcere, pepercī	*spare*
precātus, precāta, precātum	*having prayed (to)*
quantus, quanta, quantum	*how big*
quō modō?	*how? in what way?*
tūtus, tūta, tūtum	*safe*
verbum, verbī, n.	*word*
virtūs, virtūtis, f.	*courage*
vītō, vītāre, vītāvī, vītātus	*avoid*

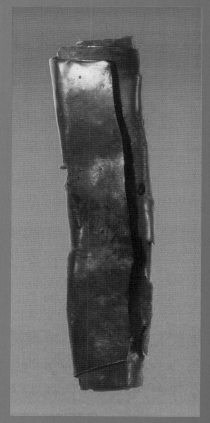

One of the Bath curse tablets, folded as it was found.

HARUSPEX

Stage 23

in thermīs

I

prope thermās erat templum, ā fabrīs Cogidubnī aedificātum.
rēx Cogidubnus cum multīs prīncipibus servīsque prō templō
sedēbat. Quīntus prope sellam rēgis stābat. rēgem prīncipēsque
manus armātōrum custōdiēbat. prō templō erat āra ingēns, quam 5
omnēs aspiciēbant. Memor, togam splendidam gerēns, prope
āram stābat.

duo sacerdōtēs, agnam nigram dūcentēs, ad āram
prōcessērunt. postquam rēx signum dedit, ūnus sacerdōs agnam
sacrificāvit. deinde Memor, quī iam tremēbat, alterī sacerdōtī,
"iubeō tē," inquit, "ōmina īnspicere. dīc mihi: quid vidēs?" 10
sacerdōs, postquam iecur agnae īnspexit, anxius,
"iecur est līvidum," inquit. "nōnne hoc mortem significat?
nōnne mortem virī clārī significat?"
Memor, quī perterritus pallēscēbat, sacerdōtī respondit,
"minimē! dea Sūlis, quae precēs aegrōtōrum audīre solet, 15
nōbīs ōmina optima mīsit."
haec verba locūtus, ad Cogidubnum sē vertit.
"ōmina sunt optima!" inquit. "ōmina tibi remedium mīrābile
significant, quod dea Sūlis Minerva tibi favet."
tum rēgem ac prīncipēs Memor in apodytērium dūxit. 20

manus armātōrum *a band of*
soldiers
aspiciēbant: aspicere
look towards
agnam: agna *lamb*

ōmina: ōmen *omen*
iecur *liver*
līvidum: līvidus *lead-colored*
significat: significāre
mean, indicate
pallēscēbat: pallēscere *grow pale*
precēs *prayers*

ac *and*

The altar at Bath. The base and the sculptured corner blocks are original; the rest of the Roman stone must have been reused elsewhere during the Middle Ages. Compare the drawing opposite. At the top left of the photograph can be seen the stone statue base which is inscribed with Memor's name.

II

deinde omnēs in eam partem thermārum intrāvērunt, ubi balneum maximum erat. Quīntus, prīncipēs secūtus, circumspectāvit et attonitus,

"hae thermae," inquit, "maiōrēs sunt quam thermae Pompēiānae!"   5

servī cum magnā difficultāte Cogidubnum in balneum dēmittere coepērunt. maximus clāmor erat. rēx prīncipibus mandāta dabat. prīncipēs lībertōs suōs vituperābant, lībertī servōs.

tandem rēx, ē balneō ēgressus, vestīmenta, quae servī   10
tulerant, induit. tum omnēs fontī sacrō appropinquāvērunt.

Cephalus, quī anxius tremēbat, prope fontem stābat, pōculum ōrnātissimum tenēns.

"domine," inquit, "pōculum aquae sacrae tibi offerō. aqua est amāra, sed remedium potentissimum."   15

haec verba locūtus, rēgī pōculum obtulit. rēx pōculum ad labra sustulit.

subitō Quīntus, pōculum cōnspicātus, manum rēgis prēnsāvit et clāmāvit,

"nōlī bibere! hoc est pōculum venēnātum. pōculum huius   20
modī in urbe Alexandrīā vīdī."

secūtus *having followed*

difficultāte: difficultās *difficulty*
dēmittere *let down, lower*

amāra: amārus *bitter*

labra: labrum *lip*
prēnsāvit: prēnsāre *take hold of, clutch*

"longē errās," respondit rēx. "nēmō mihi nocēre vult. nēmō umquam mortem mihi parāre temptāvit."

"rēx summae virtūtis es," respondit Quīntus. "sed, quamquam nūllum perīculum timēs, tūtius est tibi vērum scīre. pōculum īnspicere velim. dā mihi!"   25

tum pōculum Quīntus īnspicere coepit. Cephalus tamen pōculum ē manibus Quīntī rapere temptābat. maxima pars spectātōrum stābat immōta. sed Dumnorix, prīnceps Rēgnēnsium, saeviēbat tamquam leō furēns. pōculum rapuit   30
et Cephalō obtulit.

"facile est nōbīs vērum cognōscere," clāmāvit. "iubeō tē pōculum haurīre. num aquam bibere timēs?"

Cephalus pōculum haurīre nōluit, et ad genua rēgis
prōcubuit. rēx immōtus stābat. cēterī prīncipēs lībertum frūstrā   35
resistentem prēnsāvērunt. Cephalus, ā prīncipibus coāctus,
venēnum hausit. deinde, vehementer tremēns, gemitum
ingentem dedit et mortuus prōcubuit.

genua: genū *knee*

coāctus: cōgere *force, compel*

This sculpture was placed over the entrance to the temple of Sulis Minerva. It may be a Celtic version of the Gorgon's head that Minerva wore on her cloak or shield – a monster that could turn men to stone with a glance.

About the language 1: more about participles

1 In Stage 20, you met the present participle:

líbertus dominum **intrantem** vīdit.
*The freedman saw his master **entering**.*

2 In Stage 21, you met the perfect passive participle:

fabrī, ab architectō **laudātī**, dīligenter labōrābant.
*The craftsmen, (**having been**) **praised** by the architect, were working hard.*

3 In Stage 22, you met the perfect active participle:

Vilbia, thermās **ingressa**, clāmōrem audīvit.
*Vilbia, **having entered** the baths, heard a noise.*

4 Translate the following examples:

   a rēx, in mediā turbā sedēns, prīncipēs salūtāvit.
   b líbertus, in cubiculum regressus, Memorem excitāre temptāvit.
   c Vilbia fībulam, ā Modestō datam, Rubriae ostendit.
   d sacerdōtēs, deam precātī, agnam sacrificāvērunt.
   e templum, ā Rōmānīs aedificātum, prope fontem sacrum erat.
   f sorōrēs, in tabernā labōrantēs, mīlitem cōnspexērunt.
   g fūr rēs, in fontem iniectās, quaesīvit.
   h nōnnūllae ancillae, ā dominā verberātae, venēnum comparāvērunt.

Pick out the noun and participle pair in each sentence and state whether
the participle is present, perfect passive, or perfect active.

5 Give the case, number, and gender of each noun and participle pair
in paragraph 4.

epistula Cephalī

postquam Cephalus periit, servus eius rēgī epistulam trādidit, ā
Cephalō ipsō scrīptam:
    "rēx Cogidubne, in maximō perīculō es. Memor īnsānit.
mortem tuam cupit. iussit mē rem efficere. invītus Memorī
pāruī. fortasse mihi nōn crēdis. sed tōtam rem tibi nārrāre velim.   5
    "ubi tū ad hās thermās advēnistī, remedium quaerēns, Memor
mē ad vīllam suam arcessīvit. vīllam ingressus, Memorem
perterritum invēnī.
    "'Imperātor mortem Cogidubnī cupit,' inquit. 'iubeō tē hanc
rem administrāre. iubeō tē venēnum parāre. Cogidubnus enim   10
est homō ingeniī prāvī.'
    "Memorī respondī,
    "'longē errās. Cogidubnus est vir ingeniī optimī. tālem rem
facere nōlō.'
    "Memor īrātus,   15
    "'sceleste!' inquit, 'lībertus meus es. mandāta mea facere
dēbēs. cūr mihi obstās?'
    "rēx Cogidubne, diū recūsāvī obstinātus. diū beneficia tua
commemorāvī. tandem Memor custōdem arcessīvit, quī mē
verberāvit. ā custōde paene interfectus, Memorī tandem cessī.   20
    "ad casam meam regressus, venēnum invītus parāvī. scrīpsī
tamen hanc epistulam et servō fidēlī trādidī. iussī servum tibi
epistulam trādere. veniam petō, quamquam facinus scelestum
parāvī. Memor coēgit mē hanc rem efficere. Memorem, nōn mē,
pūnīre dēbēs."   25

īnsānit: īnsānīre
    be crazy, be insane

beneficia: beneficium
    act of kindness, favor

regressus *having returned*

facinus *crime*
coēgit: cōgere *force, compel*

About the language 2: comparison of adverbs

1 Study the following sentences:

   a Loquāx vōcem suāvem habet; **suāviter** cantāre potest.
       *Loquax has a sweet voice; he can sing **sweetly**.*
   b Melissa vōcem suāviōrem habet; **suāvius** cantāre potest.
       *Melissa has a sweeter voice; she can sing **more sweetly**.*
   c Helena vōcem suāvissimam habet; **suāvissimē** cantāre potest.
       *Helena has a very sweet voice; she can sing **very sweetly**.*

   The words in **boldface** above are adverbs. An adverb describes a verb, adjective, or other adverb.

   Study the following patterns:

   Comparative

adjective:	suāvior, suāvior, suāvius	*adverb*:	suāvius
	tardior, tardior, tardius		tardius
	celerior, celerior, celerius		celerius

   Superlative

adjective:	suāvissimus	*adverb*:	suāvissimē
	tardissimus		tardissimē
	celerrimus		celerrimē

2 Study the following sentences:

   a balneum Pompēiānum erat magnum; Quīntum **magnopere** dēlectāvit.
       *The bath at Pompeii was large; it pleased Quintus **a lot**.*
   b balneum Alexandrīnum erat maius; Quīntum **magis** dēlectāvit.
       *The bath at Alexandria was larger; it pleased Quintus **more**.*
   c balneum Britannicum erat maximum; Quīntum **maximē** dēlectāvit.
       *The bath in Britain was the largest; it pleased Quintus **the most**.*

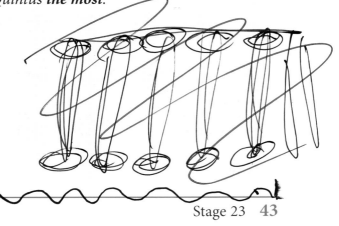

Some adverbs, like their corresponding adjectives, are compared irregularly.

positive	comparative	superlative
magnopere	magis	maximē
greatly	*more*	*most, very greatly*
bene	melius	optimē
well	*better*	*best, very well*
male	peius	pessimē
badly	*worse*	*worst, very badly*
paulum	minus	minimē
little	*less*	*least, very little*
multum	plūs	plūrimum
much	*more*	*most, very much*

For the adjectives corresponding to these adverbs, see page 266 in the Language information.

3 Notice a special meaning for the comparative:

medicus **tardius** advēnit.
*The doctor arrived **too late** (i.e. later than necessary).*

4 Notice the idiomatic use of the superlative with **quam**:

medicus **quam celerrimē** advēnit.
*The doctor arrived **as quickly as possible**.*

5 Translate the following examples:

a āthlēta Canticus celerius quam cēterī cucurrit.
b fūrēs senem facillimē superāvērunt.
c ubi hoc audīvī, magis timēbam.
d mīlitēs, quam fortissimē pugnāte!
e medicus tē melius quam astrologus sānāre potest.
f illī iuvenēs fīliam nostram avidius spectant.
g canis dominum mortuum fidēliter custōdiēbat.
h eī, quī male vīxērunt, male pereunt.

Word patterns: verbs and nouns

1 Study the form and meaning of the following verbs and nouns:

infinitive		perfect passive participle	noun	
pingere	*to paint*	pictus	pictor	*painter*
vincere	*to win*	victus	victor	*winner, victor*
līberāre	*to set free*	līberātus	līberātor	*liberator*

2 Using the pattern in paragraph 1 as a guide, complete the table below:

emere	*to buy*	ēmptus	ēmptor	. . . .
legere	. . . .	lēctus	. . . .	*reader*
spectāre	. . . .	spectātus	. . . .	. . . .

3 What do the following nouns mean?

   dēfēnsor, vēnditor, amātor, saltātor, lēctor, pugnātor

4 Many English nouns ending in **-or** are derived from Latin verbs. Which verbs do the following English nouns come from? Use the Vocabulary to help you if necessary.

   demonstrator, curator, navigator, narrator, tractor, doctor

5 Suggest what the ending **-or** indicates in Latin and English.

Britannia perdomita ^(conquered)

perdomita: perdomitus
conquered

When you have read this story, answer the questions at the end.

Salvius cum Memore anxius colloquium habet. servus ingressus ad Memorem currit.

servus:	domine, rēx Cogidubnus hūc venit. rēx togam splendidam ōrnāmentaque pretiōsa gerit. magnum numerum armātōrum sēcum dūcit.
Memor:	rēx armātōs hūc dūcit?
Salvius:	Cogidubnus, nōs suspicātus, ultiōnem petit. Memor, tibi necesse est mē adiuvāre. nōs enim Rōmānī sumus, Cogidubnus barbarus.
	(intrat Cogidubnus. in manibus epistulam tenet, ā Cephalō scrīptam.) trap prepared
Cogidubnus:	Memor, tū illās īnsidiās parāvistī. ^(you) tū iussistī Cephalum venēnum comparāre et mē necāre. sed Cephalus, lībertus tuus, mihi omnia patefēcit.
Memor:	Cogidubne, id quod dīcis absurdum est. mortuus est Cephalus.
Cogidubnus:	Cephalus homō magnae prūdentiae erat. tibi nōn crēdidit. invītus tibi pāruit. simulac mandāta ista dedistī, scrīpsit Cephalus epistulam in quā omnia patefēcit. servus, ā Cephalō missus, epistulam mihi tulit.
Memor:	epistula falsa est, servus mendācissimus.
Cogidubnus:	tū, nōn servus, es mendāx. servus enim, multa tormenta passus, in eādem sententiā mānsit.
Salvius:	Cogidubne, cūr armātōs hūc dūxistī?
Cogidubnus:	Memorem ē cūrā thermārum iam dēmōvī.
Memor:	quid dīcis? tū mē dēmōvistī? innocēns sum.
Salvius:	rēx Cogidubne, quid fēcistī? tū, quī barbarus es, haruspicem Rōmānum dēmovēre audēs? tū, summōs honōrēs ā nōbīs adeptus, numquam contentus fuistī. nunc perfidiam apertē ostendis. Imperātor Domitiānus, arrogantiam tuam diū passus, ad mē epistulam nūper mīsit. in hāc epistulā iussit mē rēgnum tuum occupāre. iubeō tē igitur ad aulam statim redīre.
Cogidubnus:	ēn iūstitia Rōmāna! ēn fidēs! nūllī perfidiōrēs sunt quam Rōmānī. stultissimus fuī, quod Rōmānīs adhūc crēdidī. nunc, ā Rōmānīs dēceptus, ista ōrnāmenta, mihi ā Rōmānīs data, humī iaciō. Salvī, mitte nūntium ad Domitiānum: "nōs tandem Cogidubnum vīcimus. Britannia perdomita est." *(senex, haec locūtus, lentē per iānuam exit.)*

Line numbers and glosses:

5 — armātōrum: armātī *armed men*

suspicātus *having suspected*
ultiōnem: ultiō *revenge*

10

īnsidiās: īnsidiae *trap, ambush*
patefēcit: patefacere *reveal*

15 — absurdum: absurdus *absurd*

20

falsa: falsus *false, untrue*

tormenta: tormentum *torture*
25 — passus *having suffered*
eādem: īdem *the same*
dēmōvī: dēmovēre *dismiss*

30

perfidiam: perfidia *treachery*
apertē *openly*

rēgnum *kingdom*
occupāre *seize, take over*
35 — ēn iūstitia! *so this is justice!*
fidēs *loyalty, trustworthiness*
perfidiōrēs: perfidus *treacherous, untrustworthy*

40 — adhūc *until now*
iaciō: iacere *throw*
vīcimus: vincere *conquer*

Questions

1. Who is described as **anxius**?
2. Read what the slave says (lines 3–5). How do Memor and Salvius know from this that Cogidubnus' visit is not an ordinary one? Make two different points.
3. What is Salvius' explanation for Cogidubnus' visit (line 7)?
4. Why does Salvius think Memor should help him?
5. What accusation does Cogidubnus make against Memor (lines 12–13)?
6. Why is Memor certain that Cogidubnus is unable to prove his accusation (lines 15–16)?
7. What proof does Cogidubnus have? How did it come into his possession (lines 18–21)?
8. Why is Cogidubnus convinced that the slave is trustworthy?
9. What question does Salvius ask Cogidubnus?
10. Why do you think that he has remained silent up to this point?
11. In line 27, why is Memor upset?
12. In lines 29–31, Salvius accuses Cogidubnus of being ungrateful. What three points does he make?
13. What order does Salvius say he has received? Who has sent it (lines 32–34)?
14. **ista ōrnāmenta … humī iaciō** (lines 38–39). What is Cogidubnus doing when he says these words? Why do you think he does this?
15. How are the attitudes or situations of Memor, Salvius, and Cogidubnus different at the end of this story from what they were at the beginning? Make one point about each character.

Britannia perdomita, *on a Roman coin.*

Practicing the language

1 Complete each sentence with the correct word. Then translate the sentence.

  a nōs ancillae fessae sumus; semper in vīllā . . . . (labōrāmus, labōrātis, labōrant)

  b "quid faciunt illī servī?" "pōcula ad mīlitēs . . . ." (ferimus, fertis, ferunt)

  c fīlius meus vōbīs grātiās agere vult, quod mē . . . . (servāvimus, servāvistis, servāvērunt)

  d quamquam prope āram . . . ., sacrificium vidēre nōn poterāmus. (stābāmus, stābātis, stābant)

  e ubi prīncipēs fontī . . . ., Cephalus prōcessit, pōculum tenēns. (appropinquābāmus, appropinquābātis, appropinquābant)

  f in maximō perīculō estis, quod fīlium rēgis . . . . (interfēcimus, interfēcistis, interfēcērunt)

  g nōs, quī fontem sacrum numquam . . . ., ad thermās cum rēge īre cupiēbāmus. (vīderāmus, vīderātis, vīderant)

  h dominī nostrī sunt benignī; nōbīs semper satis cibī . . . . (praebēmus, praebētis, praebent)

2 Complete each sentence with the most suitable perfect participle from the list below. Then translate the sentence.

  adeptus, locūtus, ingressus, missus, excitātus, superātus

  a Cogidubnus, haec verba . . . ., ab aulā discessit.

  b nūntius, ab amīcīs meīs . . . ., epistulam mihi trādidit.

  c fūr, vīllam . . . ., cautē circumspectāvit.

  d Bulbus, ā Modestō . . . ., sub mēnsā iacēbat.

  e haruspex, ā Cephalō . . . ., ē lectō surrēxit.

  f mīles, amulētum . . . ., in fontem iniēcit.

Roman religious beliefs

Sacrifices and presents to the gods

In our stories Cogidubnus sacrificed a lamb to Sulis Minerva in the hope that the goddess would be pleased with his gift and would restore him to health. This was regarded as the right and proper thing to do in such circumstances. From earliest times the Romans had believed that all things were controlled by **nūmina** (spirits or divinities). The power of numina was seen, for example, in fire or in the changing of the seasons. To ensure that the numina used their power for good rather than harm, the early Romans presented them with offerings of food and wine. After the third century BC, when Roman spirits and agricultural deities were incorporated into the Greek pantheon (system of gods), this idea of a contract between mortals and the gods persisted.

To communicate their wishes to the gods, many Romans presented an animal sacrifice, gave a gift, or accompanied their prayers with promises of offerings if the favors were granted. These promises were known as **vōta**. In this way, they thought, they could keep on good terms with the gods and stand a better chance of having their prayers answered. This was true at all levels of society. For example, if a general was going off to war, there would be a solemn public ceremony at which prayers and expensive sacrifices would be offered to

An emperor, as Chief Priest, leads a solemn procession. He covers his head with a fold of his toga. A bull, a sheep, and a pig are to be sacrificed.

the gods. Ordinary citizens would also offer sacrifices, hoping for a successful business deal, a safe voyage, or the birth of a child; and in many Roman homes, to ensure the family's prosperity, offerings of food would be made to Vesta, the spirit of the hearth, and to the lares and penates, the spirits of the household and food cupboard.

People also offered sacrifices and presents to the gods to honor them at their festivals, to thank them for some success or an escape from danger, or to keep a promise. For example, a cavalry officer stationed in the north of England set up an altar to the god Silvanus with this inscription:

> **C. Tetius Veturius Micianus, captain of the Sebosian cavalry squadron, set this up as he promised to Silvanus the unconquered, in thanks for capturing a beautiful boar, which many people before him tried to do but failed.**

Another inscription from a grateful woman in north Italy reads:

> **Tullia Superiana takes pleasure in keeping her promise to Minerva the unforgetting for giving her her hair back.**

Divination

A haruspex, like Memor, would be present at important sacrifices. He and his assistants would watch the way in which the victim fell; they would observe the smoke and flames when parts of the victim were placed on the altar fire; and, above all, they would cut the victim open and examine its entrails, especially the liver.

Above: *People kept little statues of their favorite gods in their homes, in small shrines. This model reconstructs a domestic shrine of Venus. The pipeclay statuette is original and would have been imported to Britain from Gaul (France).*

A model liver. Significant areas are labeled to help haruspices interpret any markings.

A haruspex examining a sacrificed bull.

They would look for anything unusual about the liver's size or shape, observe its color and texture, and note whether it had spots on its surface. They would then interpret what they saw and announce to the sacrificer whether the signs from the gods were favorable or not.

Such attempts to discover the future were known as divination. Another type of divination was performed by priests known as **augurēs** (augurs), who based their predictions on observations of the flight of birds. They would note the direction of flight and observe whether the birds flew together or separately, what kind of birds they were, and what noises they made.

The Roman state religion

Religion in Rome and Italy included a bewildering variety of gods, demigods, and spirits, and rituals and ceremonies whose origin and meaning were often a mystery to the worshippers themselves. The Roman state respected this variety but particularly promoted the worship of Jupiter and his family of gods and goddesses, especially Juno, Minerva, Ceres, Apollo, Diana, Mars, and Venus. They were closely linked with their equivalent Greek deities, whose characteristics and colorful mythology were readily taken over by the Romans.

A priest's ritual headdress, from Roman Britain.

In this sculpture of a sacrifice, notice the pipe player, and the attendants with the decorated victim.

The rituals and ceremonies were organized by colleges of priests and other religious officials, many of whom were senators, and the festivals and sacrifices were carried out by them on behalf of the state. Salvius, for example, was a member of the Arval Brotherhood, whose religious duties included praying for the emperor and his family. Certain priesthoods were held by women; for instance, many of the cults of Ceres were led by priestesses, while Rufilla was a priestess of the welfare of the emperors. Priestesses called the Vestal Virgins were responsible for keeping alight the flame sacred to Vesta, which was linked to the well-being of Rome. The emperor always held the position of **Pontifex Maximus** or Chief Priest. Great attention was paid to the details of worship. Everyone who watched the ceremonies had to stand quite still and silent, like Plancus in Stage 17. Every word had to be pronounced correctly; otherwise the whole ceremony had to be restarted. A pipe player was employed to drown out noises and cries, which were thought to be unlucky for the ritual.

A Vestal Virgin.

Three sculptures from Bath illustrate the mixture of British and Roman religion there.
Above: *a gilded bronze head of Sulis Minerva, presumably from her statue in the temple, shows the goddess as the Romans pictured her.*
Top right: *three Celtic mother-goddesses.*
Right: *Nemetona and the horned Loucetius Mars.*

Religion and romanization

The Roman state religion played an important part in the romanization of the provinces of the empire. The Romans generally tolerated the religious beliefs and practices of their subject peoples unless they were thought to threaten their rule or their relationship with the gods, which was so carefully fostered by sacrifices and correct rituals. They encouraged their subjects to identify their own gods with Roman gods who shared some of the same characteristics. We have seen at Aquae Sulis how the Celtic Sulis and the Roman Minerva were merged into one goddess, Sulis Minerva, and how a temple in the Roman style was built in her honor.

Another feature of Roman religion which was intended to encourage acceptance of Roman rule was the worship of the emperor, and sometimes certain members of his family such as his wife or sister. In Rome itself, emperor worship was generally discouraged, while the emperor was alive. However, the peoples of the eastern provinces of the Roman empire had always regarded their kings and rulers as divine and were equally ready to pay divine honors to the Roman emperors. Gradually the Romans introduced this idea in the west as well. The Britons and other western peoples were encouraged to worship the **genius** (protecting spirit) of the emperor, linked with the goddess Roma. Altars were erected in honor of "Rome and the emperor." When an emperor died, it was a common practice to deify him (make him a god), and temples were often built to honor the deified emperor. One such temple, that of Claudius in Camulodunum (Colchester), was destroyed, before it was even finished, during the revolt led by Queen Boudica in AD 60. The historian Tacitus tells us that this temple was a blatant stronghold of alien rule, and its observances were a pretext to make the natives appointed as its priests drain the whole country dry.

In general, however, the policy of promoting Roman religion and emperor worship proved successful in the provinces. Like other forms of romanization it became popular with the upper and middle classes, who looked to Rome to promote their careers; it helped to make Roman rule acceptable, reduced the chance of uprisings, and gave many people in the provinces a sense that they belonged to one great empire.

Often people promised to give something to the gods if they answered their prayers. Thus, Censorinus dedicated this thin silver plaque to Mars-Alator, in order to fulfill a vow.

Emperor Augustus as Pontifex Maximus.

Vocabulary checklist 23

cēdō, cēdere, cessī	give in, yield
clārus, clāra, clārum	famous, distinguished
cōnspicātus, cōnspicāta, cōnspicātum	having caught sight of
cūra, cūrae, f.	care
enim	for
gerō, gerere, gessī, gestus	wear
honor, honōris, m.	honor, official position
iaciō, iacere, iēcī, iactus	throw
immōtus, immōta, immōtum	still, motionless
locūtus, locūta, locūtum	having spoken
mandātum, mandātī, n.	instruction, order
modus, modī, m.	manner, way, kind
nimium	too much
ōrnō, ōrnāre, ōrnāvī, ōrnātus	decorate
pāreō, pārēre, pāruī	obey
regressus, regressa, regressum	having returned
scio, scīre, scīvī	know
tālis, tālis, tāle	such
umquam	ever
venēnum, venēnī, n.	poison

This bronze statuette represents a Romano-British worshipper bringing offerings to a god.

FUGA

Stage 24

in itinere

on the Journey

Modestus et Strȳthiō, ex oppidō Aquīs Sūlis ēgressī, Dēvam equitābant. in itinere ad flūmen altum vēnērunt, ubi erat pōns sēmirutus. cum ad pontem vēnissent, equus trānsīre nōluit.

"equus trānsīre timet," inquit Modestus. "Strȳthiō, tū prīmus trānsī!"

cum Strȳthiō trānsiisset, equus trānsīre etiam tum nōlēbat. Modestus igitur ex equō dēscendit. cum dēscendisset, equus statim trānsiit.

"eque! redī!" inquit Modestus. "mē dēseruistī."

equus tamen in alterā rīpā immōtus stetit. Modestus cautissimē trānsīre coepit. cum ad medium pontem vēnissent, dēcidit pōns, dēcidit Modestus. mediīs ex undīs clāmāvit,

"caudicēs, vōs pontem labefēcistis."

Dēvam *to Deva (Roman name of modern Chester)*
altum: altus *deep*
sēmirutus *rickety*
5   **cum** *when*
trānsīre *cross*

10

labefēcistis: labefacere *weaken*

A stretch of Roman road in Britain known as Wade's Causeway. In local legend, Wade was a giant who was said to have built the road by throwing stones at his wife.

Only the lower layers of road remain; the road surface has disappeared over the centuries (see page 66).

Quīntus cōnsilium capit

When you have read this story, answer the questions on the opposite page.

cum Cogidubnus trīstis īrātusque ē vīllā Memoris exiisset, Salvius quīnquāgintā mīlitēs arcessīvit. eōs iussit rēgem prīncipēsque Rēgnēnsium comprehendere et in carcere retinēre. hī mīlitēs, tōtum per oppidum missī, mox eōs invēnērunt. Dumnorix tamen, ē manibus mīlitum noctū ēlāpsus, Quīntum quaesīvit, quod eī crēdēbat.

    cubiculum Quīntī ingressus, haec dīxit:

    "amīce, tibi crēdere possum. adiuvā mē, adiuvā Cogidubnum. paucīs Rōmānīs crēdō; plūrimī sunt perfidī. nēmō quidem perfidior est quam iste Salvius quī Cogidubnum interficere nūper temptāvit. nunc Cogidubnus, ā mīlitibus Salviī comprehēnsus, in carcere iacet. rēx omnīnō dē vītā suā dēspērat.

    "tū tamen es vir summae virtūtis magnaeque prūdentiae. quamquam Salvius potentissimus est, nōlī rēgem, amīcum tuum, dēserere. nōlī eum in carcere inclūsum relinquere. tū anteā eum servāvistī. nōnne iterum servāre potes?"

    cum Dumnorix haec dīxisset, Quīntus rem sēcum anxius cōgitābat. auxilium Cogidubnō ferre volēbat, quod eum valdē dīligēbat; sed rēs difficillima erat. subitō cōnsilium cēpit.

    "nōlī dēspērāre!" inquit. "rēgī auxilium ferre possumus. hanc rem ad lēgātum Gnaeum Iūlium Agricolam clam referre dēbēmus. itaque nōbīs festīnandum est ad ultimās partēs Britanniae ubi Agricola bellum gerit. Agricola sōlus Salviō obstāre potest, quod summam potestātem in Britanniā habet. nunc nōbīs hinc effugiendum est."

    Dumnorix, cum haec audīvisset, cōnsilium audāx magnopere laudāvit. tum Quīntus servum fidēlem arcessīvit, cui mandāta dedit. servus exiit. mox regressus, cibum quīnque diērum Quīntō et Dumnorigī trādidit. illī, ē vīllā ēlāpsī, equōs cōnscendērunt et ad ultimās partēs īnsulae abiērunt.

---

comprehendere *arrest, seize*
carcere: carcer *prison*

5   **ēlāpsus** *having escaped*

quidem *indeed*

omnīnō *completely*

inclūsum: inclūsus
        shut up, imprisoned
sēcum … cōgitābat
        considered … to himself
dīligēbat: dīligere *be fond of*

nōbīs festīnandum est
        we must hurry
ultimās: ultimus *furthest*
bellum gerit: bellum gerere
        wage war, campaign
potestātem: potestās *power*
magnopere *greatly*
diērum: diēs *day*
cōnscendērunt: cōnscendere
        mount, climb on

Questions

1 **quīnquāgintā mīlitēs** (line 2). What orders did Salvius give them?

2 After Dumnorix escaped, why did he seek Quintus? Which Latin word shows why he wasn't seen by the soldiers (lines 5–6)?

3 What did Dumnorix want Quintus to do?

4 What was Dumnorix's opinion of the Romans (line 9)?

5 **nēmō quidem perfidior est quam iste Salvius** (lines 9–10). Why did Dumnorix think this?

6 In lines 13–16, how did Dumnorix try to persuade Quintus? Make three points.

7 Why was Quintus willing to help Cogidubnus? What made him at first hesitate (lines 17–19)?

8 What did Quintus suggest to Dumnorix that they should do to help the king (lines 20–22)?

9 Where was Agricola and what was he doing?

10 Why did Quintus think that Agricola could block Salvius' plans?

11 In the preparations for traveling, what indicates that the journey was likely to be a long one (lines 27–29)?

12 In line 13, Quintus is described as **vir summae virtūtis magnaeque prūdentiae**. To what extent do you think this is a good or bad description? Support your answer with three examples taken from the story.

1   Study the following sentences:

cum Modestus ad pontem **advēnisset**, equus trānsīre nōlēbat.
*When Modestus **had arrived** at the bridge, the horse did not want to cross.*

cum servī omnia **parāvissent**, mercātor amīcōs in triclīnium dūxit.
*When the slaves **had prepared** everything, the merchant led his friends into the dining room.*

The form of the verb in **boldface** is known as the subjunctive.

2   The subjunctive is often used with the word **cum** meaning *when*, as in the examples above.

3   Further examples:

a cum rēx exiisset, Salvius mīlitēs ad sē vocāvit.
b cum gladiātōrēs leōnem interfēcissent, spectātōrēs plausērunt.
c cum dominus haec mandāta dedisset, fabrī ad aulam rediērunt.
d sorōrēs, cum culīnam intrāvissent, pōcula sordida lavāre coepērunt.

4   The examples of the subjunctive in paragraphs 1 and 3 are all in the same tense, the **pluperfect subjunctive**. Compare the 3rd person of the pluperfect subjunctive with the ordinary form (called the indicative) of the pluperfect:

	PLUPERFECT INDICATIVE		PLUPERFECT SUBJUNCTIVE	
	singular	*plural*	*singular*	*plural*
first conjugation	portāverat	portāverant	portāvisset	portāvissent
second conjugation	docuerat	docuerant	docuisset	docuissent
third conjugation	trāxerat	trāxerant	trāxisset	trāxissent
fourth conjugation	dormīverat	dormīverant	dormīvisset	dormīvissent
irregular verbs				
esse (*to be*)	fuerat	fuerant	fuisset	fuissent
velle (*to want*)	voluerat	voluerant	voluisset	voluissent

Salvius cōnsilium cognōscit

postrīdiē, cum Quīntus et Dumnorix ad ultimās partēs īnsulae contenderent, mīlitēs Dumnorigem per oppidum frūstrā quaerēbant. rem dēnique Salviō nūntiāvērunt. ille, cum dē fugā Dumnorigis cognōvisset, vehementer saeviēbat. tum Quīntum quaesīvit; cum eum quoque nusquam invenīre potuisset, Belimicum, prīncipem Canticōrum, arcessīvit.

"Belimice," inquit, "iste Dumnorix ē manibus meīs effūgit; abest quoque Quīntus Caecilius. neque Dumnorigī neque Quīntō crēdō. ī nunc; dūc mīlitēs tēcum; illōs quaere in omnibus partibus oppidī. quaere servōs quoque eōrum. facile est nōbīs servōs torquēre et vērum ita cognōscere."

Belimicus, multīs cum mīlitibus ēgressus, per oppidum dīligenter quaerēbat. intereā Salvius anxius reditum eius exspectābat. cum Salvius rem sēcum cōgitāret, Belimicus subitō rediit exsultāns. servum Quīntī in medium ātrium trāxit.

Salvius ad servum trementem conversus,

"ubi est Quīntus Caecilius?" inquit. "quō fūgit Dumnorix?"

"nesciō," inquit servus quī, multa tormenta passus, vix quicquam dīcere poterat. "nihil sciō," iterum inquit.

Belimicus, cum haec audīvisset, gladium dēstrictum ad iugulum servī tenuit.

"melius est tibi," inquit, "vērum Salviō dīcere."

fugā: fuga *escape*

5 **nusquam** *nowhere*

ī: īre *go*

10

torquēre *torture*

reditum: reditus *return*

15 **exsultāns: exsultāre** *exult, be triumphant*
conversus *having turned*

quicquam *anything*
20 **dēstrictum: dēstringere** *draw*
iugulum *throat*

servus quī iam dē vītā suā dēspērābat,
"cibum quīnque diērum tantum parāvī," inquit susurrāns. "nihil aliud fēcī. dominus meus cum Dumnorige in ultimās partēs Britanniae discessit."

25

Salvius "hercle!" inquit. "ad Agricolam iērunt. Quīntus, ā Dumnorige incitātus, mihi obstāre temptat; homō tamen magnae stultitiae est; mihi resistere nōn potest, quod ego maiōrem auctōritātem habeō quam ille."

30

stultitiae: stultitia *stupidity*

Salvius, cum haec dīxisset, Belimicō mandāta dedit. eum iussit cum trīgintā equitibus exīre et fugitīvōs comprehendere. servum carnificibus trādidit. deinde scrībam arcessīvit cui epistulam dictāvit. ūnum ē servīs suīs iussit hanc epistulam quam celerrimē ad Agricolam ferre.

35

fugitīvōs: fugitīvus *fugitive*
scrībam: scrība *secretary*

intereā Belimicus, Quīntum et Dumnorigem per trēs diēs secūtus, eōs tandem in silvā invēnit. equitēs statim impetum in eōs fēcērunt. amīcī, ab equitibus circumventī, fortiter resistēbant. dēnique Dumnorix humī cecidit mortuus. cum equitēs corpus Dumnorigis īnspicerent, Quīntus, graviter vulnerātus, magnā cum difficultāte effūgit.

40

cecidit: cadere *fall*
corpus *body*

Aerial view of the Roman road followed by Quintus and Dumnorix to Deva.

About the language 2: *cum* and the imperfect subjunctive

1 In this Stage, you have met sentences with **cum** and the pluperfect subjunctive:

> senex, cum pecūniam **invēnisset**, ad vīllam laetus rediit.
> *When the old man **had found** the money, he returned happily to the villa.*

> cum rem **cōnfēcissent**, abiērunt.
> *When they **had finished** the job, they went away.*

2 Now study the following examples:

> cum custōdēs **dormīrent**, fūrēs ē carcere effūgērunt.
> *When the guards **were sleeping**, the thieves escaped from the prison.*

> Modestus, cum in Britanniā **mīlitāret**, multās puellās amābat.
> *When Modestus **was serving in the army** in Britain, he loved many girls.*

In these sentences, **cum** is being used with a different tense of the subjunctive, the **imperfect subjunctive**.

3 Further examples:

a cum hospitēs cēnam cōnsūmerent, fūr cubiculum intrāvit.
b cum prīnceps rem cōgitāret, nūntiī subitō revēnērunt.
c iuvenēs, cum bēstiās agitārent, mīlitem vulnerātum cōnspexērunt.
d puella, cum epistulam scrīberet, sonitum mīrābilem audīvit.

4 Compare the 3rd person of the imperfect subjunctive with the infinitive:

	INFINITIVE	IMPERFECT SUBJUNCTIVE	
		singular	*plural*
first conjugation	portāre	portāret	portārent
second conjugation	docēre	docēret	docērent
third conjugation	trahere	traheret	traherent
fourth conjugation	audīre	audīret	audīrent
irregular verbs			
	esse	esset	essent
	velle	vellet	vellent

Word patterns: antonyms

1 You have already met the following antonyms:

volō	*I want*	nōlō	*I do not want*
scio	*I know*	nescio	*I do not know*

Study the words in the left column and find their antonyms on the right. Then fill in their meanings.

a	umquam	*ever*	nefās	. . . .
b	homō	*man*	nusquam	. . . .
c	usquam	*anywhere*	negōtium	. . . .
d	ōtium	*leisure*	numquam	. . . .
e	fās	*morally right*	nēmō	. . . .

2 Study these further ways of forming antonyms and give the meanings of the words on the right:

a	patiēns	*patient*	impatiēns	. . . .
b	ūtilis	*useful*	inūtilis	. . . .
c	nocēns	*guilty*	innocēns	. . . .
d	cōnsentīre	*to agree*	dissentīre	. . . .
e	facilis	*easy*	difficilis	. . . .
f	similis	*similar*	dissimilis	. . . .

3 From the box choose the correct Latin words to translate the words in **boldface** in the following sentences:

sānus	fēlīx	indignus	inimīcus
dignus	īnsānus	amīcus	īnfēlīx

a Entering a room right foot first was thought to be **lucky** but a stumble was **unlucky**.
b Bulbus must be **crazy** to love Vilbia.
c Strythio is the **friend** of Modestus, but Bulbus is his **enemy**.
d I am **worthy** of Vilbia's love; Modestus is **unworthy**.

4 Work out the meanings of the following words:

immōtus, incertus, dissuādeō, incrēdibilis, inīquus, ignōtus, neglegō, ingrātus.

Practicing the language

1 Complete each sentence with the correct form of the adjective. Then translate the sentence.

    a medicus puellae . . . . pōculum dedit. (aegram, aegrae)
    b hospitēs coquum . . . . laudāvērunt. (callidum, callidō)
    c faber mercātōrī . . . . dēnāriōs reddidit. (īrātum, īrātō)
    d ancillae dominō . . . . pārēre nōlēbant. (crūdēlem, crūdēlī)
    e centuriō mīlitēs . . . . vituperābat. (ignāvōs, ignāvīs)
    f puer stultus nautīs . . . . crēdidit. (mendācēs, mendācibus)
    g stolās . . . . emēbat fēmina. (novās, novīs)
    h . . . . amīcīs pecūniam obtulī. (omnēs, omnibus)

2 With the help of paragraph 4 on page 272 in the Language information section, replace the words in **boldface** with the correct form of the pronoun **is**. Then translate the sentence. For example:

    Rūfilla in hortō ambulābat. Quīntus **Rūfillam** salūtāvit.
    This becomes:
    Rūfilla in hortō ambulābat. Quīntus **eam** salūtāvit.
    *Rufilla was walking in the garden. Quintus greeted **her**.*

In sentences **g** and **h**, you may need to look up the gender of a noun in the Vocabulary at the end of the book.

    a Quīntus mox ad aulam advēnit. ancilla **Quīntum** in ātrium dūxit.
    b Salvius in lectō recumbēbat. puer **Salviō** plūs cibī obtulit.
    c Rūfilla laetissima erat; marītus **Rūfillae** tamen nōn erat contentus.
    d Britannī ferōciter pugnāvērunt, sed Rōmānī tandem **Britannōs** vīcērunt.
    e barbarī impetum in nōs fēcērunt. **barbarīs** autem restitimus.
    f multae fēminae prō templō conveniēbant. līberī **fēminārum** quoque aderant.
    g prope templum est fōns sacer; **fontem** saepe vīsitāvī.
    h in oppidō Aquīs Sūlis erant thermae maximae; architectus Rōmānus **thermās** exstrūxit.

Travel and communication

Judged by modern standards, traveling in the Roman world was neither easy nor comfortable; nevertheless, people traveled extensively and there was much movement of goods throughout the provinces of the empire. This was made possible by a great network of straight, well-surfaced roads – estimated at 56,000 miles (92,000 kilometers) at the peak of the empire – which covered the Roman world using the shortest possible routes. The roads, with tunnels and bridges as necessary, crossed plains, forests, mountains, rivers, valleys, marshes, and deserts.

A Roman road was laid out by military surveyors who used a **grōma** to achieve a straight line. Where trees or hills were in the way, the surveyors took sightings from high points using smoke from fires to ensure that each section of road took the shortest practical route between the points. River valleys and impassable mountains forced the surveyors to make diversions, but once past the obstructions, the roads usually continued along their original line.

Vitruvius, a Roman architect and engineer, gives us a description of roadbuilding which utilizes local resources and adjusts to local terrain. After the line was chosen, a cut was made the width of the planned road and deep enough to hold the filling. If the earth was soft at that depth, piles were driven in to strengthen it. On this base the road was built up in four layers up to 5 feet (1.5 meters) thick and between 6 and 20 feet (2 and 6 meters) wide. At the bottom was a footing of large stones. This was covered with a layer of smaller stones, concrete, or rubble, and then a layer of rolled sand concrete. The surface or **pavīmentum** was made of local materials, usually large, flat paving stones dressed on the top side. This final surface was curved or "cambered" to provide effective drainage. The Romans liked to raise their roadways on an embankment of earth, called

Rubble layer and curbstones in northern Britain (see page 57).

Road surface with large flat stones on the Appian Way in Italy.

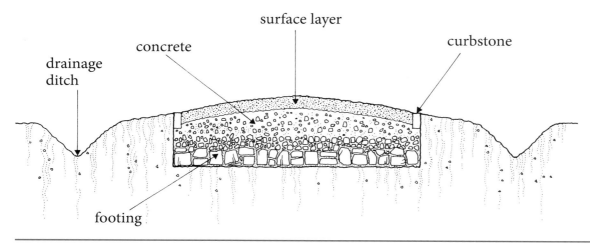

drainage ditch

concrete

surface layer

curbstone

footing

an **agger**, which was raised about 3 feet (1 meter) both to aid drainage and to give marching troops a good view of the territory. Ditches on either side of the agger also provided drainage.

Roman roadbuilding was generally carried out with great skill and thoroughness: a fully paved Roman road lasted 80–100 years before it had to be renewed. The roads were so well made that some are still in use today. Many modern roads in Europe still follow the Roman routes and these can be seen very clearly on maps. Only in the last hundred years, with the advent of heavy vehicle traffic, have nations begun to return to roadbuilding methods like those used by the Romans.

The roads' original purpose was to allow rapid movement of Roman troops and supplies and so ensure military control of the provinces. However, roads were a vital part of the empire, since

Three forms of transport: a light carriage with two horses, passing a milestone; an enclosed coach of the Imperial Post with seating inside and on top, drawn by two mules; and an agricultural wagon carrying a skin full of wine, drawn by two eager oxen.

they extended the civilization as well as the power of Rome. Government correspondence and government officials made use of a system known as the Imperial Post (**cursus pūblicus**). A government warrant (**diplōma**) indicated that the bearer was on official business and was entitled to secure fresh horses at posting stations (**mutātiōnēs**), and to stay at the resthouses (**mansiōnēs**) which were situated at frequent intervals along all main roads. It has been estimated that an official courier could average 50 miles (80 kilometers) a day; in an emergency, by traveling night and day, he could triple this distance. Private letters, either carried by a person's own slave or sent with a traveler, took much longer but even so letters came and went in all directions.

A traveler in a hooded cloak, from a relief. An inscription found with it shows that he is paying the innkeeper's wife for a meal for himself and his mule.

Travelers walked, used carriages or carts, or rode, generally on mules or ponies. Horses were ridden mainly by cavalrymen or government officials. Journey times were affected by many factors, such as the freshness of animals and travelers, the time of year, and the gradients of the road. In good conditions a traveler might cover 20 miles (32 kilometers) on foot, 25–30 miles (40–48 kilometers) by carriage, perhaps a little more by mule.

Wealthy travelers would make arrangements, wherever possible, to break long journeys by staying at their family houses or with friends, acquaintances, even business associates. Ordinary travelers, however, with no estates, wealthy friends, or letters of introduction, would have to stay at roadside inns, where they were at the mercy of the **caupōnēs** (innkeepers), who were often dishonest. The inns were, for the most part, small, dirty, and uncomfortable and were frequented by thieves, prostitutes, and drunks. The Roman poet Horace, traveling on the Appian Way from Rome to Brundisium, writes of the "wicked innkeepers" and Pliny complains of the bedbugs. The graffiti found on the walls also testify to a lower-class clientele: "Innkeeper, I urinated in the bed. Want to know why? There was no mattress!" It is no wonder that respectable travelers tried to avoid such inns.

Travelers, both military and civilian, could also use flat-bottomed river and canal barges for transportation. Some of these barges had oars but most, especially when going upstream, were propelled by men or mules hauling towropes along towpaths. In an effort to avoid the unsavory people and inns one night, Horace and his traveling party boarded a canal barge, arranging to be towed to their next major stop while they slept. Imagine their disgust to awake the next morning at the same dock with the mule unhitched and the shiftless sailors snoring!

Traveling by sea was generally more popular, although it was restricted to the sailing season (March to November) and was subject to danger from pirates, storms, and shipwrecks. Most sea journeys were undertaken on merchant ships; passenger shipping as we know it did not exist, except for the occasional ferry. A traveler would have to wait until a merchant ship was about to put to sea and bargain with the captain for an acceptable fare.

The ship would not set sail until the winds were favorable and an animal had been sacrificed to the gods. There were also certain days which were considered unlucky, rather like our Friday the 13th, when no ship would leave port. When at last all was ready, the passenger would come on board with his slaves, bringing enough food and wine to last them until the next port of call. No cabins were provided, except for the very wealthy, and passengers would sleep on deck, perhaps in a small portable shelter, which would be taken down during the day.

When the ship came safely to port, the captain would thank the gods. Then a tugboat, manned by rowers, would tow the ship to her berth at the dockside.

A tugboat.

A merchant ship in a harbor. On the left is a lighthouse approached by a causeway. The stern of the ship can be seen, with a carved swan's head, one of the large oars used for steering, and a small shelter to the left of the sail.

Vocabulary checklist 24

auctōritās, auctōritātis, f.	*authority*
audāx, audāx, audāx, *gen.* audācis	*bold, daring*
carcer, carceris, m.	*prison*
comprehendō, comprehendere, comprehendī, comprehēnsus	*arrest, seize*
cum	*when*
dēserō, dēserere, dēseruī, dēsertus	*desert*
ēgressus, ēgressa, ēgressum	*having gone out*
eques, equitis, m.	*horseman*
flūmen, flūminis, n.	*river*
humī	*on the ground*
intereā	*meanwhile*
maximē	*very greatly, most of all*
neque ... neque	*neither ... nor*
oppugnō, oppugnāre, oppugnāvī, oppugnātus	*attack*
passus, passa, passum	*having suffered*
patefaciō, patefacere, patefēcī, patefactus	*reveal*
pōns, pontis, m.	*bridge*
trānseō, trānsīre, trānsiī	*cross*
trīstis, trīstis, trīste	*sad*
vērum, vērī, n.	*the truth*

A Roman milestone.

MILITES

Stage 25

Dēvae

1   mīles legiōnis secundae per castra ambulābat. subitō
    iuvenem ignōtum prope horreum latentem cōnspexit.
        "heus tū," clāmāvit mīles, "quis es?"
        iuvenis nihil respondit. mīles iuvenem iterum rogāvit quis
    esset. iuvenis fūgit.

2   mīles iuvenem petīvit et facile superāvit.
        "furcifer!" exclāmāvit. "quid prope horreum facis?"
        iuvenis dīcere nōlēbat quid prope horreum faceret. mīles
    eum ad centuriōnem dūxit.

3   centuriō, iuvenem cōnspicātus,
        "hunc agnōscō!" inquit. "explōrātor Britannicus est, quem
saepe prope castra cōnspexī. quō modō eum cēpistī?"
        tum mīles explicāvit quō modō iuvenem cēpisset.

4   centuriō, ad iuvenem conversus,
        "cūr in castra vēnistī?" rogāvit.
        iuvenis tamen tacēbat. centuriō, ubi cognōscere nōn
poterat cūr iuvenis in castra vēnisset, mīlitem iussit eum ad
carcerem dūcere.

        iuvenis, postquam verba centuriōnis audīvit,
        "ego sum Vercobrix," inquit, "fīlius prīncipis
Deceanglōrum. vōbīs nōn decōrum est mē in carcere tenēre."
        "fīlius prīncipis Deceanglōrum?" exclāmāvit centuriō.
"libentissimē tē videō. nōs tē diū quaerimus, cellamque
optimam tibi in carcere parāvimus."

Strӯthiō

optiō per castra ambulat. Strӯthiōnem, iam Dēvam regressum, cōnspicit.

optiō: heus Strӯthiō! hūc venī! tibi aliquid dīcere volō.

Strӯthiō: nōlī mē vexāre! occupātus sum. Modestum quaerō, quod puella eum exspectat.

optiō: mī Strӯthiō, quamquam occupātissimus es, dēbēs maximā cum dīligentiā mē audīre. centuriō tē iubet ad carcerem statim festīnāre.

Strӯthiō: īnsānit centuriō! innocēns sum.

optiō: tacē! centuriō Modestum quoque iussit ad carcerem festīnāre.

Strӯthiō: deōs testēs faciō. innocentēs sumus. nūllum facinus commīsimus.

optiō: caudex! tacē! centuriō vōs ambōs carcerem custōdīre iussit.

Strӯthiō: nōlī mē vituperāre! rem nunc intellegō! centuriō nōs vult custōdēs carceris esse. decōrum est centuriōnī nōs ēligere, quod fortissimī sumus.

optiō: *(susurrāns)* difficile est mihi hoc crēdere.

Strӯthiō: quid dīcis?

optiō: quamquam fortissimī estis, dīligentiam quoque maximam praestāre dēbētis. nam inter captīvōs est Vercobrix, iuvenis magnae dignitātis, cuius pater est prīnceps Deceanglōrum. necesse est vōbīs Vercobrigem dīligentissimē custōdīre.

Strӯthiō: nōlī anxius esse, mī optiō. nōbīs nihil difficile est, quod fortissimī sumus, ut anteā dīxī. ego et Modestus, cum in Āfricā mīlitārēmus, nōn ūnum hominem, sed tōtam prōvinciam custōdiēbāmus.

exeunt. optiō centuriōnem quaerit, Strӯthiō amīcum.

optiō *optio (military officer, ranking below centurion)*
castra *military camp*
commīsimus: committere *commit*
ambōs: ambō *both*
praestāre *show, display*
captīvōs: captīvus *prisoner, captive*
cuius *whose (genitive of* **quī***)*
prōvinciam: prōvincia *province*

Legionary helmet from the river Thames, with shield boss from the Eighth Legion, found in the river Tyne.

Modestus custōs

Modestus et Strȳthiō, carcerem ingressī, cellās in quibus captīvī
erant īnspiciēbant. habēbat Strȳthiō tabulam in quā nōmina
captīvōrum scrīpta erant. Modestus eum rogāvit in quā cellā
Vercobrix inclūsus esset. Strȳthiō, tabulam īnspiciēns, cognōvit
ubi Vercobrix iacēret, et Modestum ad cellam dūxit. Modestus,
cum ad portam cellae advēnisset, incertus cōnstitit.

Strȳthiō "cūr cellam intrāre timēs?" inquit. "vīnctus est fīlius
prīncipis Deceanglōrum. tē laedere nōn potest."

cum Strȳthiō haec dīxisset, Modestus īrātus exclāmāvit,
"caudex, prīncipis fīlium nōn timeō, cōnstitī quod tē
exspectābam. volō tē mihi portam aperīre." stop

cum portam Strȳthiō aperuisset, Modestus rūrsus haesitāvit.
"obscūra est cella," inquit Modestus anxius, "fer mihi
lucernam."

Strȳthiō, vir summae patientiae, lucernam tulit amīcōque
trādidit. ille, cellam ingressus, ē cōnspectū discessit.

in angulō cellae iacēbat Vercobrix. Modestus, cum eum
vīdisset, gladium dēstrīnxit. tum, ad mediam cellam prōgressus,
Vercobrigem vituperāre coepit. Vercobrix tamen contumēliās
Modestī audīre nōn poterat, quod graviter dormiēbat.

subitō arānea, ē tēctō cellae lāpsa, in nāsum Modestī incidit et
trāns ōs cucurrit. Modestus, ab arāneā territus, ē cellā fūgit,
vehementer clāmāns.

Strȳthiō, quī extrā cellam stābat, attonitus erat. nesciēbat
enim cūr Modestus clāmāret.

"Strȳthiō! Strȳthiō!" clāmāvit Modestus. "claude portam
cellae. nōbīs necesse est summā cum dīligentiā Vercobrigem
custōdīre. etiam arāneae eum adiuvant!"

Strȳthiō, cum portam clausisset, Modestum territum rogāvit
quid accidisset.

"Modeste," inquit, "quam pallidus es! num captīvum timēs?"

"minimē! pallidus sum, quod nōn cēnāvī," respondit.

"vīsne mē ad culīnam īre et tibi cēnam ferre?" rogāvit Strȳthiō.

"optimum cōnsilium est!" inquit alter. "tū tamen hīc manē.
melius est mihi ipsī ad culīnam īre, quod coquus decem dēnāriōs
mihi dēbet."

haec locūtus, ad culīnam statim cucurrit.

cellās: cella *cell*

incertus *uncertain*
cōnstitit: cōnsistere *halt, stop*
vīnctus: vincīre *bind, tie up*

haesitāvit: haesitāre *hesitate*
obscūra: obscūrus *dark, gloomy*
lucernam: lucerna *lamp*
patientiae: patientia *patience*
cōnspectū: cōnspectus *sight*
angulō: angulus *corner*
prōgressus *having advanced*
contumēliās: contumēlia
insult, abuse
arānea *spider*
tēctō: tēctum *ceiling, roof*
lāpsa: lāpsus *having fallen*
trāns *across*
ōs *face*

pallidus *pale*

hīc *here*

About the language 1: indirect questions

1 In Unit 1, you met sentences like this:

"quis clāmōrem audīvit?"   "ubi habitat rēx?"
"Who heard the shout?"   *"Where does the king live?"*

In each example, a question is being asked. These examples are known as **direct questions**.

2 In Stage 25, you have met sentences like this:

centuriō nesciēbat **quis clāmōrem audīvisset**.
*The centurion did not know **who had heard the shout**.*

equitēs cognōvērunt **ubi rēx habitāret**.
*The horsemen found out **where the king was living**.*

In each of these examples, the question is *referred to*, but not asked directly. These examples are known as **indirect questions**. The verb in an indirect question in Latin is subjunctive.

3 Compare the following examples:

direct questions	*indirect questions*
"quid Vercobrix fēcit?"	mīlitēs intellēxērunt quid Vercobrix fēcisset.
"What has Vercobrix done?"	*The soldiers understood what Vercobrix had done.*
"quis appropinquat?"	custōs nesciēbat quis appropinquāret.
"Who is approaching?"	*The guard did not know who was approaching.*
"ubi sunt barbarī?"	Rōmānī cognōvērunt ubi barbarī essent.
"Where are the barbarians?"	*The Romans found out where the barbarians were.*

4 Further examples of direct and indirect questions:

a "quis puerum interfēcit?"
b nēmō sciēbat quis puerum interfēcisset.
c "ubi pecūniam invēnērunt?"
d iūdex mē rogāvit ubi pecūniam invēnissent.
e Salvius nesciēbat cūr Quīntus rēgem adiuvāret.
f Cogidubnus cognōvit quō modō Cephalus venēnum comparāvisset.
g Quīntus scīre voluit quid in templō esset.
h Salvius tandem intellēxit quō Quīntus et Dumnorix fugerent.

In each of the *indirect* questions state whether the subjunctive is imperfect or pluperfect.

Modestus perfuga

perfuga *deserter*

I

Modestus, ēgressus ē culīnā ubi cēnam optimam cōnsūmpserat,
ad carcerem lentē redībat.

    ubi carcerī appropinquāvit, portam apertam vīdit. permōtus,

    "dī immortālēs!" inquit. "Strȳthiō, num portam carceris
apertam relīquistī? nēminem neglegentiōrem quam tē nōvī."   5

    carcerem ingressus, portās omnium cellārum apertās invēnit.
cum hoc vīdisset,

    "ēheu!" inquit. "omnēs portae apertae sunt! captīvī, ē cellīs
ēlāpsī, omnēs fūgērunt!"

    Modestus rem anxius cōgitāvit. nesciēbat enim quō captīvī   10
fūgissent; intellegere nōn poterat cūr Strȳthiō abesset.

    "quid facere dēbeō? perīculōsum est hīc manēre ubi mē
centuriō invenīre potest. mihi fugiendum est. ō Strȳthiō,
Strȳthiō! coēgistī mē statiōnem dēserere. mē perfugam fēcistī.
sed deōs testēs faciō. invītus statiōnem dēserō."   15

permōtus *alarmed, disturbed*

mihi fugiendum est *I must flee*

statiōnem: statiō *post*

II

Modestus, haec locūtus, subitō sonitum audīvit. aliquis portam
cellae Vercobrigis aperīre et exīre temptābat!

    "mihi ē carcere fugiendum est," aliquis ē cellā clāmāvit.

    Modestus, cum haec audīvisset, ad portam cellae cucurrit et
clausit.   5

    "Vercobrix, tibi in cellā manendum est!" clāmāvit Modestus.
"euge! nōn effūgit Vercobrix! eum captīvum habeō! euge! nunc
mihi centuriō nocēre nōn potest, quod captīvum summae
dignitātis in carcere retinuī."

    Modestus autem anxius manēbat; nesciēbat enim quid   10
Strȳthiōnī accidisset. subitō pugiōnem humī relictum cōnspexit.

    "heus, quid est? hunc pugiōnem agnōscō! est pugiō
Strȳthiōnis! Strȳthiōnī dedī, ubi diem nātālem celebrābat. ēheu!
cruentus est pugiō. ō mī Strȳthiō! nunc rem intellegō. mortuus
es! captīvī, ē cellīs ēlāpsī, tē necāvērunt. ēheu! cum ego tuam   15
cēnam in culīnā cōnsūmerem, illī tēcum pugnābant! ō Strȳthiō!
nēmō īnfēlīcior est quam ego. nam tē amābam sīcut pater fīlium.
Vercobrix, quī in hāc cellā etiam nunc manet, poenās dare dēbet.
heus! Vercobrix, mē audī! tibi moriendum est, quod Strȳthiō
meus mortuus est."   20

Marginal glosses:
aliquis *someone*
nocēre *harm*
relictum: relinquere *leave*
cruentus *bloodstained*
tibi moriendum est *you must die*

III

Modestus in cellam furēns irrumpit. captīvum, quī intus latet,
verberāre incipit.

captīvus: Modeste! mī Modeste! dēsine mē verberāre! nōnne
              mē agnōscis? Strȳthiō sum, quem tū amās sīcut pater
              fīlium.   5

Modestus: Strȳthiō? Strȳthiō! num vīvus es? cūr vīvus es?
              sceleste! furcifer! ubi sunt captīvī quōs custōdiēbās?

Strȳthiō: fūgērunt, Modeste. mē dēcēpērunt. coēgērunt mē
              portās omnium cellārum aperīre.

Modestus: ēheu! quid facere dēbēmus?   10

Strȳthiō: nōbīs statim ē carcere fugiendum est; centuriōnem
              appropinquantem audiō.

Modestus: ō Strȳthiō! ō, quam īnfēlīx sum!

amīcī ē carcere quam celerrimē fugiunt.

Marginal gloss:
vīvus *alive, living*

About the language 2: more about the imperfect and pluperfect subjunctive

1 In Stages 24 and 25, you have met the 3rd person singular and plural ("he," "she," "it," and "they") of the imperfect and pluperfect subjunctive. For example:

> nēmō sciēbat ubi Britannī **latērent**.
> *Nobody knew where the Britons were lying hidden.*

> centuriō, cum hoc **audīvisset**, saeviēbat.
> *When the centurion had heard this, he was furious.*

2 Now study the forms of the 1st person ("I," "we") and the 2nd person ("you") of the imperfect and pluperfect subjunctive.

SINGULAR	IMPERFECT	PLUPERFECT
1st person	portārem	portāvissem
2nd person	portārēs	portāvissēs
3rd person	portāret	portāvisset

PLURAL		
1st person	portārēmus	portāvissēmus
2nd person	portārētis	portāvissētis
3rd person	portārent	portāvissent

3 Translate the following examples:

a custōdēs nōs rogāvērunt cūr clāmārēmus.
b nesciēbam quō fūgissēs.
c cum in Britanniā mīlitārem, oppidum Aquās Sūlis saepe vīsitāvī.
d cum cēnam tuam cōnsūmerēs, centuriō tē quaerēbat.
e rēx nōbīs explicāvit quō modō vītam suam servāvissētis.
f cum nōmina recitāvissem, hospitēs ad rēgem dūxī.
g amīcus meus cognōscere voluit ubi habitārētis.
h puella nōs rogāvit cūr rem tam difficilem suscēpissēmus.

In each sentence state whether the subjunctive is 1st or 2nd person singular or plural and whether it is imperfect or pluperfect.

Word patterns: male and female

1   Study the following nouns:

   dominus, leaena, dea, domina, fīlia, captīvus, fīlius, captīva, leō, deus.

   Organize these nouns in pairs and write them out in two columns headed *male* and *female*.

2   Add the following nouns to your columns. Some meanings are given to help you.

   saltātrīx (*dancing girl*), vēnātor (*hunter*), avus (*grandfather*), vēnātrīx, victor, avia, victrīx, ursus (*bear*), lupa (*she-wolf*), lupus, ursa, saltātor

3   Which two endings here indicate the masculine form of a Latin noun? What are the feminine equivalents for those two endings?

Practicing the language

1   This exercise is based on the story **Modestus custōs** on page 75. Read the story again. Complete each of the sentences below with one of the following groups of words. Then translate the sentence. Use each group of words once only.

   cum Modestus extrā cellam haesitāret
   cum Modestus ad culīnam abiisset
   cum carcerem intrāvissent
   cum arānea in nāsum dēcidisset
   cum lucernam tulisset
   cum Modestus vehementer clāmāret

   a   Modestus et Strȳthiō, ..., cellās captīvōrum īnspiciēbant.
   b   . . . ., Strȳthiō eum rogāvit cūr timēret.
   c   Strȳthiō, ..., Modestō trādidit.
   d   . . . ., Vercobrix graviter dormiēbat.
   e   . . . ., Modestus fūgit perterritus.
   f   . . . ., Strȳthiō in carcere mānsit.

2 Complete each sentence with the correct participle from the list below. Then translate the sentence.

> missōs, līberātī, territa, regressam, tenentēs, passus

a captīvī, ē cellīs subitō . . . . , ad portam carceris ruērunt.
b Britannī, hastās in manibus . . . . , castra oppugnāvērunt.
c ancilla, ā dominō īrātō . . . . , respondēre nōn audēbat.
d Cogidubnus, tot iniūriās . . . . , Rōmānōs vehementer vituperāvit.
e māter puellam, ē tabernā tandem . . . . , pūnīvit.
f centuriō mīlitēs, ex Ītaliā nūper ab Imperātōre . . . . , īnspexit.

3 Translate each English sentence into Latin by selecting correctly from the list of Latin words.

a *The kind citizens had provided help.*
| cīvis | benignī | auxilium | praebuērunt |
| cīvēs | benignōs | auxiliī | praebuerant |

b *They arrested the soldier in the kitchen of an inn.*
| mīlitem | per culīnam | tabernae | comprehendunt |
| mīlitis | in culīnā | tabernārum | comprehendērunt |

c *Master! Read this letter!*
| domine | haec | epistula | lege |
| dominus | hanc | epistulam | legis |

d *The words of the soothsayer frightened him.*
| verbum | haruspicis | eum | terruit |
| verba | haruspicī | eōs | terruērunt |

e *The old men departed, praising the brave messenger.*
| senēs | discēdunt | fortem | nūntium | laudāns |
| senum | discessērunt | fortī | nūntiōs | laudantēs |

f *How can we avoid the punishments of the gods?*
| quō modō | poenae | deōrum | vītantēs | possumus |
| quis | poenās | deīs | vītāre | poterāmus |

The legionary soldier

The soldiers who served in the legions formed the elite of the Roman army (**exercitus**). Each soldier (**mīles**) was a Roman citizen and full-time professional who had signed on for twenty-five years. Roman soldiers were highly trained in the skills of infantry warfare and were often specialists in other fields as well. In fact a Roman legion, consisting normally of about 5,000 foot soldiers, was a miniature army in itself, capable of constructing forts and camps, manufacturing its weapons and equipment, and building roads. On its staff were engineers, architects, carpenters, smiths, doctors, medical orderlies, clerks, and accountants.

Building camps and erecting bridges were among the skills required of the army. In this picture, auxiliary soldiers stand guard while soldiers from the legions do engineering work.

Recruitment

An investigating board (**inquīsītiō**) would first ensure that a new recruit was a Roman citizen and that he was given a medical examination. Vegetius, who wrote a military manual in the fourth century AD, laid down guidelines for choosing recruits:

> **A young soldier should have alert eyes and should hold his head upright. The recruit should be broad-chested with powerful shoulders and brawny arms. His fingers should be long rather than short. He should**

not be pot-bellied or have a fat bottom. His calves and feet should not be flabby; instead they should be made entirely of tough sinew. Smiths, carpenters, butchers, and hunters of deer and wild boar are the most suitable kind of recruit. The whole well-being of the Roman state depends on the kind of recruits you choose; so you must choose men who are outstanding not only in body but also in mind.

Training, armor, and weapons

After being accepted and sworn in, the new recruit was sent to his unit to begin training. This was thorough, systematic, and physically hard. First the young soldier had to learn to march at the regulation pace for distances of up to 24 Roman miles (about 22 statute miles or 35 kilometers). Physical fitness was further developed by running, jumping, swimming, and carrying heavy packs. Next came weapons training, starting with a wooden practice-sword, wicker shield, and dummy targets and progressing to actual equipment. Vegetius again:

> They are also taught not to cut with their swords but to thrust. The Romans find it so easy to defeat people who use their swords to cut rather than thrust that they laugh in their faces. For a cutting stroke, even when made with full force, rarely kills. The vital organs are protected by the armor as well as by the bones of the body. On the other hand, a stab even two inches deep is usually fatal.

Besides the short stabbing sword (**gladius**) worn on the right, the legionary was armed with a dagger (**pugiō**) worn on the left, and a javelin (**pīlum**). The legionary shield (**scūtum**) was a 3-foot-long (1 meter), curved rectangle made of strips of wood glued together and covered with hide. Soldiers learned to handle their shields correctly and to attack dummy targets with the point of their swords.

Another phase of weapons training was to learn to throw the pilum. This had a wooden shaft 5 feet (1.5 meters) long and a pointed iron head of 2 feet (60 centimeters). The head was cleverly constructed so that the first 10 inches (25 centimeters) of tempered metal penetrated the target, but the rest, untempered, was fairly soft and liable to bend. When the javelin was hurled at an enemy, from a distance of 25–30 yards (23–28 meters), its point penetrated and stuck into his shield, while the neck of the metal head bent and the shaft hung down. This not only made

A centurion, a legionary, and the aquilifer (eagle-bearer) of the legion.

the javelin unusable, so that it could not be thrown back, but also made the encumbered shield so difficult to manage that the enemy might have to abandon it altogether.

By the time of our stories, the legionary soldier was wearing segmented armor of metal strips (**lōrīca segmentāta**) with leather straps and buckle fastenings over a woolen tunic. The military belt (**cingulum**) was worn at all times, even without the armor. At first the Roman soldier did not wear trousers, but short leggings were gradually adopted. The legionary helmet was padded on the inside and designed to protect the head, face, and neck without obstructing hearing or vision. Strong military sandals (**caligae**) with very thick soles and iron hobnails were designed to withstand weight and miles of marching.

When the recruit could handle his weapons competently and was physically fit, he was ready to leave the barracks for training in the open countryside. This began with route marches on which he carried not only his body armor and weapons but also a heavy pack which weighed about 90 pounds (40 kilograms), and which included dishes, water bottle, woolen cloak, several days' ration of food, and equipment for making an overnight camp, such as a saw, an axe, and a basket for moving earth. Much importance was attached to the proper construction of the camp at the end of the day's march, and the young soldier was given careful instruction and practice. Several practice camps and forts have been found in Britain.

Soldiers marching with their equipment slung from stakes.

Life and work of a soldier

The fully trained legionary did not spend all or even much of his time on combat duty. Most of it was spent on peacetime duties, such as building or roadmaking, and he was given free time and leave. During the first century AD at least, he had good prospects of surviving until his term of service expired. He was generally stationed in a large legionary fortress somewhere near the frontiers of the empire in places such as Deva (Chester), Eboracum (York), Bonna (Bonn), and Vindobona (Vienna) which were key points in the Roman defenses against the barbarians.

A carving of a legionary soldier, employed on harvesting duties.

Many of the daily duties and activities were the same wherever the soldier was stationed. Inscriptional evidence gives us insights into the everyday life of a soldier. A duty roster, written on papyrus and covering the first ten days in October possibly in the year AD 87, lists the names of thirty-six soldiers in the same unit in a legion stationed in Egypt. C. Julius Valens, for example, was to spend October 2nd on guard duty, October 5th and 6th in the armory, and October 7th in the bathhouse, probably stoking the furnace.

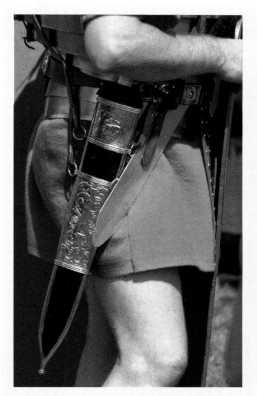

*The Ermine Street Guard demonstrating legionaries'
training. Clockwise from top left: replica of a sword found
in Britain; swords were used to thrust, not slash; the pilum;
practice with wooden swords and wicker shields.*

Pay and promotion

In both war and peacetime the soldier received the same rate of pay. In the first century AD, up to the time of the Emperor Domitian (AD 81–96), this amounted to 225 denarii per annum; Domitian improved the rate to 300 denarii. These amounts were gross pay; before any money was handed to the soldier certain deductions were made. Surprising though it may seem, he was obliged to pay for his food, clothing, and equipment. He would also leave some money in the military savings bank. What he actually received in cash may have been only a quarter or a fifth of his gross pay. Whether he felt badly treated is difficult to say. Certainly we know of cases of discontent and – very occasionally – mutiny, but pay and conditions of service were apparently not bad enough to discourage recruits.

Any soldier could hope for promotion, in which case his life began to change in several ways. He was paid more and he was exempted from many of the duties performed by the ordinary soldier. In addition, any soldier could look forward to an honorable discharge at the end of twenty to twenty-five years of service with a lump sum of 3,000 denarii or an allocation of land.

Each centurion was assisted by an **optiō** or deputy who would take control of the century if the centurion were absent or lost in battle. There was also in each century a **signifer** (standard-bearer) and a **tesserārius**, who organized the guards and distributed the passwords, and one or two clerks. The centurions were the backbone of the legion. Most of them had long experience in the army and had risen from the ranks because of their courage and ability. There were sixty of them, each responsible for the training and discipline of a century. As a symbol of rank, each centurion carried a **vītis** or cane with which he could punish his soldiers. The importance of the centurions was reflected in their pay, which was probably about 1,500 denarii per annum. The most senior centurion of the legion was the **prīmus pīlus**, a highly respected figure; he was at least fifty years old and had worked his way up through the various grades of centurion. He held office for one year, then received a large payment and was allowed to retire; or he might go on still further to become the **praefectus castrōrum** (the commander of the camp), the highest-ranking officer to serve his entire career in the army.

Centurion in the Ermine Street Guard, wearing his decorations and his helmet with transverse plume and leaning on his vine-wood staff (vītis).

Diagram of a legion

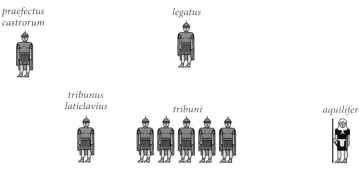

praefectus castrorum

legatus

tribunus laticlavius

tribuni

aquilifer

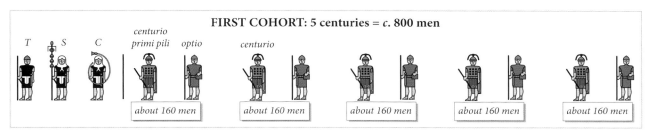

FIRST COHORT: 5 centuries = c. 800 men

T S C

centurio primi pili optio centurio

about 160 men   about 160 men   about 160 men   about 160 men   about 160 men

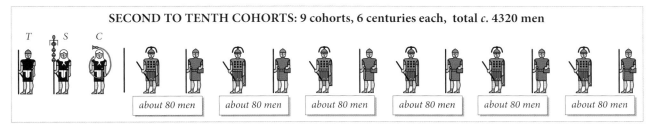

SECOND TO TENTH COHORTS: 9 cohorts, 6 centuries each, total c. 4320 men

T S C

about 80 men   about 80 men   about 80 men   about 80 men   about 80 men   about 80 men

HORSEMEN: about 120

Key
T = tesserarius
S = signifer
C = cornicen (horn player)
Each cohort had one of each of these.
Each century had a centurion and an optio.

The auxiliaries

The heavily armed legionaries formed the best-trained fighting force in the Roman army but they needed to be supplemented by large numbers of specialized troops. These were provided by men from different parts of the empire who had developed particular skills, for example, archers from Arabia and slingers from Majorca and Minorca. The most important and prestigious were the cavalry, who were regularly used in battle to support the infantry. They were usually positioned on each side of the legionaries from where they could protect the center, launch attacks themselves, or pursue defeated enemy forces.

Auxiliaries were paid less than legionary soldiers. However, when they completed their service, those who were not already Roman citizens were granted citizenship. This was another way of making people in the provinces feel loyalty to Roman rule.

Vocabulary checklist 25

accidō, accidere, accidī	*happen*
aliquis	*someone*
aperiō, aperīre, aperuī, apertus	*open*
autem	*but*
castra, castrōrum, n. pl.	*military camp*
cōgō, cōgere, coēgī, coāctus	*force, compel*
cōnfīdō, cōnfīdere	*trust*
dignitās, dignitātis, f.	*importance, prestige*
explicō, explicāre, explicāvī, explicātus	*explain*
extrā	*outside*
lateō, latēre, latuī	*lie hidden*
nescio, nescīre, nescīvī	*not know*
nōmen, nōminis, n.	*name*
perītus, perīta, perītum	*skillful*
poena, poenae, f.	*punishment*
poenās dare	*pay the penalty, be punished*
rūrsus	*again*
scelestus, scelesta, scelestum	*wicked*
suāvis, suāvis, suāve	*sweet*
testis, testis, m. f.	*witness*

A Roman soldier's dagger.

AGRICOLA

Stage 26

adventus Agricolae

mīlitēs legiōnis secundae, quī Dēvae in castrīs erant, diū et
strēnuē labōrābant. nam Gāius Iūlius Sīlānus, lēgātus legiōnis,
adventum Agricolae exspectābat. mīlitēs, ā centuriōnibus iussī,
multa et varia faciēbant. aliī arma poliēbant; aliī aedificia
pūrgābant; aliī plaustra reficiēbant. Sīlānus neque quiētem neque   5
commeātum mīlitibus dedit.

    mīlitēs, ignārī adventūs Agricolae, rem graviter ferēbant. trēs
continuōs diēs labōrāvērunt; quārtō diē Sīlānus adventum
Agricolae nūntiāvit. mīlitēs, cum hoc audīvissent, maximē
gaudēbant quod Agricolam dīligēbant.   10

    tertiā hōrā Sīlānus mīlitēs in ōrdinēs longōs īnstrūxit, ut
Agricolam salūtārent. mīlitēs, cum Agricolam castra intrantem
vīdissent, magnum clāmōrem sustulērunt:

    “iō, Agricola! iō, iō, Agricola!”

tantus erat clāmor ut nēmō iussa centuriōnum audīret.   15

    Agricola ad tribūnal prōcessit ut pauca dīceret. omnēs statim
tacuērunt ut Agricolam audīrent.

    “gaudeō,” inquit, “quod hodiē vōs rūrsus videō. nūllam
legiōnem fidēliōrem habeō, nūllam fortiōrem. disciplīnam
studiumque vestrum valdē laudō.”   20

    mīlitēs ita hortātus, per ōrdinēs prōcessit ut eōs īnspiceret.
deinde prīncipia intrāvit ut colloquium cum Sīlānō habēret.

adventus *arrival*
legiōnis: legiō *legion*
Dēvae *at Deva*
strēnuē *hard, energetically*
aliī … aliī … aliī
        some … others … others
arma *arms, weapons*
poliēbant: polīre *polish*
pūrgābant: pūrgāre *clean*
quiētem: quiēs *rest*
commeātum: commeātus
        (military) leave
trēs … diēs *for three days*
continuōs: continuus
        continuous, in a row
quārtō diē *on the fourth day*
gaudēbant: gaudēre
        be pleased, rejoice
tertiā hōrā *at the third hour*
iō! *hurrah!*
tribūnal *platform*

disciplīnam: disciplīna
        discipline, orderliness
studium *enthusiasm, zeal*
vestrum: vester *your*
hortātus *having encouraged*
prīncipia *headquarters*

How we know about Agricola

The two inscriptions below both contain the name of Gnaeus Julius Agricola. The first is on a lead water pipe found at Chester.

With the abbreviated words written out, this reads:

**Imperatore Vespasiano VIIII Tito Imperatore VII consulibus
Cnaeo Iulio Agricola legato Augusti propraetore**

This shows that the pipe was made in AD 79, when Vespasian and Titus were consuls and Agricola was governor of Britain.

The inscription drawn below was found in the forum of Verulamium (Roman name of modern St Albans, 25 miles or 40 kilometers north of London). Only fragments have survived, giving us the letters in red. But it is possible to guess at the rest of the first five lines because they contain only the names and titles of the Emperor Titus, his brother and successor Domitian, and Agricola. There is not enough left to reconstruct the last line.

> IMP·TITVS·CAESAR·DIVI·VESPASIANI·F·VESPASIANVS·AVG
> P·M·TR·PVIIII·IMPXV·COSVIIDESIG·VIII·CENSOR·PATER·PATRIAE
> ET·CAESAR·DIVI·VESPASIANI·F·DOMITIANVS·COS·VI·DESIG·VII
> PRINCEPS·IVVENTVTIS·COLLEGIORVM·OMNIVM·SACERDOS
> CN·IVLIO·AGRICOLA·LEG·AVG·PRO·PR
> VE   NATA

These inscriptions might have been virtually all that we knew about Agricola if his life history had not been written by his son-in-law, the historian Tacitus.

in prīncipiīs

When you have read this story, answer the questions on the opposite page.

Salvius ipse paulō prius ad castra advēnerat. iam in legiōnis secundae prīncipiīs sedēbat, Agricolam anxius exspectāns. sollicitus erat quod in epistulā, quam ad Agricolam mīserat, multa falsa scrīpserat. in prīmīs Cogidubnum sēditiōnis accūsāverat. in animō volvēbat num Agricola sibi crēditūrus esset. Belimicum sēcum dūxerat ut testis esset.

    subitō Salvius, Agricolam intrantem cōnspicātus, ad eum festīnāvit ut salūtāret. deinde commemorāvit ea quae in epistulā scrīpserat. Agricola, cum haec audīvisset, diū tacēbat. dēnique maximē commōtus,

    "quanta perfidia!" inquit. "quanta īnsānia! id quod mihi patefēcistī, vix intellegere possum. īnsānīvit Cogidubnus. īnsānīvērunt prīncipēs Rēgnēnsium. numquam nōs oportet barbarīs crēdere; tūtius est eōs omnēs prō hostibus habēre. semper nōs prōdunt. nunc mihi necesse est rēgem opprimere quem quīnque annōs prō amīcō habeō."

    haec locūtus, ad Sīlānum, lēgātum legiōnis, sē vertit.

    "Sīlāne," inquit, "nōs oportet rēgem prīncipēsque Rēgnēnsium quam celerrimē opprimere. tibi statim cum duābus cohortibus proficīscendum est."

    Sīlānus, ē prīncipiīs ēgressus, centuriōnibus mandāta dedit. eōs iussit cohortēs parāre. intereā Agricola plūra dē rēgis perfidiā rogāre coepit. Salvius eī respondit,

    "ecce Belimicus, vir ingeniī optimī summaeque fideī, quem iste Cogidubnus corrumpere temptābat. Belimicus autem, quī blanditiās rēgis spernēbat, omnia mihi patefēcit."

    "id quod Salvius dīxit vērum est," inquit Belimicus. "rēx Rōmānōs ōdit. Rōmānōs ē Britanniā expellere tōtamque īnsulam occupāre cupit. nāvēs igitur comparat. mīlitēs exercet. etiam bēstiās saevās colligit. nūper bēstiam in mē impulit ut mē interficeret."

    Agricola tamen hīs verbīs diffīsus, Salvium dīligentius rogāvit quae indicia sēditiōnis vīdisset. cognōscere voluit quot essent armātī, num Britannī cīvēs Rōmānōs interfēcissent, quās urbēs dēlēvissent.

    subitō magnum clāmōrem omnēs audīvērunt. per iānuam prīncipiōrum perrūpit homō squālidus. ad Agricolam praeceps cucurrit genibusque eius haesit.

    "cīvis Rōmānus sum," inquit. "Quīntum Caecilium Iūcundum mē vocant. ego multās iniūriās passus hūc tandem advēnī. hoc ūnum dīcere volō. Cogidubnus est innocēns."

    haec locūtus humī prōcubuit exanimātus.

paulō prius *a little earlier*

falsa: falsum *lie, untruth*
in prīmīs *in particular*
sēditiōnis: sēditiō *rebellion*
in animō volvēbat: in animō   **volvere** *wonder, turn over in the mind*
5
10 **num** *whether*
crēditūrus *going to believe*
īnsānia *insanity, madness*
nōs oportet *we must*
prō hostibus habēre *consider as enemies*
15
prōdunt: prōdere *betray*
opprimere *crush*

tibi ... proficīscendum est *you must set out*
20
cohortibus: cohors *cohort*

25 **corrumpere** *corrupt*
blanditiās: blanditiae *flatteries*
spernēbat: spernere *despise, reject*

30 **colligit: colligere** *collect*

diffīsus *having distrusted*
indicia: indicium *sign, evidence*
quot *how many, how numerous*
35

perrūpit: perrumpere *burst through, burst in*
squālidus *covered with dirt, filthy*
40

Questions

1 Why was Salvius in the headquarters?
2 Why is he described as **sollicitus** (lines 3–4)?
3 What particular accusation had he made?
4 Why had he brought Belimicus with him?
5 **Agricola ... diū tacēbat** (line 9). What is there in his subsequent comments which would explain his hesitation?
6 What conclusion did he come to about the proper treatment for barbarians?
7 What did Agricola tell Silanus they had to do? What order was Silanus given?
8 After Silanus left, what did Agricola try to find out?
9 How did Salvius describe Belimicus' character? According to Salvius, how had Belimicus helped him?
10 From Belimicus' information in lines 27–31, find one thing that Agricola might have believed and one thing about which he might have had doubts.
11 In lines 32–35 Agricola asked Salvius for evidence of the rebellion. What three details did he want to find out?
   What do you think of Agricola for not asking these questions before sending out the cohorts?
12 What happened before Salvius could answer Agricola?
13 What two things did the **homō squālidus** do (lines 37–38)?
14 What did he say first? Why? What were his final words?
15 **haec locūtus humī prōcubuit exanimātus** (line 42). Which three Latin words in his speech explain why he suddenly collapsed?

About the language 1: purpose clauses

1 Study the following examples:

> mīlitēs ad prīncipia convēnērunt **ut Agricolam audīrent**.
> *The soldiers gathered at the headquarters **in order that they might hear Agricola**.*

> per tōtam noctem labōrābat medicus **ut vulnera mīlitum sānāret**.
> *The doctor worked all night **in order that he might treat the soldiers' wounds**.*

The groups of words in **boldface** are known as **purpose clauses**, because they indicate the purpose for which an action was done. The verb in a purpose clause in Latin is always subjunctive.

2 Further examples:

   a omnēs cīvēs ad silvam contendērunt ut leōnem mortuum spectārent.
   b dominus stilum et cērās poposcit ut epistulam scrīberet.
   c dēnique ego ad patrem rediī ut rem explicārem.
   d rēx iter ad fontem fēcit ut aquam sacram biberet.
   e equōs celeriter cōnscendimus ut ex oppidō fugerēmus.
   f vīllam intrāvistī ut pecūniam nostram caperēs.

3 Instead of translating **ut** and the subjunctive as *in order that I (you, s/he, etc.) might …*, it is often possible to use a simpler form of words:

> mīlitēs ad prīncipia convēnērunt ut Agricolam audīrent.
> *The soldiers gathered at the headquarters in order to hear Agricola.*
> Or, simpler still:
> *The soldiers gathered at the headquarters to hear Agricola.*

tribūnus

Agricola, ubi hoc vīdit, custōdēs iussit Quīntum auferre medicumque arcessere. tum ad tribūnum mīlitum, quī adstābat, sē vertit.

"mī Rūfe," inquit, "prūdentissimus es omnium tribūnōrum quōs habeō. tē iubeō hunc hominem summā cum cūrā interrogāre." 5

Salvius, cum Rūfus exiisset, valdē commōtus,

"omnia explicāre possum," inquit. "nōtus est mihi hic homō. nūper in vīllā mē vīsitāvit, quamquam nōn invītāveram. trēs mēnsēs apud mē mānsit, opēs meās dēvorāns. duōs tripodas argenteōs habēbam, quōs abstulit ut Cogidubnō daret. sed eum nōn accūsāvī, quod hospes erat. ubi tamen Aquās Sūlis mēcum advēnit, facinus scelestum committere temptāvit. venēnum parāvit ut Memorem, haruspicem Rōmānum, necāret. postquam rem nōn effēcit, mē ipsum accūsāvit. nōlī eī crēdere. multō perfidior est quam Britannī." 15

haec cum audīvisset, Agricola respondit,

"sī haec fēcit, eī moriendum est."

mox revēnit Rūfus valdē attonitus.

"Quīntus Caecilius," inquit, "est iuvenis summae fideī. patrem meum, quem Alexandrīae relīquī, bene nōverat. hoc prō certō habeō quod Quīntus hanc epistulam mihi ostendit, ā patre ipsō scrīptam." 20

Agricola statim Quīntum ad sē vocāvit, cēterōsque dīmīsit. Salvius, Quīntum dētestātus, anxius exiit. Agricola cum Quīntō colloquium trēs hōrās habēbat. 25

tribūnus *tribune (high-ranking officer)*

adstābat: adstāre *stand by*

prūdentissimus: prūdēns *shrewd, intelligent*

opēs *money, wealth*
dēvorāns: dēvorāre *devour, eat up*

multō perfidior *much more treacherous*

sī *if*

Alexandrīae *at Alexandria*
prō certō habeō: prō certō habēre *know for certain*

dētestātus *having cursed*

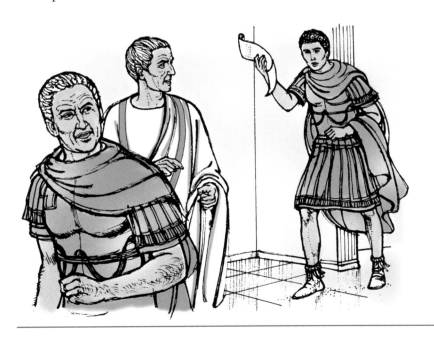

Deva was founded at the highest point on the river Dee that seagoing ships could reach. Part of the Roman quayside can be seen today.

About the language 2: gerundives

1 From Stage 14 on, you have met sentences of this kind:

necesse est mihi ad castra contendere.
I must hurry to the camp.

necesse est vōbīs labōrāre.
You must work.

2 You have now met another way of expressing the same idea:

necesse est nōbīs currere.
nōbīs **currendum** est.
We must run.

necesse est eī revenīre.
eī **reveniendum** est.
He must come back.

The word in **boldface** is known as the **gerundive**.

3 Further examples:

a mihi fugiendum est.
b nōbīs ambulandum est.
c tibi hīc manendum est.
d servīs dīligenter labōrandum est.
e omnibus cīvibus tacendum est quod sacerdōtēs appropinquant.
f sī Imperātōrem vidēre volunt, eīs festīnandum est.

contentiō

Agricola, cum Quīntum audīvisset, Salvium furēns arcessīvit.
quī, simulatque intrāvit, aliquid dīcere coepit. Agricola tamen,
cum silentium iussisset, Salvium vehementer accūsāvit.

"dī immortālēs! Cogidubnus est innocēns, tū perfidus. cūr
tam īnsānus eram ut tibi crēderem? simulatque ad hanc   5
prōvinciam vēnistī, amīcī mē dē calliditāte tuā monuērunt. nunc
rēs ipsa mē docuit. num Imperātor Domitiānus hanc tantam
perfidiam ferre potest? ego sānē nōn possum. in hāc prōvinciā
summam potestātem habeō. iubeō tē hās inimīcitiās dēpōnere.
iubeō tē ad Cogidubnī aulam īre, veniamque ab eō petere.   10
praetereā Imperātōrī ipsī rem explicāre dēbēs."

haec ubi dīxit Agricola, Salvius respondit īrātus,

"quam caecus es! quam longē errās! tē ipsum oportet
Imperātōrī id quod in Britanniā facis explicāre. tū enim in
ultimīs Britanniae partibus bellum geris et victōriās inānēs ē   15
Calēdoniā refers; sed Imperātor pecūniam opēsque accipere
cupit. itaque rēgnum Cogidubnī occupāre cōnstituit;
Calēdoniam nōn cūrat. tū sānē hoc nescīs. in magnō
perīculō es, quod cōnsilium meum spernis. nōn sōlum mihi
sed Imperātōrī ipsī obstās."   20

cum hanc contentiōnem inter sē habērent, subitō nūntius
prīncipia ingressus exclāmāvit,

"mortuus est Cogidubnus!"

inimīcitiās: inimīcitia *feud,*
dispute

caecus *blind*
tē oportet *you must*
victōriās: victōria *victory*
inānēs: inānis *empty,*
meaningless
Calēdoniā: Calēdonia *Scotland*
cōnstituit: cōnstituere *decide*

Word patterns: verbs and nouns

1 Some verbs and nouns are closely connected. For example:

Imperātor Cogidubnum **honōrāre** volēbat.
The Emperor wanted to honor Cogidubnus.

magnōs **honōrēs** ab Imperātōre accēpit.
He received great honors from the Emperor.

terra valdē **tremere** coepit.
The earth began to shake violently.

cīvēs magnum **tremōrem** sēnsērunt.
The citizens felt a great shaking.

2 Further examples:

verbs		nouns	
amāre	*to love*	amor	*love*
clāmāre	*to shout*	clāmor	*a shout, shouting*
terrēre	*to terrify*	terror	*terror*

3 Now complete the table below:

timēre	*to fear*	timor	. . . .
dolēre	(1) *to hurt, to be in pain*	dolor	(1) . . . .
dolēre	(2) *to grieve*	dolor	(2) . . . .
favēre	. . . .	favor	*favor*
furere	. . . .	furor	*rage*
labōrāre	. . . .	. . . .	. . . .

1 Complete each sentence with the correct form of the noun. Then translate the sentence.

 a Agricola, ubi verba . . . . audīvit, Salvium arcessīvit. (Quīntum, Quīntī, Quīntō)
 b omnēs hospitēs . . . . saltātrīcis laudāvērunt. (artem, artis, artī)
 c iter nostrum difficile erat, quod tot cīvēs . . . . complēbant. (viās, viārum, viīs)
 d prō prīncipiīs stābat magna turba . . . . (mīlitēs, mīlitum, mīlitibus)
 e lēgātus, postquam mandāta . . . . dedit, legiōnem ad montem proximum dūxit. (centuriōnēs, centuriōnum, centuriōnibus)
 f iūdex, quī . . . . nōn crēdēbat, īrātissimus erat. (puerōs, puerōrum, puerīs)

2 Complete each sentence with the correct form of the subjunctive. Then translate the sentence.

 a cum Sīlānus legiōnem . . . ., Agricola ē prīncipiīs prōcessit. (īnstrūxisset, īnstrūxissent)
 b mīlitēs in flūmen dēsiluērunt ut hostēs . . . . (vītāret, vītārent)
 c senātor scīre voluit num pater meus Imperātōrī . . . . (fāvisset, fāvissent)
 d cum senex . . . ., fūrēs per fenestram tacitē intrāvērunt. (dormīret, dormīrent)
 e nōs, cum in Britanniā . . . ., barbarōs saepe vīcimus. (essem, essēmus)
 f intellegere nōn poteram cūr cīvēs istum hominem . . . . (laudāvisset, laudāvissent)
 g latrōnem interfēcī ut īnfantem . . . . (servārem, servārēmus)
 h māter tua mē rogāvit quid in tabernā . . . . (fēcissēs, fēcissētis)

3 Complete each sentence with the correct word from the list below. Then translate the sentence.

   epistulam, audīvisset, ēgressus, invēnērunt, equīs, captī

 a Salvius, ē prīncipiīs . . . ., Belimicum quaesīvit.
 b Agricola, cum haec verba . . . ., ad Rūfum sē vertit.
 c dominus . . . . ē manibus servī furēns rapuit.
 d custōdēs nūntium sub aquā iacentem . . . .
 e quattuor Britannī, in pugnā . . . ., vītam dūrissimam in carcere agēbant.
 f aliī mīlitēs . . . . aquam dabant, aliī frūmentum in horrea īnferēbant.

The senior officers in the Roman army

The officer commanding a legion was called a **lēgātus**. He was a member of the senate in Rome and usually in his middle thirties. He was assisted by six military tribunes. Of these, one was usually a young man of noble birth, serving his military apprenticeship before starting a political career. After holding civilian posts in Rome or one of the provinces, he might be appointed as legatus and spend three or four years commanding his legion. Then he would usually resume his civilian career.

The other five tribunes were members of a slightly lower social class and they would also be in their thirties. They were generally able, wealthy, and educated men, often aiming at important posts in the imperial administration. Some of them returned to the army later to command auxiliary cavalry units.

The senior officers usually spent only short periods in the army, unlike the centurions and the legionaries who served for the whole of their working lives. They had therefore to rely heavily on the expertise and experience of the centurions for advice. Because the army was highly trained and well organized, the appointment of relatively inexperienced officers rarely affected the success of its operations.

Some officers like Agricola proved themselves to be extremely competent and were promoted to become governors of provinces like Britain where military skill and powers of leadership were required.

The god Mars, wearing the helmet, breastplate, and greaves of a senior officer.

Agricola, governor of Britain

Agricola was born in AD 40 in the Roman colony of Forum Iulii (modern Fréjus) in southeast Gaul. His father had been made a senator by the Emperor Tiberius, but later fell out of favor with the Emperor Gaius Caligula and was executed shortly after Agricola was born.

Agricola went to school at Massilia (Marseilles), which was the cultural and educational center of southern Gaul. He followed the normal curriculum for the young sons of upper-class Roman families: public speaking and philosophy. He enjoyed the latter, but the historian Tacitus, Agricola's son-in-law and biographer, records his mother's reaction:

I remember that Agricola often told us that in his youth he was more enthusiastic about philosophy than a Roman and a senator was expected to be and that his mother thought it wise to restrain such a passionate interest.

At the age of eighteen, Agricola served in the Roman army in Britain with the rank of **tribūnus**. He used this opportunity to become familiar with the province. The soldiers under his command had a similar opportunity to get to know him. Two years later, during the revolt of Boudica in AD 60, he witnessed the grim realities of warfare. Agricola was by now very knowledgeable about the province of Britain and this knowledge was very useful during his governorship some eighteen years later.

Back in Rome, he continued his political career. In AD 70, he returned to Britain to take command of the Twentieth Legion, which was stationed at Viroconium (Wroxeter) in the west of England and had become undisciplined and troublesome. His success in handling this difficult task was rewarded by promotion to the governorship of Aquitania (the central region in modern France) in Gaul. He then became consul in Rome and in AD 78 returned to Britain for a third time, as **prōpraetor** (governor) of the province. The political experience and military skill which he had acquired by then equipped him to face an exciting and demanding situation.

An antefix (a kind of roof tile) made by the Twentieth Legion. The boar was their badge.

Agricola fought the fierce tribes of Scotland. This boar's head is part of one of their war trumpets (reconstruction).

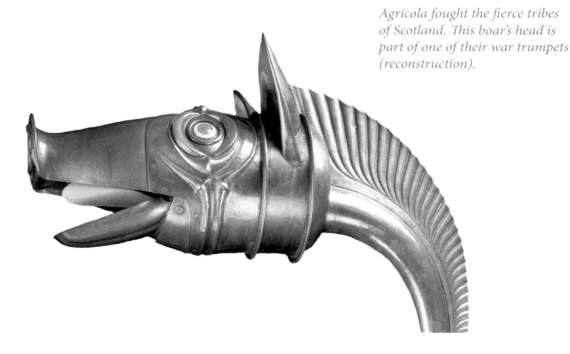

Agricola rose to the challenge in many different ways. He completed the conquest of Wales and then fought a series of successful campaigns in Scotland, culminating in a great victory at Mons Graupius in the north of the Grampian mountains. He extended the network of roads and forts across northern Britain and established the legionary fortress at Chester.

In addition to his military exploits Agricola carried out an extensive program of romanization. Tacitus tells us that he "encouraged individuals and helped communities to build temples, fora, and houses in the Roman style" and that he made the people realize that under good laws it was better to live at peace with the Romans than to rebel against them. Tacitus also tells us of his plans to improve the education of the British:

Agricola arranged for the sons of British chiefs to receive a broad education. He made it clear that he preferred the natural abilities of the British to the skill and training of the Gauls. As a result, instead of hating the language of the Romans, they became very eager to learn it.

The earthworks of Chew Green, one of the camps first built by Agricola on his way to conquer the Caledonians of Scotland.

Agricola was governor of Britain for seven years, an unusual length of time and longer than any other imperial Roman governor. During this time Britain was circumnavigated and the area under direct Roman control was nearly doubled. The rapid expansion of urban life in Britain in the second century may have owed as much to Agricola's civil policies and provincial sympathies as to his military successes. Agricola was recalled from Britain in AD 85, possibly because of the jealousy of Domitian. When he returned to Rome, Agricola was given the honors due to a successful general – a statue and a citation; but this was the end of his career. He retired into the safety of private life. Any hopes he may have had of a further governorship were not fulfilled, and he lived in retirement until his death in AD 93.

A Roman cavalryman triumphing over Caledonians: a sculpture put up on a later Roman frontier in Scotland, the Antonine Wall.

Vocabulary checklist 26

auferō, auferre, abstulī, ablātus	*take away, steal*
bellum, bellī, n.	*war*
bellum gerere	*wage war, campaign*
commōtus, commōta, commōtum	*moved, excited, upset*
doceō, docēre, docuī, doctus	*teach*
falsus, falsa, falsum	*false, dishonest*
fidēs, fideī, f.	*loyalty, trustworthiness*
īnstruō, īnstruere, īnstrūxī, īnstrūctus	*draw up*
lēgātus, lēgātī, m.	*commander*
legiō, legiōnis, f.	*legion*
nōtus, nōta, nōtum	*known, well-known, famous*
num	*whether*
praebeō, praebēre, praebuī, praebitus	*offer, provide*
quot?	*how many?*
referō, referre, rettulī, relātus	*bring back, carry*
rēgnum, rēgnī, n.	*kingdom*
saevus, saeva, saevum	*savage, cruel*
sī	*if*
ultimus, ultima, ultimum	*furthest*
ut	*that, in order that*

A small figure of a teacher reading from a scroll. Agricola encouraged the British to learn Latin.

IN CASTRIS

Stage 27

1 "fuge mēcum ad horreum!"

extrā carcerem, Modestus et Strȳthiō
sermōnem anxiī habēbant.
    Modestus Strȳthiōnem monēbat ut ad
horreum sēcum fugeret.

2 "invenīte Modestum Strȳthiōnemque!"

prō prīncipiīs, centuriō mīlitibus mandāta
dabat.
    centuriō mīlitibus imperābat ut
Modestum Strȳthiōnemque invenīrent.

3 "castra Rōmāna oppugnāte! horrea
incendite!"

in silvā proximā, Vercobrix ōrātiōnem apud
Britannōs habēbat.
    Vercobrix Britannōs incitābat ut castra
Rōmāna oppugnārent et horrea incenderent.

in horreō

Modestus et Strȳthiō, ē carcere ēgressī, ad horreum fūgērunt. per aditum angustum rēpsērunt et in horreō cēlātī manēbant. centuriō, cum portās cellārum apertās carceremque dēsertum vīdisset, īrātissimus erat. mīlitibus imperāvit ut Modestum et Strȳthiōnem caperent. mīlitēs tamen, quamquam per tōta castra quaerēbant, eōs invenīre nōn poterant. illī duōs diēs mānsērunt cēlātī. tertiō diē Modestus tam miser erat ut rem diūtius ferre nōn posset.

Modestus: quam īnfēlīx sum! mālim in illō carcere esse potius quam in hōc horreō latēre. ēheu! mē taedet huius vītae. ubīque frūmentum videō, sed cōnsūmere nōn possum. quālis est haec vīta?

Strȳthiō: mī Modeste, difficile est nōbīs hīc diūtius manēre. nunc tamen advesperāscit. vīsne mē, ex horreō ēgressum, cibum quaerere? hominibus miserrimīs cibus spem semper affert.

Modestus: id est cōnsilium optimum. nōbīs cēnandum est. Strȳthiō, ī prīmum ad coquum. eum iubē cēnam splendidam coquere et hūc portāre. deinde quaere Aulum et Pūblicum, amīcōs nostrōs! invītā eōs ad cēnam! iubē Aulum amphoram vīnī ferre, Pūblicum lucernam. tum curre ad vīcum; Nigrīnam quaere! optima est saltātrīcum; mihi saltātrīcēs semper sōlācium afferunt.

Strȳthiō: quid dīcis? vīsne mē saltātrīcem in castra dūcere?

Modestus: abī, caudex!

Strȳthiō, ut mandāta Modestī efficeret, celeriter discessit. coquō persuāsit ut cēnam splendidam parāret; Aulō et Pūblicō persuāsit ut vīnum lucernamque ferrent; Nigrīnam ōrāvit ut in castra venīret, sed eī persuādēre nōn poterat.

aditum: **aditus** *entrance*
angustum: **angustus** *narrow*
rēpsērunt: **rēpere** *crawl*
imperāvit: **imperāre**
             order, command

5

mālim *I would prefer*
potius *rather*
mē taedet *I am tired, I am*
                bored

10

advesperāscit:
    advesperāscere
        get dark, become dark
spem: **spēs** *hope*
affert: **afferre** *bring*
prīmum *first*

15

vīcum: **vīcus** *town, village*

20

sōlācium *comfort*

25

ōrāvit: **ōrāre** *beg*

30

Reconstruction of a granary.

About the language 1: indirect commands

1 In Unit 1, you met sentences like this:

"redīte!"   "pecūniam trāde!"
"Go back!"   *"Hand over the money!"*

In each example, an order or command is being given. These examples are known as **direct commands**.

2 In Stage 27, you have met sentences like this:

lēgātus mīlitibus imperāvit **ut redīrent**.
*The commander ordered his soldiers **that they should go back**.*
Or, in more natural English:
*The commander ordered his soldiers **to go back**.*

latrōnēs mercātōrī imperāvērunt **ut pecūniam trāderet**.
*The robbers ordered the merchant **that he should hand over the money**.*
Or, in more natural English:
*The robbers ordered the merchant **to hand over the money**.*

In each of these examples, the command is not being given directly, but is being *reported* or *referred to*. These examples are known as **indirect commands**. The verb in an indirect command in Latin is usually subjunctive.

3 Compare the following examples:

direct commands	*indirect commands*
"contendite!"	iuvenis amīcīs persuāsit ut contenderent.
"Hurry!"	*The young man persuaded his friends to hurry.*
"dā mihi aquam!"	captīvus custōdem ōrāvit ut aquam sibi daret.
"Give me water!"	*The prisoner begged the guard to give him water.*
"fuge!"	mē monuit ut fugerem.
"Run away!"	*He warned me to run away.*

4 Further examples of direct and indirect commands:

a "tacē!"
b centuriō mihi imperāvit ut tacērem.
c "parcite mihi!"
d senex nōs ōrābat ut sibi parcerēmus.
e nēmō ancillae persuādēre poterat ut saltāret.
f coquus servīs imperāvit ut vīnum in mēnsam pōnerent.
g vōs saepe monēbam ut dīligenter labōrārētis.
h mīlitēs mercātōrem monuērunt ut ab oppidō celeriter discēderet.

Modestus prōmōtus

prōmōtus: prōmovēre *promote*

I

cum Strȳthiō cēnam et amīcōs quaereret, decem Britannī, ā
Vercobrige ductī, castrīs cautē appropinquābant. Vercobrix
enim eīs persuāserat ut castra oppugnārent. Britannī, postquam
custōdēs vītāvērunt, castra intrāvērunt. in manibus facēs
tenēbant ut horrea incenderent. celeriter ad horrea advēnērunt   5
quod prius cognōverant ubi sita essent.

    Modestus, ignārus adventūs Britannōrum, in horreō sedēbat.
adeō ēsuriēbat ut dē vītā paene dēspērāret. per aditum
prōspiciēbat, reditum Strȳthiōnis exspectāns.

    "trēs hōrās Strȳthiōnem iam exspectō. quid eī accidit?"   10
subitō manum hominum per tenebrās cōnspexit.

    "euge! tandem vēnērunt amīcī! heus, amīcī, hūc venīte!"

    Britannī, cum Modestī vōcem audīvissent, erant tam attonitī
ut immōtī stārent. respondēre nōn audēbant. Vercobrix tamen,
quī raucam Modestī vōcem agnōverat, ad comitēs versus,   15

    "nōlīte timēre," inquit susurrāns. "nōtus est mihi hic mīles.
stultior est quam asinus. nōbīs nocēre nōn potest."

    tum Britannī per aditum tacitī rēpsērunt. simulatque
intrāvērunt, Modestus eīs obviam iit, ut salūtāret.

    "salvēte, amīcī! nunc nōbīs cēnandum ac bibendum est."   20

    tum Britannus quīdam, vir ingēns, in Modestum incurrit.

    "ō Nigrīna, dēliciae meae!" inquit Modestus. "tē nōn agnōvī!
quam longī sunt capillī tuī! age! cōnsīde prope mē! dā mihi
ōsculum! quis lucernam habet?"

facēs: fax *torch*

ignārus *not knowing, unaware*

prōspiciēbat: prōspicere *look out*

comitēs: comes *comrade,*
companion
versus *having turned*

obviam iit: obviam īre *meet,*
go to meet
incurrit: incurrere *bump into*

Vercobrix, cum Modestum lucernam rogantem audīvisset,   *25*
Britannīs imperāvit ut facēs incenderent. Modestus,
Vercobrigem Britannōsque cōnspicātus, palluit.

"dī immortālēs!" inquit. "abiit Nigrīna, appāruērunt Britannī!
mihi statim effugiendum est."

II

When you have read this part of the story, answer the questions at
the end.

Vercobrix tamen suīs imperāvit ut Modestum comprehenderent.   **suīs: suī** *his men*
ūnus ē Britannīs Modestō appropinquāvit ut dēligāret. fax,
tamen, quam tenēbat, tunicam Modestī forte incendit.

"ēheu!" ululāvit ille. "ardeō! mē dēvorant flammae!"

tum ē manibus Britannōrum ēlāpsus fūgit praeceps. simulac   *5*
per aditum ērūpit, Strȳthiōnī amīcīsque occurrit. amphoram vīnī   **occurrit: occurrere** *meet*
ē manibus Aulī ēripuit et vīnum in tunicam fūdit.   **ēripuit: ēripere** *snatch, tear*

"īnsānit Modestus!" clāmāvit Strȳthiō attonitus.

Modestus tamen, Strȳthiōnis clāmōrum neglegēns,
amphoram in aditum impulit. tum in amphoram innīxus,   *10*   **innīxus** *having leaned*
magnōs clāmōrēs sustulit.

"subvenīte! subvenīte! Britannōs cēpī!"   **subvenīte: subvenīre**
      help, come to help
tantī erant clāmōrēs Modestī ut tōta castra complērent. statim   **causam: causa** *reason, cause*
manus mīlitum, ā centuriōne ducta, ad horrea contendit ut
causam strepitūs cognōsceret.   *15*   **strepitūs: strepitus** *noise, din*

Modestus exsultāns "īnsidiās Britannīs parāvī," inquit.
"Vercobrix ipse multīs cum Britannīs in horreō inclūsus est."

breve erat certāmen. tantus erat numerus mīlitum
Rōmānōrum ut Britannōs facile superārent. Rōmānī Britannōs
ex horreō extractōs ad carcerem redūxērunt. tum lēgātus
legiōnis ipse Modestum arcessītum laudāvit.

"Modeste," inquit, "mīlitem fortiōrem quam tē numquam
anteā vīdī. nōs decet praemium tibi dare."

Modestus, ā lēgātō ita laudātus, adeō gaudēbat ut vix sē
continēre posset. pecūniam laetus exspectābat.

"carcerī tē praeficiō," inquit lēgātus.

breve: brevis *short, brief*
certāmen *struggle, fight*
20 **redūxērunt: redūcere** *lead back*

nōs decet *it is proper for us*
continēre *contain*
25 **praeficiō: praeficere**
put in charge of

Questions

1 What order did Vercobrix give his men?

2 Explain how Modestus' tunic caught fire (lines 2–3).

3 What had Modestus just done to make Strythio exclaim "**īnsānit Modestus**" (line 8)?

4 Pick out and translate the Latin words which show that Modestus took no notice of Strythio.

5 What did Modestus do next with the amphora (lines 9–10)?

6 What success did he then claim?

7 Why did the centurion and the soldiers hasten to the granaries (lines 13–15)?

8 **breve erat certāmen** (line 18). Explain why this was so.

9 What happened to the Britons?

10 How did the **lēgātus** congratulate Modestus (lines 22–23)?

11 **nōs decet praemium tibi dare** (line 23). What reward did Modestus expect? What reward did he actually get?

12 Do you think the reward was a suitable one for Modestus? Give a reason.

About the language 2: result clauses

1 Study the following examples:

   tanta erat multitūdō **ut tōtam aulam complēret**.
   *So great was the crowd **that it filled the whole palace**.*

   iuvenis gladium adeō cupiēbat **ut pecūniam statim trāderet**.
   *The young man wanted the sword so much **that he handed over the
   money immediately**.*

   The groups of words in **boldface** are known as result clauses,
   because they indicate a result. The verb in a result clause in Latin is
   always subjunctive.

2 Further examples:

   a tam stultus erat dominus ut omnēs servī eum dērīdērent.
   b tantus erat clāmor ut nēmō iussa centuriōnum audīret.
   c Agricola tot mīlitēs ēmīsit ut hostēs fugerent.
   d centuriōnem adeō timēbam ut ad castra redīre nōn audērem.
   e tot servōs habēbās ut eōs numerāre nōn possēs.
   f ancillae nostrae tam dīligenter labōrābant ut eās saepe
   laudārēmus.

3 Notice that in the first part of each sentence there is a word that
   signals that a result clause is coming. For example, study the first
   sentence in paragraph 1. **tanta**, *so great*, is a signal for the result
   clause **ut tōtam aulam complēret**. In the last three sentences in
   paragraph 2, what are the signal words? What do they mean?

Word patterns: adjectives and nouns

1 Study the form and meaning of the following adjectives and nouns:

adjectives		*nouns*	
longus	*long*	longitūdō	*length*
sollicitus	*worried*	sollicitūdō	*worry, anxiety*
altus	*deep*	altitūdō	*depth*

2 Now complete the table below:

sōlus	*alone, lonely*	solitūdō	....
magnus	....	magnitūdō	....
lātus	*wide*	....	....
mānsuētus	*tame*	mānsuētūdō	....

3 Give the meaning of the following nouns:

   fortitūdō, pulchritūdō, multitūdō.

4 How many of the Latin nouns in paragraphs 1–3 can be translated into English by a noun ending in -tude? If you are unsure, use an English dictionary to help you.

5 Notice some slightly different examples:

cupere	*to desire*	cupīdō	*desire*
		Cupīdō	*Cupid, the god of desire*
valēre	*to be well*	valētūdō	*health*
			(1) *good health*
			(2) *bad health*

The imperative of **valēre** has a special meaning which you have met before:

   valē   *be well*, i.e. *farewell, good-bye*

Practicing the language

1 Translate the following examples:

    a faber, prope iānuam tabernae stāns, pugnam spectābat.
    b Vilbia, ē culīnā ēgressa, sorōrem statim quaesīvit.
    c fūrēs, ad iūdicem ductī, veniam petīvērunt.
    d centuriō, amphoram vīnī optimī adeptus, ad amīcōs celeriter rediit.
    e subitō equōs appropinquantēs audīvimus.
    f puer callidus pecūniam, in terrā cēlātam, invēnit.

Pick out the participle in each sentence and say whether it is present, perfect passive, or perfect active. Then write down the noun described by each participle.

2 Change the words in **boldface** from singular to plural. Then translate the new sentences.

    a Imperātor **īnsulam** vīsitābat.
    b **nauta** pecūniam **poscēbat**.
    c haec verba **senem** terrēbant.
    d iuvenēs **captīvum** custōdiēbant.
    e fūr **pōculum** īnspiciēbat.
    f **leō** ad pāstōrem **contendēbat**.
    g equī **flūmen** trānsīre nōlēbant.
    h **templum** in forō **erat**.

3 With the help of the table of nouns on pages 262–263, complete the sentences of this exercise with the correct case of each unfinished noun. Then translate the sentence.

    a puella tabernam meam intrāvit. puell. . . multōs ānulōs ostendī.
    b puerī per viam currēbant. clāmōrēs puer. . . mē excitāvērunt.
    c Salvius ad aulam rēg. . . quam celerrimē contendit.
    d servī prope iānuam stābant. serv. . . pecūniam dedimus.
    e Memor, ubi nōm. . . tuum audīvit, perterritus erat.
    f in hāc viā sunt duo templ. . . .
    g mercātor ad fundum meum herī vēnit. frūmentum meum mercātōr. . . vēndidī.
    h magna multitūdō cīv. . . nōbīs obstābat.
    i barbarī prōvinciam oppugnāvērunt, multāsque urb. . . dēlēvērunt.
    j iūdex mercātōr. . . , quī fēminam dēcēperat, pūnīvit.

The legionary fortress

If the legion itself was like a miniature army, the fortress in which it lived when not on campaign could be compared to a fortified town. It covered about 50–60 acres (20–25 hectares), about one third of the area of Pompeii. The design of the fortress was based on a standard pattern (see below).

The chief buildings, grouped in the center, were the **prīncipia** (headquarters), the **praetōrium** (the living-quarters of the commanding officer), the **valētūdinārium** (the hospital), and the **horrea** (granaries). Numerous streets and alleyways were laid out in an orderly grid pattern throughout the fortress, but there were three main streets: the **via praetōria** ran from the main gate to the front entrance of the principia; the **via prīncipālis** extended across the whole width of the fortress, making a T-junction with the via praetoria just in front of the principia; the **via quīntāna** passed behind the principia and also extended across the width of the fortress. The fortress was surrounded by a ditch, a rampart (**vallum**), which was an earth wall or mound, and battlements, with towers at the corners and at intervals along the sides. Each side had a fortified gateway.

The principia was a large and impressive building at the heart of the fortress. A visitor would first enter a flagstone courtyard surrounded on three sides by a colonnade and storerooms. On the far side of the courtyard was a surprisingly large **basilica** or a great hall, where the commander

Plan of a legionary fortress.

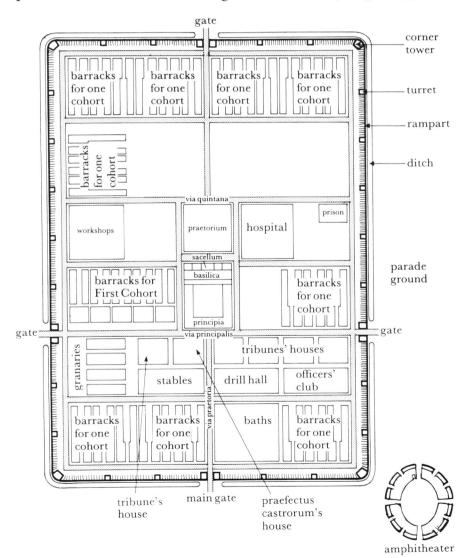

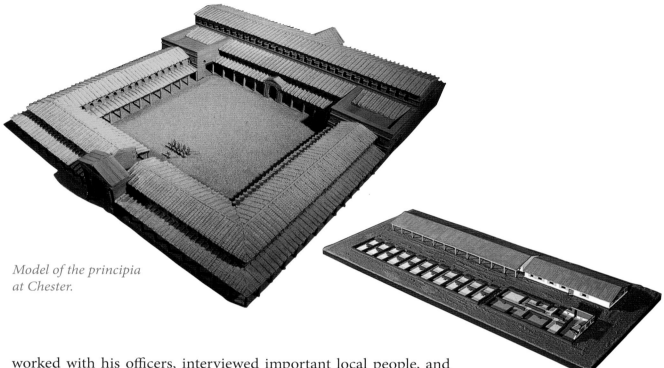

Model of the principia at Chester.

Cutaway model of a pair of barracks blocks.

worked with his officers, interviewed important local people, and administered military justice. The one at Deva, for example, was about 240 feet (73 meters) long; its central nave, bounded by tall columns supporting a vaulted roof, was 40 feet (12 meters) wide and flanked by two aisles each 20 feet (6 meters) wide.

In the center of the far long wall of the basilica and directly facing the main gate was the most sacred place in the fortress, the **sacellum** or chapel. This housed the standard of the legion, the **aquila**, an image of an eagle perched with outspread wings on the top of a pole. It was made of gold and in its talons it clutched a bundle of golden darts that represented the thunderbolts of Jupiter. The aquila represented the spirit of the legion and aroused feelings of intense loyalty and an almost religious respect. To lose it in battle was the worst possible disgrace and misfortune; this rarely happened. The soldier who looked after the aquila and carried it in battle was called the **aquilifer** (eagle-bearer). He was always a soldier of the first cohort.

On either side of the sacellum were the rooms where the clerks kept the payrolls and attended to all the paperwork that was needed to run a large organization. Close by and usually underground was the legion's strong room, in which pay and savings were kept safely locked.

The praetorium was situated by the side of or just behind the principia. It was a luxurious house in the style of an Italian **domus urbāna** and it provided the legatus and his family with those comforts

aquilifer

which they would expect and regard as necessary for a civilized life: central heating, a garden, and a private suite of baths. The very high standard of the commander's quarters would demonstrate the attractions of Roman civilization to any local civilian leaders entertained in the praetorium. However, whether this display of wealth made them any happier about the taxes which they had to pay to the Romans is another question.

The valetudinarium or hospital contained many small wards which were designed to ensure peace and quiet for the sick and injured. There was also a large reception hall to accommodate an influx of casualties from the battlefield and a small operating theater equipped with running water.

The horrea were skillfully designed to keep grain dry and cool for long periods. In the first century AD, like many other buildings in the fortress, they were built mainly of wood, but from the second century stone was the regular material. A granary was a long, narrow building; to carry the rainwater away from the walls the roof had wide, overhanging eaves; and to prevent damp rising from the ground the floor was supported on small piers or low walls which allowed air to circulate freely underneath. There were several of these granaries in a fortress, often arranged side by side in pairs, and they could contain stocks of grain sufficient for at least one year and possibly two.

The barracks, housing 5,000–6,000 men, occupied the largest area. These long, narrow, rectangular buildings were divided into pairs of rooms, each pair providing accommodation for an eight-man

A stone-built granary at a camp near Hadrian's Wall.

section (**contubernium**). Along the front of each building ran a colonnaded veranda. Each section cooked for itself on a hearth in the front living room, which was slightly the smaller of the two rooms, and slept in the larger room at the back. Each block housed a century (80 men). At the end of the block a larger suite of rooms was provided for the centurion, who may have shared it with his optio. The blocks themselves were arranged in pairs facing each other across an alleyway.

The bathhouse was important both for hygienic reasons and because it provided a social center for the troops; every fortress and many smaller forts had one. Like the civilian baths, it consisted of a tepidarium, caldarium, and frigidarium. Sometimes it was outside the fortress, by a nearby stream or river, sometimes inside.

One other building, always outside, should be mentioned: the amphitheater. It had the same shape and layout as the civilian amphitheater and could seat the whole legion. It was used for ceremonial parades, weapon training, and displays of tactics, as well as for occasional gladiatorial shows.

Not surprisingly, civilians also tended to gather around military bases. At first they were traders who set up little bars to sell appetizing food and drink to supplement the plain rations served in the barracks. Naturally, too, these bars gave soldiers opportunities to meet the local girls. Unlike their senior officers, whose wives, children, and sometimes even mothers and sisters lived in the fortress, legionary soldiers were not legally allowed to marry. However, the army tolerated unofficial unions. While the father lived in barracks, his family grew up just outside, and his sons often followed his profession and enlisted when they were eighteen or nineteen. Many such settlements (**vīcī**) developed gradually into

A centurion's quarters, based on remains of a wooden barrack block with painted plaster found at Chester.

Barrack blocks and the amphitheater.

The remains of the Chester amphitheater today.

towns. A few became large, self-governing cities, such as Eboracum (York). Thus the military fortress, which had begun as a means of holding down newly conquered territory, ended by playing an important part in the development of civilian town life.

The Roman fortress

The Romans built their fortresses of wood, for speed, and later rebuilt them in stone. The top picture shows a reconstruction of a wooden gate at a fort in central England (seen from the inside). Below is a stone gateway (seen from the outside) rebuilt at a fortress used as a supply base for Hadrian's Wall.

Vocabulary checklist 27

adeō	*so much, so greatly*
anteā	*before*
appāreō, appārēre, appāruī	*appear*
ardeō, ardēre, arsī	*burn, be on fire*
comes, comitis, m. f.	*comrade, companion*
gaudeō, gaudēre	*be pleased, rejoice*
ignārus, ignāra, ignārum	*not knowing, unaware*
imperō, imperāre, imperāvī	*order, command*
incendō, incendere, incendī, incēnsus	*burn, set fire to*
īnsidiae, īnsidiārum, f. pl.	*trap, ambush*
iussum, iussī, n.	*order, instruction*
manus, manūs, f.	*hand, band (of men)*
noceō, nocēre, nocuī	*hurt*
praeceps, praeceps, praeceps, *gen.* praecipitis	*headlong*
praemium, praemiī, n.	*prize, reward*
proximus, proxima, proximum	*nearest*
quālis, quālis, quāle	*what sort of*
sub	*under, beneath*
tacitus, tacita, tacitum	*silent, quiet*
tantus, tanta, tantum	*so great, such a great*

An eagle and other standards.

IMPERIUM

Stage 28

ultiō Rōmāna

post mortem Cogidubnī, Salvius rēgnum eius occupāvit.
pecūniam ā Britannīs extorquēre statim coepit. Salvium
adiuvābat Belimicus, prīnceps Canticōrum.

prope aulam habitābat agricola Britannicus, quī Salviō
pecūniam trādere nōluit. Salvius igitur mīlitibus imperāvit ut
casam agricolae dīriperent. centuriōnem mīlitibus praefēcit.

1 mīlitēs, gladiīs hastīsque armātī, casam
agricolae oppugnāvērunt.

2 agricola, gladiō centuriōnis vulnerātus,
exanimātus dēcidit.

3 servī, clāmōribus territī,
fūgērunt.

4 fīlius agricolae, fūste armātus, frūstrā
restitit.

5 Belimicus, spē praemiī adductus, mīlitēs
Rōmānōs adiuvābat et incitābat.

6 mīlitēs casam intrāvērunt et arcam,
pecūniā complētam, abstulērunt.

7   deinde mīlitēs fēminās, catēnīs vīnctās, ad
    castra dūxērunt.

8   postrēmō mīlitēs casam incendērunt.
    flammae, ventō auctae, casam celeriter
    cōnsūmpsērunt.

9   pāstōrēs, quī prope casam habitābant, immōtī stābant,
    spectāculō attonitī.
          casam vīdērunt, flammīs cōnsūmptam.
          fīlium agricolae vīdērunt, hastā graviter vulnerātum.
          agricolam ipsum vīdērunt, gladiō centuriōnis interfectum.
          tandem abiērunt, īrā commōtī, Belimicum Rōmānōsque
    vituperantēs.

testāmentum

ego, Tiberius Claudius Cogidubnus, rēx magnus Britannōrum, morbō gravī afflīctus, hoc testāmentum fēcī.

ego Titum Flāvium Domitiānum, optimum Imperātōrum, hērēdem meum faciō. mandō T. Flāviō Domitiānō rēgnum meum cīvēsque Rēgnēnsēs. iubeō cīvēs Rēgnēnsēs lēgibus pārēre et vītam quiētam agere. nam prīncipēs Rēgnēnsium mē saepe vexāvērunt. aliī, spē praedae adductī, inter sē pugnāvērunt; aliī, īnsāniā affectī, sēditiōnem contrā Rōmānōs facere temptāvērunt. nunc tamen eōs omnēs oportet discordiam huius modī dēpōnere.

dō lēgō Cn. Iūliō Agricolae statuam meam, ā fabrō Britannicō factam. sīc Agricola mē per tōtam vītam in memoriā habēre potest.

dō lēgō C. Salviō Līberālī, fidēlissimō amīcōrum meōrum, duōs tripodas argenteōs. Salvius vir summae prūdentiae est.

dō lēgō L. Marciō Memorī vīllam meam prope Aquās Sūlis sitam. L. Marcius Memor, ubi aeger ad thermās vēnī, ut auxilium ā deā Sūle peterem, benignē mē excēpit.

dō lēgō Dumnorigī, prīncipī Rēgnēnsium, quem sīcut fīlium amāvī, mīlle aureōs aulamque meam. sī forte Dumnorix mortuus est, haec C. Salviō Līberālī lēgō.

dō lēgō Belimicō, prīncipī Canticōrum, quīngentōs aureōs et nāvem celerrimam. Belimicus enim mē ab ursā ōlim servāvit, quae per aulam meam saeviēbat.

mandō C. Salviō Līberālī cūram fūneris meī. volō Salvium corpus meum sepelīre. volō eum mēcum sepelīre gemmās meās, paterās aureās, omnia arma quae ad bellum vēnātiōnemque comparāvī.

mandō C. Salviō Līberālī hoc testāmentum, manū meā scrīptum ānulōque meō signātum. dolus malus ab hōc testāmentō abestō!

5 **lēgibus: lēx** *law*

spē: spēs *hope*
praedae: praeda *booty, plunder, loot*
10 **adductī: addūcere** *lead on, encourage*
affectī: afficere *affect*
contrā *against*
discordiam: discordia *strife*
15 **sīc** *thus, in this way*
in memoriā habēre *keep in mind, remember*
benignē *kindly*
excēpit: excipere *receive*
20 **mīlle** *a thousand*
quīngentōs: quīngentī *five hundred*
celerrimam: celer *quick, fast*
fūneris: fūnus *funeral*
25 **sepelīre** *bury*
gemmās: gemma *gem, jewel*
ad bellum *for war*
signātum: signāre *sign, seal*
dolus … abestō! *may … trickery keep away!*
30 **malus** *evil, bad*

in aulā Salviī

When you have read this story, answer the questions on the opposite page.

Salvius, cum dē morte Cogidubnī audīvisset, ē castrīs discessit.
per prōvinciam iter fēcit ad aulam quam ē testāmentō accēperat.
ibi novem diēs manēbat ut rēs Cogidubnī administrāret. decimō
diē, iterum profectus, pecūniam opēsque ā Britannīs extorquēre
incēpit. nōnnūllī prīncipēs, avāritiā et metū corruptī, Salvium
adiuvābant.

Belimicus, quamquam multa praemia honōrēsque ā Salviō
accēpit, haudquāquam contentus erat. rēx enim Rēgnēnsium
esse cupiēbat. hāc spē adductus, cum paucīs prīncipibus
coniūrāre coepit. quī tamen, Belimicō diffīsī, rem Salviō
rettulērunt.

Salvius, audāciā Belimicī incēnsus, eum interficere cōnstituit.
amīcōs igitur, quibus maximē cōnfīdēbat, ad sē vocāvit; eōs in
aulam ingressōs rogāvit utrum vim an venēnum adhibēret.

ūnus ex amīcīs, vir callidissimus,
"venēnum," inquit, "Belimicō, hostī īnfestō, aptissimum est."
"sed quō modō tālem rem efficere possumus?" inquit Salvius.
"nam Belimicus, vir magnae prūdentiae, nēminī cōnfīdit."
"hunc homunculum dēcipere nōbīs facile est," inquit ille.
"venēnum cibō mixtum multōs virōs callidiōrēs quam
Belimicum iam fefellit. ipse sciō venēnum perītē dare."
"euge!" inquit Salvius, cōnsiliō amīcī dēlectātus. "facillimum
est mihi illum ad cēnam sūmptuōsam invītāre. mē oportet
epistulam blandam eī mittere. verbīs enim mollibus ac blandīs
resistere nōn potest."

Salvius igitur Belimicum ad aulam sine morā invītāvit. quī,
epistulā mendācī dēceptus neque ūllam fraudem suspicātus, ad
aulam nōnā hōrā vēnit.

decimō: decimus *tenth*
profectus *having set out*
5 avāritiā: avāritia *greed*
metū: metus *fear*

haudquāquam *not at all*

10
rettulērunt: referre *tell, report*
audāciā: audācia *boldness, audacity*
incēnsus *inflamed, angered*
15 utrum ... an *whether ... or*
adhibēret: adhibēre *use*
īnfestō: īnfestus *dangerous*
aptissimum: aptus *suitable*

20 mixtum: miscēre *mix*
fefellit: fallere *deceive*
sūmptuōsam: sūmptuōsus *expensive, lavish*
blandam: blandus *flattering*
25 mollibus: mollis *soft*
morā: mora *delay*
neque *and not*
ūllam: ūllus *any*
fraudem: fraus *trick*
nōnā: nōnus *ninth*

Questions

1 Where was Salvius when he heard of Cogidubnus' death? Where did he then travel to (lines 1–2)?

2 How long did Salvius stay there? Why?

3 After setting out again, what did Salvius do next (lines 3–5)?

4 What motivated some chieftains to help him?

5 Why would you have expected Belimicus to be satisfied? Why did he start plotting (lines 7–10)?

6 How did Salvius find out about Belimicus' plot (lines 10–11)?

7 What decision did Salvius take when he heard of Belimicus' treachery? What question did Salvius put to his friends?

8 What did one of the friends suggest? Why did Salvius feel doubtful about it?

9 The friend gave reasons in support of his suggestion (lines 19–21). Give two of them.

10 What did Salvius say would be very easy to do (lines 22–23)?

11 How did Salvius say he would lure Belimicus into his trap? Why was he certain of success (lines 23–25)?

12 Pick out and translate one group of Latin words in the last sentence to show that Belimicus fell into the trap.

About the language 1: more on the ablative case

1   In this Stage, you have seen sentences like this:

> Salvius, cum dē **morte** rēgis audīvisset, ē **castrīs** discessit.
> *When Salvius had heard about the death of the king, he left the camp.*

The words in **boldface** are in the ablative case. The ablative case is used with a number of prepositions in Latin.

2   Study the following sentences:

> mīles, **vulnere** impedītus, tandem cessit.
> *The soldier, hindered by his wound, gave in at last.*

> iuvenis, **gladiō** armātus, ad castra contendit.
> *The young man, armed with a sword, hurried to the camp.*

> servī, **catēnīs** vīnctī, in fundō labōrābant.
> *The slaves, bound in chains, were working on the farm.*

The words in **boldface** are in the ablative case, but there is no preposition ahead of them in Latin. Notice the various ways of translating these words into English.

3   Further examples:

   a   Salvius, audāciā Belimicī attonitus, nihil dīxit.
   b   mercātor, fūstibus verberātus, in fossā exanimātus iacēbat.
   c   mīlitēs, mūrō dēfēnsī, barbarīs diū resistēbant.
   d   uxor mea ānulum, gemmīs ōrnātum, ēmit.
   e   hospitēs, arte ancillae dēlectātī, plausērunt.

cēna Salviī

Belimicum aulam intrantem Salvius benignē excēpit et in
triclīnium addūxit. ibi sōlī sūmptuōsē atque hilarē cēnābant.
Belimicus, Salvium rīdentem cōnspicātus vīnōque solūtus,
audācter dīcere coepit:

"mī Salvī, multa et magna beneficia ā mē accēpistī. postquam
effūgērunt Quīntus et Dumnorix, ego sōlus tē adiūvī; multōs
continuōs diēs eōs persecūtus, Dumnorigem occīdī; multa falsa
Agricolae dīxī ut Cogidubnum perfidiae damnārem. prō hīs
tantīs beneficiīs praemium meritum rogō."

Salvius, ubi haec audīvit, arrogantiā Belimicī incēnsus, īram
tamen cēlāvit et cōmiter respondit:

"praemium meritum iam tibi parāvī. sed cūr nihil cōnsūmis,
mī amīce? volō tē garum exquīsītissimum gustāre quod ex
Hispāniā importāvī. puer! fer mihi et Belimicō illud garum!"

cum servus garum ambōbus dedisset, Salvius ad hospitem
versus,

"dīc mihi, Belimice," inquit, "quid prō hīs tantīs beneficiīs
repetis?"

"iam ex testāmentō Cogidubnī," respondit ille, "quīngentōs
aureōs accēpī. id haudquāquam satis est. rēgnum ipsum repetō."

quod cum audīvisset, Salvius "ego," inquit, "nōn Cogidubnus,
aureōs tibi dedī. cūr haud satis est?"

"quid dīcis?" exclāmāvit Belimicus. "hoc nōn intellegō."

"illud testāmentum," respondit Salvius, "est falsum. nōn
Cogidubnus sed ego scrīpsī."

sūmptuōsē *lavishly*
atque *and*
hilarē *in high spirits*
5   vīnō . . . solūtus *relaxed by the*
               wine
audācter *boldly*
persecūtus *having pursued*
damnārem: damnāre *condemn*
10 meritum: meritus *well-deserved*
īram: īra *anger*

Hispāniā: Hispānia *Spain*

15

repetis: repetere *claim*

20

haud *not*

25

About the language 2: expressions of time

1 Study the following examples:

> lēgātus sermōnem cum Quīntō **duās hōrās** habēbat.
> *The commander talked with Quintus for two hours.*

> **quattuor diēs** fugitīvus in silvā latēbat.
> *For four days, the fugitive lay hidden in the wood.*

In these sentences, the words in **boldface** indicate how long something went on; for this, Latin uses the accusative case.

2 Now study the following:

> **tertiā hōrā** nūntiī advēnērunt.
> *At the third hour, the messengers arrived.*

> **decimō diē** Agricola pugnāre cōnstituit.
> *On the tenth day, Agricola decided to fight.*

In these sentences, the words in **boldface** indicate when something happened; for this, Latin uses the ablative case.

3 Further examples:

a hospitēs trēs hōrās cēnābant.
b quartō diē revēnit rēx.
c Agricola prōvinciam septem annōs administrāvit.
d secundā hōrā lībertus Memorem excitāre temptāvit.
e mediā nocte hostēs castra nostra oppugnāvērunt.
f sex diēs nāvigābāmus; septimō diē ad portum advēnimus.

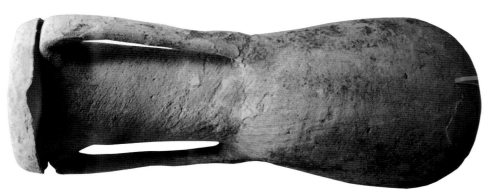

An amphora that brought garum from Spain to Deva.

Belimicus rēx

Belimicus, cum haec audīvisset, adeō attonitus erat ut nihil respondēre posset. Salvius autem haec addidit rīdēns,
"mī amīce, cūr tam attonitus es? tū et Cogidubnus semper inimīcī erātis. num quicquam ab illō spērāvistī? nōs autem in amīcitiā sumus. tibi multum dēbeō, ut dīxistī. itaque rēgem tē creāre in animō habeō. sed rēgnum quod tibi dēstinō multō maius est quam Cogidubnī. heus! puer! plūs garī!"
servus, cui Salvius hoc imperāvit, statim exiit. brevī regressus, garum venēnō mixtum intulit atque in Belimicī pateram effūdit. tam laetus erat ille, ubi verba Salviī audīvit, ut garum cōnsūmeret, ignārus perīculī mortis.
"quantum est hoc rēgnum quod mihi prōmīsistī? ubi gentium est?" rogāvit Belimicus.
Salvius cachinnāns "multō maius est," inquit, "quam imperium Rōmānum."
Belimicus hīs verbīs permōtus,
"nimium bibistī, mī amīce," inquit. "nūllum rēgnum nōvī maius quam imperium Rōmānum."
"rēgnum est, quō omnēs tandem abeunt," respondit Salvius. "rēgnum est, unde nēmō redīre potest. Belimice, tē rēgem creō mortuōrum."
Belimicus, metū mortis pallidus, surrēxit. haerēbat lingua in gutture; tintinābant aurēs. ventrem, quī iam graviter dolēbat, prēnsāvit. metū īrāque commōtus exclāmāvit,
"tū mihi nocēre nōn audēs, quod omnia scelera tua Agricolae dēnūntiāre possum."
"mē dēnūntiāre nōn potes, Belimice, quod nunc tibi imminet mors. nunc tibi abeundum est in rēgnum tuum. avē atque valē, mī Belimice!"
Belimicus, venēnō excruciātus, magnum gemitum dedit et humī cecidit mortuus. servī corpus Belimicī ē triclīniō extractum in hortō incendērunt. flammae, ventō auctae, corpus celerrimē cōnsūmpsērunt. sīc Belimicus arrogantiae poenās dedit; sīc Salvius cēterīs prīncipibus persuāsit ut in fidē manērent.

5   spērāvistī: spērāre *hope for, expect*
amīcitiā: amīcitia *friendship*
creāre *make, create*
dēstinō: dēstināre *intend*

10   effūdit: effundere *pour out*

ubi gentium? *where in the world?*

15

20   lingua *tongue*
gutture: guttur *throat*
tintinābant: tintināre *ring*
ventrem: venter *stomach*
graviter dolēbat: graviter dolēre *be extremely painful*

25   scelera: scelus *crime*
dēnūntiāre *denounce, reveal*
imminet: imminēre *hang over*
tibi abeundum est *you must go away*

30   avē atque valē *hail and farewell*
excruciātus: excruciāre *torture, torment*
ventō: ventus *wind*
auctae: augēre *increase*

About the language 3: impersonal verbs

1 In Stage 11, you met the verb **placet**. Notice again how it is used:

> mihi **placet** hoc dōnum accipere.
> *It pleases me to receive this present.*

Or, in more natural English:

> *I am glad to receive this present.*

> nōbīs **placet**.
> *It pleases us.*

Or, in more natural English:

> *We like it.*

2 The following verbs are used in a similar way:

> nōs **decet** praemium Modestō dare.
> *It is proper for us to give a reward to Modestus.*

Or, more naturally:

> *We ought to give a reward to Modestus.*

> mē **taedet** huius vītae.
> *It makes me tired of this life.*

Or, more naturally:

> *I am tired of this life.*

> Rōmānōs numquam **oportet** hostibus crēdere.
> *It is never right for Romans to trust the enemy.*

Or, more naturally:

> *Romans must never trust the enemy.*

3 These verbs are known as **impersonal verbs**. Their literal English equivalent always involves the general idea of "it."

4 Further examples:

   a tibi placet?
   b saltātrīcem spectāre volō! mē taedet cibī et vīnī!
   c semper pluit!
   d Britannōs decet extrā aulam manēre.
   e nunc advesperāscit.
   f nōs oportet rēgnum Cogidubnī occupāre.

Word patterns: adjectives and nouns

1 Study the form and meaning of the following adjectives and nouns:

adjectives		nouns	
avārus	*greedy, miserly*	avāritia	*greed*
laetus	*happy*	laetitia	*happiness*
īnsānus	*mad*	īnsānia	*madness*

2 Now complete the table below:

superbus	*proud*	superbia	. . . .
trīstis	. . . .	trīstitia	. . . .
perītus	. . . .	perītia	*skill, experience*
prūdēns	*shrewd, sensible*	prūdentia	. . . .
sapiēns	. . . .	. . . .	. . . .
ēlegāns	. . . .	ēlegantia	. . . .

3 Give the meaning of the following nouns:

audācia, amīcitia, arrogantia, potentia, perfidia, absentia, neglegentia.

Practicing the language

1 Complete each of the sentences below with the correct person of the subjunctive verb. Then translate each sentence. For example:

> tam perterritī erāmus ut ex urbe fugerē. . . .
> tam perterritī erāmus ut ex urbe **fugerēmus**.
> *We were so frightened that we fled from the city.*

a Quīntus nesciēbat quō modō Cogidubnus periisse. . . .
b cīvēs, cum tabernam intrāvisse. . . , vīnum poposcērunt.
c Agricola mīlitibus imperāvit ut ad castra redīre. . . .
d tantus erat clāmor ut nēmō centuriōnem audīre. . . .
e nōs, cum Agricolam vīdissē. . . , maximē gaudēbāmus.
f rēxne tibi persuāsit ut sēcum templum vīsitārē. . . ?
g domum rediī ut parentēs meōs adiuvāre. . . .
h cūr dīcere nōlēbātis ubi illō diē mātrem vestram vīdissē. . . ?

2 Complete each sentence with the correct ablative from the box below. Then translate the sentence.

audāciā	vīnō	gladiō	fūstibus	īrā	catēnīs

a nūntius, ... graviter vulnerātus, effugere nōn poterat.
b Salvius, ... eius attonitus, diū tacēbat.
c captīvī, ... vīnctī, in longīs ōrdinibus stābant.
d Britannī, ... armātī, pugnāre volēbant.
e dominus, ... commōtus, omnēs servōs carnificibus trādidit.
f hospitēs, ... solūtī, clāmāre et iocōs facere coepērunt.

Interpreting the evidence: our knowledge of Roman Britain

Our knowledge of the Roman occupation of Britain is based on different types of evidence:

1 **literary** evidence: what the Greeks and Romans wrote about Britain;

2 **archaeological** evidence: what archaeologists have discovered from excavations, including:

3 **inscriptional** evidence: inscriptions in Latin (and sometimes Greek) from tombstones, altars, public buildings and monuments, and from private objects such as writing tablets, defixiones, etc.

Julius Caesar.

Literary evidence

A picture of Roman Britain is given in two well-known Latin texts. One is Julius Caesar's account of his brief reconnaissance mission to the southeast coast of Britain in 55 BC and his return in greater force the following year when he stormed the fortress of a British king before withdrawing again. The other is Tacitus' biography of his father-in-law, Agricola. Much of this is devoted to Agricola's career in the army in Roman Britain and to his campaigns as governor of the province. The account of Agricola's life in Stage 26 is almost entirely based on Tacitus' description.

Both pieces of writing are to some extent biased. Caesar wrote his account in order to justify his actions to the senate in Rome and place himself in a favorable light; Tacitus was anxious to honor the memory of his father-in-law and to praise his success as a soldier and a governor. Agricola appears almost too good to be true, in strong contrast to the Emperor Domitian, who is portrayed as jealous of Agricola's success and anxious to bring about his downfall.

Tacitus' Agricola *in an English translation.*

A rescue excavation: a Roman bathhouse in London, England. This excavation was undertaken during the construction of a new rail link.

An excavation in London on the site of the temple of Mithras has uncovered 10,000 Roman artifacts including fences, clothing, documents, and even this woven basket.

Archaeological evidence

The task of archaeologists is to uncover and explain the remains of the past. First they must locate a suitable site to excavate. Some sites are already known but have not been completely excavated; others are found by accident. In 1960 a workman digging a drain came across fragments of a mosaic floor and this chance discovery led to the excavation of the palace at Fishbourne. When sites are needed for roadbuilding or other kinds of development, archaeologists may have limited time in which to excavate before the bulldozers move in or the remains are reburied.

Once the site has been located, archaeologists have to plan and carry out a careful scientific survey and excavation of the area. As the earth is removed from a site, they will watch for two things: the existence and position of any building foundations, and the way in which the various levels or layers of earth change color and texture. In this way they build up a picture of the main features on the site.

At the same time they carefully examine the soil for smaller pieces of evidence such as bones, pottery, jewelry, coins, and other small objects. The aim is not simply to find precious objects but to discover as much as possible about the people who used the buildings, what their lives were like, when they lived there, and even perhaps what happened to them. For such work the archaeologist needs some of the same kind of training and skills as a detective.

Certain finds are useful for dating the site. Roman coins can usually be dated accurately because they have emperors' heads and names stamped on them. These in turn can help date the level of soil being excavated. Fairly accurate dates can also be obtained from a study of the styles and patterns of pottery found on a site. Large quantities have survived, as pottery is a durable material which does not rot, and broken pieces (shards) are found in very large numbers on many sites.

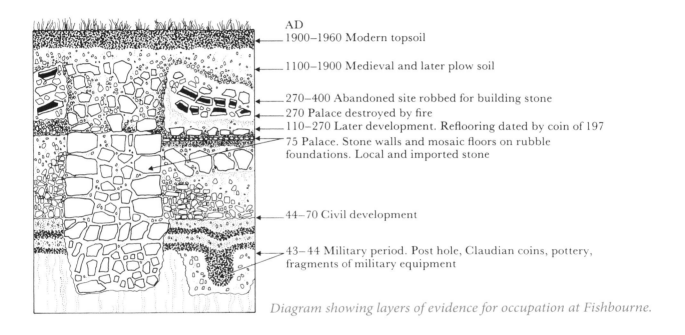

AD
1900–1960 Modern topsoil

1100–1900 Medieval and later plow soil

270–400 Abandoned site robbed for building stone
270 Palace destroyed by fire
110–270 Later development. Reflooring dated by coin of 197
75 Palace. Stone walls and mosaic floors on rubble foundations. Local and imported stone

44–70 Civil development

43–44 Military period. Post hole, Claudian coins, pottery, fragments of military equipment

Diagram showing layers of evidence for occupation at Fishbourne.

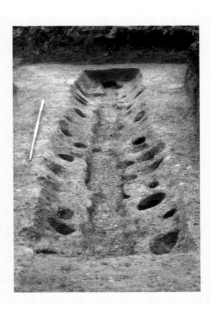

A field belonging to a Roman villa was found to contain a system of trenches. Very careful attention to difference of color and texture of soil revealed a planting trench with holes at the sides for posts to support the plants. Microscopic examination of pollen in the trench showed that these were grape vines.

Pottery is also one of the clues that can reveal trade and travel patterns. The presence on a British site of pottery which has come from Italy or Gaul shows that, at the time the site was occupied, goods were imported from those areas. In addition, the owner of the villa was wealthy enough to pay for such imported goods.

By painstaking excavation archaeologists have been able to reconstruct a remarkably detailed picture of the Roman occupation of Britain. Layers of ash, charred pottery, and other burned objects indicate a destruction by fire; a mass of broken rubble may suggest that a building was demolished, perhaps to make way for a larger, better one. Many sites in Britain show a gradual development from a simple timber-framed farmhouse building to a larger stone house to a grander, multi-roomed mansion with baths, mosaic pavements, and colonnades. The fact that most of the Romano-British villas were in the southeast, whereas the military fortresses were established in the north and west, suggests that Britain was largely peaceful and prosperous in the southeast but still troubled by the threat of hostile tribes in the northwest. Traces of a vast network of Roman roads have been found, showing just how numerous and effective communications must have been. Parts of many Romano-British towns have been excavated, revealing how advanced urban life was. It is not uncommon to find the remains of an extensive forum, carefully laid out grids of streets, the foundations of many large buildings including temples with altars and inscriptions, sometimes a theater and an amphitheater, and substantial city walls.

The excavation of military sites, such as forts, marching camps, and legionary fortresses, has shown how important the army was in maintaining peace and protection for the province. It has also shown very clearly the movements of the legions and auxiliaries around the country and told us much about the lives of Roman soldiers.

Finds of coins and pottery are useful in dating levels, but need careful interpretation. This denarius of the Emperor Vespasian, who sent Agricola to govern Britain, was minted in AD 73. But coins circulated for many years; this was found with other coins issued a century later.

This small fragment of a pottery bowl can be dated by the style of decoration. It was made in central Gaul about AD 240–270. However, it would have been an expensive import and so could have been treasured for generations before it eventually broke and was thrown away.

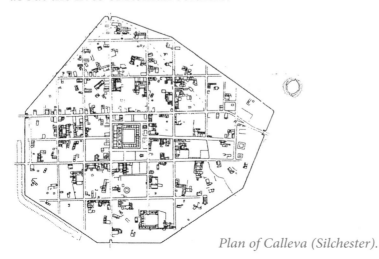

Plan of Calleva (Silchester).

Britain in the later first century AD

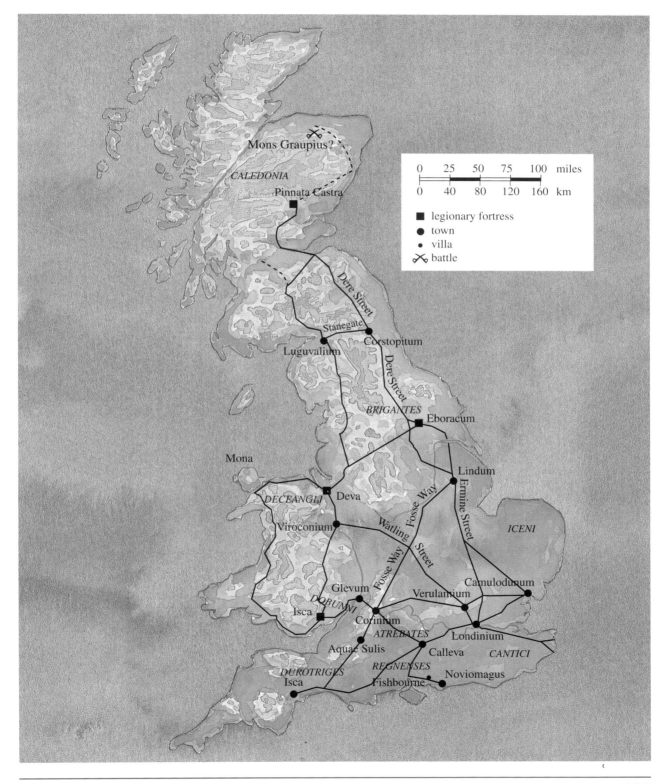

Mons Graupius?

CALEDONIA

Pinnata Castra

0	25	50	75	100	miles
0	40	80	120	160	km

■ legionary fortress
● town
· villa
⚔ battle

Dere Street

Stanegate

Corstopitum

Luguvalium

Dere Street

BRIGANTES

Eboracum

Mona

Lindum

DECEANGLI   Deva

Ermine Street

Viroconium

ICENI

Fosse Way

Watling Street

Camulodunum

Glevum

Verulamium

Isca

DOBUNNI

Corinium

Londinium

ATREBATES

Aquae Sulis

Calleva

CANTICI

DUROTRIGES

REGNENSES

Noviomagus

Isca

Fishbourne

Inscriptional evidence

Some important evidence about the Roman occupation of Britain comes from inscriptions, particularly on the tombstones of soldiers. Here is the inscription on the tombstone of a soldier who was buried at Deva.

At first sight, this looks difficult to decipher. The task, however, is made easier by the fact that most of these inscriptions follow a standard pattern. The items are usually arranged in the following order:

```
       D M
 L LICINIUS L F
   TER VALENS
  ARE VETERAN
LEG XX VV AN VL
      H S E
```

1 The dedication at the top of the stone – D M – abbreviation for **Dīs Mānibus** (to the spirits of the departed).

2 The praenomen. This is the first of a citizen's three names and is usually abbreviated to a single letter, as here – L for **Lūcius**.

3 The nomen. Always given in full, as here – **Licinius**.

4 The father's name. It is usually only the father's praenomen that is given, and this can be recognized in abbreviated form by the single letter which comes before an F representing **fīlius**. The son often had the same praenomen as his father, as here L F for **Lūciī fīlius**.

5 Tribe. Roman soldiers were Roman citizens and were therefore enrolled in one of the thirty-five Roman tribes which were used for voting purposes. The name of the tribe is abbreviated, as here – TER for **Teretīna**.

6 The cognomen. This is the last of the three names, usually placed after the father's name and the voting tribe in which the soldier was enrolled. It is always given in full, as here – **Valēns**. Three names were a mark of Roman citizenship and therefore an important indication of status.

7 Birthplace. This can usually be identified as a town in the Roman empire, thus ARE for **Arelātē** (modern Arles in the south of France).

8 Rank and legion. They are usually both abbreviated – VETERAN for **veterānus** (a retired soldier or one coming up to retirement); LEG XX VV for **legiōnis XX Valeriae Victrīcis** (Twentieth Legion Valeria Victrix).

9 Age. This is represented by AN or ANN for **annōrum**, followed by a number. This number is often rounded off to a multiple of 5. Sometimes VIX for **vīxit** (lived) is placed before AN.

10 Length of service (not included in the inscription above). This is represented by STIP followed by a number, e.g. STIP X for **stipendia X** (ten years' service).

11 The final statement. This is abbreviated, and usually takes the form of H S E for **hīc situs est** (is buried here) or H F C for **hērēs faciendum cūrāvit** (his heir had this stone set up).

The inscription can therefore be interpreted as follows:

D(IS) M(ANIBUS)
L(UCIUS) LICINIUS L(UCII) F(ILIUS)
TER(ETINA) VALENS
ARE(LATE) VETERAN(US)
LEG(IONIS) XX V(ALERIAE) V(ICTRICIS)
AN(NORUM) VL
H(IC) S(ITUS) E(ST)

This stone is dedicated to the spirits of the departed. Lucius Licinius Valens, son of Lucius, of the Teretine tribe, from Arelate, veteran of the Twentieth Legion Valeria Victrix, aged forty-five, is buried here.

On the right is the inscription on another soldier's tombstone, also found at Chester.

Try to find out from it the following information:

1 The soldier's name
2 His rank
3 His legion
4 His age at death
5 The length of his service

In the same way, find as much information as you can from the following inscription:

Vocabulary checklist 28

ac, atque	*and*
cōnstituō, cōnstituere, cōnstituī, cōnstitūtus	*decide*
corpus, corporis, n.	*body*
doleō, dolēre, doluī	*hurt, be in pain*
gemitus, gemitūs, m.	*groan*
īra, īrae, f.	*anger*
malus, mala, malum	*evil, bad*
mandō, mandāre, mandāvī, mandātus	*order, entrust, hand over*
metus, metūs, m.	*fear*
occīdō, occīdere, occīdī, occīsus	*kill*
opēs, opum, f. pl.	*money, wealth*
quicquam (*also spelt* quidquam)	*anything*
sīc	*thus, in this way*
spēs, speī, f.	*hope*
suspicātus, suspicāta, suspicātum	*having suspected*
ut	*as*
ventus, ventī, m.	*wind*
ūnus	*one*
duo	*two*
trēs	*three*
quattuor	*four*
quīnque	*five*
sex	*six*
septem	*seven*
octō	*eight*
novem	*nine*
decem	*ten*
vīgintī	*twenty*
trīgintā	*thirty*
quadrāgintā	*forty*
quīnquāgintā	*fifty*
sexāgintā	*sixty*
septuāgintā	*seventy*
octōgintā	*eighty*
nōnāgintā	*ninety*
centum	*a hundred*
mīlle	*a thousand*
mīlia	*thousands*

An altar at Chester dedicated to the Holy Genius (Guardian Spirit) of his century by Aelius Claudianus, optio. VS stands for VOTUM SOLVIT, "fulfilled his vow." Aelius had promised to set up the altar if a prayer of his was answered. On the right are carved a sacrificial axe and a knife used in religious ceremonies at the altar. (Modern copy.)

ROMA

Stage 29

1 in mediā Rōmā est mōns nōtissimus, quī Capitōlium
appellātur.
in summō Capitōliō stat templum, ubi deus Iuppiter adōrātur.

2 sub Capitōliō iacet Forum Rōmānum.
forum ab ingentī multitūdine cīvium cotīdiē complētur.
aliī negōtium agunt; aliī in porticibus stant et ab amīcīs
salūtantur; aliī per forum in lectīcīs feruntur. ubīque magnus
strepitus audītur.

3 aliquandō pompae splendidae per forum dūcuntur.

4 prope medium forum est templum Vestae, ubi ignis sacer ā Virginibus Vestālibus cūrātur.

5 in extrēmō forō stant Rōstra, ubi ōrātiōnēs apud populum habentur.

6 prope Rōstra est carcer, ubi captīvī populī Rōmānī custōdiuntur.

nox

I

nox erat. lūna stēllaeque in caelō serēnō fulgēbant. tempus erat
quō hominēs quiēscere solent. Rōmae tamen nūlla erat quiēs,
nūllum silentium.

magnīs in domibus, ubi dīvitēs habitābant, cēnae splendidae
cōnsūmēbantur. cibus sūmptuōsus ā servīs offerēbātur; vīnum   5
optimum ab ancillīs fundēbātur; carmina ā citharoedīs
perītissimīs cantābantur.

in altīs autem īnsulīs, nūllae cēnae splendidae
cōnsūmēbantur, nūllī citharoedī audiēbantur. ibi pauperēs, famē
paene cōnfectī, vītam miserrimam agēbant. aliī ad patrōnōs   10
epistulās scrībēbant ut auxilium eōrum peterent, aliī scelera
committere parābant.

prope forum magnus strepitus audiēbātur. nam arcus
magnificus in Viā Sacrā exstruēbātur. ingēns polyspaston arcuī
imminēbat. fabrī, quī arcum exstruēbant, dīligentissimē   15
labōrābant. aliī figūrās in arcū sculpēbant; aliī titulum in
fronte arcūs īnscrībēbant; aliī marmor ad summum arcum
tollēbant. omnēs strēnuē labōrābant ut arcum ante lūcem
perficerent. nam Imperātor Domitiānus hunc arcum frātrī Titō
postrīdiē dēdicāre volēbat. Titum vīvum ōderat; sed Titum   20
mortuum honōrāre cupiēbat. Domitiānus enim populum
Rōmānum, quī Titum maximē dīlēxerat, nunc sibi favēre
volēbat.

serēnō: serēnus *calm, clear*
fulgēbant: fulgēre *shine*
tempus *time*
Rōmae *in Rome*
quiēs *rest*
domibus: domus *house, home*
carmina: carmen *song*
altīs: altus *high*
īnsulīs: īnsula *apartment
  building*
famē: famēs *hunger*
cōnfectī: cōnfectus *worn out,
  exhausted*
patrōnōs: patrōnus *patron*
arcus *arch*
Viā Sacrā: Via Sacra *the Sacred
  Way (road running through
  the Forum)*
polyspaston *crane*
fabrī: faber *craftsman, workman*
figūrās: figūra *figure, shape*
sculpēbant: sculpere *carve*
titulum: titulus *inscription*
fronte: frōns *front*
īnscrībēbant: īnscrībere *write,
  inscribe*
marmor *marble*
ante *before*
lūcem: lūx *light, daylight*
perficerent: perficere *finish*
dēdicāre *dedicate*

II

praeerat huic operī Quīntus Haterius Latrōniānus, redēmptor
nōtissimus. eā nocte ipse fabrōs furēns incitābat. aderat quoque
Gāius Salvius Līberālis, Hateriī patrōnus, quī eum invicem
incitābat ut opus ante lūcem perficeret. anxius enim erat Salvius
quod Imperātōrī persuāserat ut Haterium operī praeficeret. hic   5
igitur fabrīs, quamquam omnīnō fessī erant, identidem
imperāvit nē labōre dēsisterent.

Glitus, magister fabrōrum, Haterium lēnīre temptābat.
"ecce, domine!" inquit. "fabrī iam arcum paene perfēcērunt.
ultimae litterae titulī nunc īnscrībuntur; ultimae figūrae   10
sculpuntur; ultimae marmoris massae ad summum arcum
tolluntur."

operī: opus *work, construction*
redēmptor *contractor, builder*
invicem *in turn*

identidem *repeatedly*

lēnīre *soothe, calm down*

ultimae: ultimus *last*
litterae: littera *letter*
massae: massa *block*

paulō ante hōram prīmam, fabrī labōre cōnfectī arcum
perfēcērunt. paulīsper urbs silēbat.

ūnus faber tamen, domum per forum rediēns, subitō trīstēs
fēminārum duārum clāmōrēs audīvit. duae enim captīvae,
magnō dolōre affectae, in carcere cantābant:

"mī Deus! mī Deus! respice mē! quārē mē dēseruistī?"

paulīsper *for a short time*
15 **silēbat: silēre** *be silent*

dolōre: dolor *grief*
affectae: affectus *overcome*
respice: respicere *look at, look*
                                            upon
quārē? *why?*

SENATVS
POPVLVSQVEROMANV
DIVOTITODIVIVESPAS
VESPASIANOAVGVST

"ecce, domine! fabrī iam
arcum paene perfēcērunt."

The origins of Rome

No one knows the source or the meaning of the name "Rome." However, the Romans themselves claimed that the name of their city came from that of its mythical founder, Romulus, who, according to tradition, drew the sacred city boundary line on the Palatine hill with his plow in 753 BC. The discovery of archaic huts confirms the presence of an eighth-century settlement on the Palatine. This settlement, like the rest of the district of Latium at this time, was inhabited by the **Latīnī**, who were shepherds and farmers. The geographical position of the Palatine settlement was ideal. It was bounded on the western side by a bend of the river Tiber where the river encircling the Tiber Island was narrow enough to be bridged; there was a ford nearby where sea, river, and land travel and trade converged from Etruria in the north, from Magna Graecia in the south, and from the Tyrrhenian Sea in the west toward the mountains along the Great Salt Way, the **Via Salāria**; and there were seven hills in the area providing strategic defense positions for an expanding population.

From the sixth century onward a continuous process of expansion transformed the agricultural settlements into one **urbs** extending over all seven hills. The marshy valley-lands were drained by canals, including the great sewer, the **Cloāca Maxima**, into which all the water flowed. There was constant building activity and the city was crowded with temples, public squares, baths, and basilicas.

Even as the city expanded, its form of government also changed. According to legend, Romulus had been followed by six other kings. The last of these, Tarquinius Superbus, was driven out, and the Roman Republic was established in 509 BC. The kings were replaced by annually elected magistrates. The most senior of these were the two consuls, who presided over the senate. During the time of Augustus (63 BC–AD 14), the Roman Republic in effect became an empire, with an emperor at its head.

Archaic cinerary urn in the form of a hut.

Romulus and Remus and the wolf.

About the language 1: active and passive voice

1 In Unit 1, you met sentences like these:

> puer clāmōrem **audit**.　　　ancilla vīnum **fundēbat**.
> *A boy **hears** the shout.*　　*A slave girl **was pouring** wine.*

The words in **boldface** are active forms of the verb.

2 In Stage 29, you have met sentences like these:

> clāmor ā puerō **audītur**.　　vīnum ab ancillā **fundēbātur**.
> *The shout **is heard** by a boy.*　*Wine **was being poured** by a slave girl.*

The words in **boldface** are passive forms of the verb.

3 Compare the following active and passive forms:

PRESENT TENSE

present active	*present passive*
portat	portātur
s/he carries, s/he is carrying	*s/he is carried*, or *s/he is being carried*
portant	portantur
they carry, they are carrying	*they are carried*, or *they are being carried*

IMPERFECT TENSE

imperfect active	*imperfect passive*
portābat	portābātur
s/he was carrying	*s/he was being carried*
portābant	portābantur
they were carrying	*they were being carried*

4 Further examples of the present passive:

   a cēna nostra ā coquō nunc parātur.
   b multa scelera in hāc urbe cotīdiē committuntur.
   c laudantur; dūcitur; rogātur; mittuntur.

Further examples of the imperfect passive:

   d candidātī ab amīcīs salūtābantur.
   e fābula ab āctōribus in theātrō agēbātur.
   f audiēbantur; laudābātur; necābantur; tenēbātur.

Masada

I

ex carcere, ubi captīvī custōdiēbantur, trīstēs clāmōrēs
audiēbantur. duae enim fēminae Iūdaeae, superstitēs eōrum quī
contrā Rōmānōs rebellāverant, fortūnam suam lūgēbant. altera
erat anus septuāgintā annōrum, altera mātrōna trīgintā annōs
nāta. ūnā cum eīs in carcere erant quīnque līberī, quōrum Simōn   5
nātū maximus sōlācium mātrī et aviae ferre temptābat.
    "māter, cūr tū lacrimīs opprimeris? nōlī lūgēre! decōrum est
Iūdaeīs fortitūdinem in rēbus adversīs praestāre."
    māter fīlium amplexa,
    "melius erat," inquit, "cum patre vestrō perīre abhinc annōs   10
novem. cūr tum ā morte abhorruī? cūr vōs servāvī?"
    Simōn, hīs verbīs commōtus, mātrem rogāvit quō modō
periisset pater atque quārē rem prius nōn nārrāvisset. eam ōrāvit
ut omnia explicāret. sed tantus erat dolor mātris ut prīmō nihil
dīcere posset. mox, cum sē collēgisset, ad līberōs conversa,   15
    "dē morte patris vestrī," inquit, "prius nārrāre nōlēbam nē vōs
quoque perīrētis, exemplum eius imitātī. nam tū frātrēsque
obstinātiōne iam nimium afficiminī. nunc tamen audeō vōbīs
tōtam rem patefacere quod nōs omnēs crās moritūrī sumus.

Iūdaeae: Iūdaeus *Jewish*
superstitēs: superstes *survivor*
rebellāverant: rebellāre *rebel,
    revolt*
lūgēbant: lūgēre *lament, mourn*
altera … altera *one … the other*
… annōs nāta *…years old*
ūnā cum *together with*
nātū maximus *eldest*
aviae: avia *grandmother*
opprimeris: opprimere
    overwhelm
rēbus adversīs: rēs adversae
    misfortune
praestāre *show, display*
amplexa: amplexus *having
    embraced*
abhinc *ago*
abhorruī: abhorrēre *shrink
    (from)*
exemplum *example*
imitātī: imitātus *having
    imitated*
obstinātiōne: obstinātiō
    stubbornness
afficiminī: afficere *affect*
crās *tomorrow*

The rock of Masada, showing the Roman siege ramp built on the west (right) side.

"nōs Iūdaeī contrā Rōmānōs trēs annōs pugnāre cōgēbāmur. annō 20
quārtō iste Beelzebub, Titus, urbem Ierosolymam expugnāvit.
numquam ego spectāculum terribilius vīdī: ubīque aedificia
flammīs cōnsūmēbantur; ubīque virī, fēminae, līberī
occīdēbantur; Templum ipsum ā mīlitibus dīripiēbātur; tōta
urbs ēvertēbātur. in illā clāde periērunt multa mīlia Iūdaeōrum; 25
sed nōs, quamquam ā mīlitibus īnfestīs circumveniēbāmur, cum
circiter mīlle superstitibus effūgimus. duce Eleazārō, ad rūpem
Masadam prōcessimus; quam ascendimus et occupāvimus. tū,
Simōn, illō tempore vix quīnque annōs nātus erās.

"rūpēs Masada est alta et praerupta, prope lacum Asphaltītēn 30
sita. ibi nōs, mūnītiōnibus undique dēfēnsī, Rōmānīs diū
resistēbāmus. intereā dux hostium, Lūcius Flāvius Silva, rūpem
castellīs multīs circumvēnit. deinde mīlitēs, iussū Silvae,
ingentem aggerem usque ad summam rūpem exstrūxērunt.
postrēmō aggerem ascendērunt, magnamque partem 35
mūnītiōnum ignī dēlēvērunt. tandem, cum nox appropinquāret,
Silva mīlitēs ad castra redūxit ut proximum diem victōriamque
exspectārent."

II

"illā nocte Eleazārus Iūdaeīs cōnsilium dīrum prōposuit.

"'magnō in discrīmine sumus,' inquit. 'nōs Iūdaeī, Deō
cōnfīsī, Rōmānīs adhūc resistimus; nunc illī nōs in servitūtem
trahere parant. nūlla spēs salūtis nōbīs ostenditur. nōnne melius
est perīre quam Rōmānīs cēdere? ego ipse mortem meā manū 5
īnflīctam accipiō, servitūtem spernō.'

"hīs verbīs Eleazārus tantum ardōrem in Iūdaeīs excitāvit ut
ad mortem statim festīnārent. virī uxōrēs līberōsque amplexī
occīdērunt. cum hanc dīram et saevam rem cōnfēcissent, decem
eōrum sorte ductī cēterōs interfēcērunt. tum ūnus ex illīs, sorte 10
invicem ductus, postquam novem reliquōs interfēcit, sē ipsum
gladiō trānsfīxit."

"quō modō nōs ipsī effūgimus?" rogāvit Simōn.

"ego Eleazārō pārēre nōn potuī," respondit māter. "amōre
līberōrum meōrum plūs quam timōre servitūtis afficiēbar. 15
vōbīscum in locō subterrāneō latēbam."

"ignāva!" clāmāvit Simōn. "ego mortem haudquāquam timeō.
ego, patris exemplī memor, eandem fortitūdinem praestāre
volō."

Beelzebub *Beelzebub, devil*
Ierosolymam: Ierosolyma
          Jerusalem
expugnāvit: expugnāre
          storm, take by storm

circiter *about*
duce: dux *leader*
rūpem: rūpēs *rock, crag*
praerupta: praeruptus *sheer,*
          steep
lacum Asphaltītēn: lacus
     Asphaltītēs *Lake*
     Asphaltites (the Dead Sea)
mūnītiōnibus: mūnītiō
          defense, fortification
undique *on all sides*
castellīs: castellum *fort*
iussū Silvae *at Silva's order*
aggerem: agger *ramp, mound*
          of earth
usque ad *right up to*
ignī, *abl*: ignis *fire*

discrīmine: discrīmen *crisis*
cōnfīsī: cōnfīsus *having*
     trusted, having put
     trust in
servitūtem: servitūs *slavery*
īnflīctam: īnflīgere *inflict*
ardōrem: ardor *spirit,*
          enthusiasm
sorte ductī *chosen by lot*
reliquōs: reliquus *remaining*
trānsfīxit: trānsfīgere *stab*

timōre: timor *fear*
subterrāneō: subterrāneus
          underground
haudquāquam *not at all*
memor *remembering,*
          mindful of
eandem *the same*

1   Study the following examples:

ego dē cōnsiliō dīrō nārrāre **cōgor**.
*I **am forced** to talk about a dreadful plan.*

cūr tū lacrimīs **opprimeris**?
*Why **are** you **overwhelmed** by tears?*

nōs ā mīlitibus īnfestīs **circumveniēbāmur**.
*We **were being surrounded** by hostile soldiers.*

tū frātrēsque obstinātiōne nimium **afficiminī**.
*You and your brothers **are affected** too much by stubbornness.*

2   You have now met many of the passive forms for the present and imperfect tenses. Compare all the passive forms with the active forms.

PRESENT TENSE

present active		*present passive*	
portō	*I carry, I am carrying*	portor	*I am (being) carried*
portās	*you carry (are carrying)*	portāris	*you are (being) carried*
portat	*s/he carries (is carrying)*	portātur	*s/he is (being) carried*
portāmus	*we carry (are carrying)*	portāmur	*we are (being) carried*
portātis	*you carry (are carrying)*	portāminī	*you are (being) carried*
portant	*they carry (are carrying)*	portantur	*they are (being) carried*

IMPERFECT TENSE

imperfect active		*imperfect passive*	
portābam	*I was carrying*	portābar	*I was being carried*
portābās	*you were carrying*	portābāris	*you were being carried*
portābat	*s/he was carrying*	portābātur	*s/he was being carried*
portābāmus	*we were carrying*	portābāmur	*we were being carried*
portābātis	*you were carrying*	portābāminī	*you were being carried*
portābant	*they were carrying*	portābantur	*they were being carried*

3   Further examples:

   a   cūr ad carcerem redūcimur? ab hostibus circumvenīris.
   b   tū et amīcus ā captīvīs dēcipiminī. tacēre iubeor.
   c   accūsor; īnstruuntur; docēmur; laediminī; comprehenderis; oppugnātur.
   d   ā comitibus dēserēbar. in fossās iaciēbāminī.
   e   identidem monēbāris ut domī manērēs.
   f   ēligēbantur; vītābāris; extrahēbāmur; adiuvābāminī; arcessēbātur; līberābar.

arcus Titī

I

postrīdiē māne ingēns Rōmānōrum multitūdō ad arcum Titī
undique conveniēbat. diēs fēstus ab omnibus cīvibus
celebrābātur. Imperātor Domitiānus eō diē frātrī Titō arcum
dēdicātūrus erat. iussū Imperātōris pompa magnifica tōtam per
urbem dūcēbātur.   5

    multae sellae ā servīs prope arcum pōnēbantur. illūc multī
senātōrēs, spē favōris Domitiānī, conveniēbant. inter eōs Salvius,
togam splendidam gerēns, locum quaerēbat ubi cōnspicuus
esset. inter equitēs, quī post senātōrēs stābant, aderat Haterius
ipse. favōrem Imperātōris avidē spērābat, et in animō volvēbat   10
quandō ā Salviō praemium prōmissum acceptūrus esset.

    āra ingēns, prō arcū exstrūcta, ā servīs flōribus ōrnābātur.
circum āram stābant vīgintī sacerdōtēs. aderant quoque
haruspicēs quī exta victimārum īnspicerent.

    intereā pompa lentē per Viam Sacram dūcēbātur. prīmā in   15
parte incēdēbant tubicinēs, tubās īnflantēs. post eōs vēnērunt
iuvenēs, quī trīgintā taurōs corōnīs ōrnātōs ad sacrificium
dūcēbant. tum multī servī, quī gāzam Iūdaeōrum portābant,
prīmam pompae partem claudēbant. huius gāzae pars
pretiōsissima erat mēnsa sacra, tubae, candēlābrum, quae omnia   20
aurea erant.

    septem captīvī Iūdaeī, quī mediā in pompā incēdēbant, ā
spectātōribus vehementer dērīdēbantur. quīnque līberī, serēnō
vultū incēdentēs, clāmōrēs et contumēliās neglegēbant, sed duae
fēminae plūrimīs lacrimīs spectātōrēs ōrābant ut līberīs   25
parcerent.

    post captīvōs vēnit Domitiānus ipse, currū magnificō vectus.
post Imperātōrem ībant ambō cōnsulēs, quōrum alter erat L.
Flāvius Silva. magistrātūs nōbilissimī effigiem Titī in umerīs
portābant. ā mīlitibus pompa claudēbātur.   30

undique *from all sides*

dēdicātūrus *going to dedicate*

favōris: favor *favor*
cōnspicuus *conspicuous, easily
seen*
equitēs *equites (wealthy
men ranking below senators)*
quandō *when*
acceptūrus *going to receive*
exta *entrails*

incēdēbant: incēdere *march, stride*

gāzam: gāza *treasure*
claudēbant: claudere *conclude,
complete*

vultū: vultus *expression, face*
currū: currus *chariot*
vectus: vehere *carry*
cōnsulēs: cōnsul *consul (senior
magistrate)*
magistrātūs: magistrātus
*magistrate (elected official
of Roman government)*

*Carving on the arch of Titus,
showing the treasures of the
Temple at Jerusalem carried in
triumph through the streets of
Rome.*

II

When you have read this part of the story, answer the questions on the next page.

ad arcum pompa pervēnit. Domitiānus, ē currū ēgressus ut sacrificium faceret, senātōrēs equitēsque salūtāvit. tum oculōs in arcum ipsum convertit. admīrātiōne affectus, Imperātor Salvium ad sē arcessītum valdē laudāvit. eī imperāvit ut Hateriō grātiās ageret. inde ad āram prōgressus, cultrum cēpit quō victimam sacrificāret. servus eī iugulum taurī obtulit. deinde Domitiānus victimam sacrificāvit, haec locūtus:

"tibi, dīve Tite, haec victima nunc sacrificātur; tibi hic arcus dēdicātur; tibi grātiae maximae ā populō Rōmānō aguntur."

subitō, dum Rōmānī oculōs in sacrificium intentē dēfīgunt, Simōn occāsiōnem nactus prōsiluit. mediōs in sacerdōtēs irrūpit; cultrum rapuit. omnēs spectātōrēs immōtī stābant, audāciā eius attonitī. Domitiānus, pavōre commōtus, pedem rettulit. nōn Imperātōrem tamen Simōn petīvit. cultrum in manū tenēns clāmāvit,

"nōs, quī superstitēs Iūdaeōrum rebellantium sumus, Rōmānīs servīre nōlumus. mortem obīre mālumus."

haec locūtus, facinus dīrum commīsit. mātrem et aviam amplexus cultrō statim occīdit. tum frātrēs sorōrēsque, haudquāquam resistentēs, eōdem modō interfēcit. postrēmō magnā vōce populum Rōmānum dētestātus sē ipsum cultrō trānsfīxit.

admīrātiōne: admīrātiō
    admiration
5 inde *then*
cultrum: culter *knife*

dīve: dīvus *divine*

10 dum *while*
dēfīgunt: dēfīgere *fix*
occāsiōnem: occāsiō *opportunity*
nactus *having seized*
prōsiluit: prōsilīre *leap forward, jump*
15 pavōre: pavor *panic*
pedem rettulit: pedem referre
    step back
servīre *serve (as a slave)*
20 mālumus: mālle *prefer*
eōdem modō *in the same way*
dētestātus *having cursed*

Questions

1 What was Domitian's purpose when he left his chariot (lines 1–2)?
2 What did he do next (line 2)?
3 **admīrātiōne** (line 3). What caused this feeling? What did it prompt the emperor to do?
4 What order did the emperor give to Salvius?
5 Why do you think the emperor did not wish to meet Haterius personally?
6 **inde … obtulit** (lines 5–6). Describe how the victim was to be sacrificed.
7 To whom were the emperor's words addressed (lines 8–9)?
8 What three points did he make in his speech (lines 8–9)?
9 **subitō … prōsiluit** (lines 10–11). Why did Simon's action at first pass unnoticed?
10 **mediōs in sacerdōtēs irrūpit** (line 11). Why did he do this?
11 Write down the Latin phrase that explains the reaction of the spectators (lines 12–13).
12 Why do you think Domitian was **pavōre commōtus** (line 13)?
13 **mātrem … interfēcit** (lines 18–20). Describe Simon's actions.
14 Describe Simon's death (lines 20–22).
15 Look back at lines 16–22. In what ways did Simon's words and actions copy those of Eleazarus at Masada (Masada II, lines 2–12)?

About the language 3: more about purpose clauses

1   In Stage 26, you met purpose clauses used with **ut**:

senex īnsidiās parāvit **ut fūrēs caperet**.
*The old man set a trap **in order that he might catch the thieves**.*
Or, in more natural English:
The old man set a trap to catch the thieves.

2   In Stage 29, you have met purpose clauses used with forms of the relative pronoun **quī**:

fēmina servum mīsit **quī cibum emeret**.
*The woman sent a slave **who was to buy food**.*
Or, in more natural English:
The woman sent a slave to buy food.

You have also met purpose clauses used with **ubi**:

locum quaerēbāmus **ubi stārēmus**.
*We were looking for a place **where we might stand**.*
Or, in more natural English:
We were looking for a place to stand.

3   Further examples:

a   sacerdōs haruspicem arcessīvit quī victimam īnspiceret.
b   lībertus dōnum quaerēbat quod patrōnum dēlectāret.
c   Haterius quīnque fabrōs ēlēgit quī figūrās in arcū sculperent.
d   domum emere volēbam ubi fīlius meus habitāret.
e   senātor gemmam pretiōsam ēmit quam uxōrī daret.
f   fēminae līberīque locum invēnērunt ubi latērent.

The Emperor Titus was enormously
popular but reigned less than three years.

Word patterns: compound verbs 1

1 Study the following verbs and their translations.

currere	dēcurrere	excurrere	recurrere
to run	*to run down*	*to run out*	*to run back*
iacere	dēicere	ēicere	reicere
to throw	*to throw down*	*to throw out*	*to throw back*

2 Verbs may have their meaning extended by placing **dē**, **ex**, or **re** at the beginning of the word. Such verbs are known as **compound verbs**.

3 Using the pattern above, complete the table below:

trahere	dētrahere	extrahere	retrahere
to pull, drag	. . . .	. . . .	. . . .
cadere	dēcidere	excidere	recidere
to fall	. . . .	. . . .	. . . .
mittere	. . . .	ēmittere	. . . .
to send	. . . .	. . . .	. . . .

4 Complete the following sentences with the correct compound verb. Then translate the sentences.

> dēpōnerent   ēdūcēbantur   revēnērunt

   a fabrī, postquam domum . . . ., diū dormīvērunt.
   b lēgātus hostibus imperāvit ut arma . . . .
   c mīlitēs ē castrīs . . . . ut rūpem Masadam oppugnārent.

5 Explain the connection between the following Latin verbs and the English verbs derived from them.

dēpōnere	*depose*	ērumpere	*erupt*	retinēre	*retain*
dēspicere	*despise*	ēicere	*eject*	referre	*refer*

Practicing the language

1 Complete each sentence with the correct form of the imperfect subjunctive, using the verb in parentheses. Then translate the sentence.

For example: Domitiānus ad āram prōcessit ut victimam . . . .(sacrificāre)
Answer: Domitiānus ad āram prōcessit ut victimam **sacrificāret**.
Domitian advanced to the altar in order to sacrifice the victim.

The forms of the imperfect subjunctive are given on page 278.

  a equitēs īnsidiās parāvērunt ut ducem hostium . . . . (capere)
  b ad forum contendēbāmus ut pompam . . . . (spectāre)
  c barbarī facēs in manibus tenēbant ut templum . . . . (incendere)
  d extrā carcerem stābam ut captīvōs . . . . (custōdīre)
  e Haterī, quam strēnuē labōrāvistī ut arcum . . . .! (perficere)
  f rūpem Masadam occupāvimus ut Rōmānīs . . . .(resistere)

2 Complete each sentence with the most suitable participle from the lists below, using the correct form. Then translate the sentence. Do not use any participle more than once.

dūcēns	labōrāns	sedēns	incēdēns	clāmāns
dūcentem	labōrantem	sedentem	incēdentem	clāmantem
dūcentēs	labōrantēs	sedentēs	incēdentēs	clāmantēs

  a videō Salvium prope arcum . . . .
  b fabrī, in Viā Sacrā . . . ., valdē dēfessī erant.
  c nōnne audīs puerōs . . . .?
  d iuvenis, victimam . . . ., ārae appropinquāvit.
  e spectātōrēs captīvōs, per viās . . . ., dērīdēbant.

3 Translate each English sentence into Latin by selecting correctly from the list of Latin words.

  a *The citizens, having been delighted by the show, applauded.*

cīvis	spectāculum	dēlectātī	plaudunt
cīvēs	spectāculō	dēlectātus	plausērunt

  b *I recognized the slave girl who was pouring the wine.*

ancilla	quī	vīnum	fundēbat	agnōvī
ancillam	quae	vīnō	fundēbant	agnōvit

  c *Having returned to the bank of the river, the soldiers halted.*

ad rīpam	flūmine	regressī	mīlitēs	cōnstitērunt
ad rīpās	flūminis	regressōs	mīlitum	cōnstiterant

d *The woman, sitting in prison, told a sad story.*

fēmina	in carcerem	sedēns	fābulam	trīstis	nārrat
fēminae	in carcere	sedentem	fābulae	trīstem	nārrāvit

e *We saw the altar, decorated with flowers.*

āram	flōrī	ōrnāta	vīdī
ārās	flōribus	ōrnātam	vīdimus

f *They killed the sleeping prisoners with swords.*

captīvī	dormientem	gladiōs	occīdērunt
captīvōs	dormientēs	gladiīs	occīdit

The arch of Titus, looking toward the Forum.

The Roman Forum

The Palatine may have been the birthplace of Rome but the commercial, cultural, social, and political heart of the city was the **Forum Rōmānum**, which, in turn, was the center of the whole empire. To symbolize this, the Emperor Augustus placed the **mīliārium aureum** (golden milestone) in the Forum Romanum to mark the starting-point of the roads that radiated from the city to all the corners of the empire. The Forum Romanum was not the only forum in the city. By the time of our stories, two other fora had been built by Julius Caesar and Augustus. Then a third in the line of imperial fora was built by Vespasian; it contained the great temple of Peace. Later, two more fora were added: one by Domitian, completed by Nerva, and one by Trajan. The most splendid of the new fora was Trajan's forum, which contained the famous column commemorating Trajan's victories over the Dacians. But none of these other fora replaced the Forum Romanum as the center of city life.

Ordinary people came in great numbers to the Forum Romanum, to visit its temples and public buildings, to listen to speeches, to watch a procession, and sometimes just to meet their friends and stroll idly about, pausing at times to gossip, listen to an argument, or bargain with a passing street-vendor.

In the basilicas lawyers pleaded their cases in front of large and often noisy audiences, and merchants and bankers negotiated their business deals. Senators made their way to the **cūria** (the senate-house) to conduct the affairs of government under the

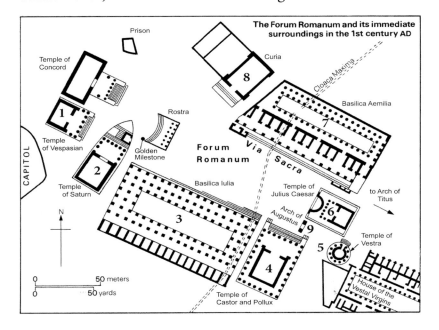

The Forum Romanum seen from the Palatine hill.
1, **2** Columns belonging to the temples of Vespasian and Saturn;
3 Corner of the Basilica Iulia;
4 Base and three columns of the temple of Castor and Pollux;
5 Remains of the temple of Vesta;
6 Foundations of the temple of Julius Caesar;
7 A white archway leading into the Basilica Aemilia;
8 Curia. Near it is the arch of Severus built in the third century AD.
9 Arch of Augustus.

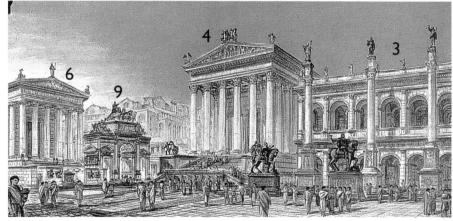

Right: *A reconstruction of the Forum looking the opposite way to the photograph, toward the Palatine hill:*
6 *Temple of Julius Caesar;*
9 *Arch of Augustus;*
4 *Temple of Castor and Pollux;*
3 *Basilica Iulia.*
The columns with statues on top were built in the fourth century AD.

leadership of the emperor. Sometimes a funeral procession wound its way through the Forum, accompanied by noisy lamentations and loud music; sometimes the crowd was forced to make way for a wealthy noble, who was carried through the Forum in a sedan-chair by his slaves and escorted by a long line of citizens.

The Forum lay on low ground between two of Rome's hills, the Capitoline and the Palatine. On the Capitoline at the western end of the Forum stood the temple of Jupiter Optimus Maximus, the center of the Roman state religion. Here the emperor came to pray for the continued safety of the Roman people, and here the consuls took their solemn vows on January 1st each year at the beginning of their consulship. On the Palatine stood the emperor's residence. In the time of Augustus, this had been a small and simple house; later emperors built palaces of steadily increasing splendor.

Near the foot of the Capitoline stood the **Rōstra**, a platform from which public speeches were made to the people. It took its name from the **rōstra** (ships' prows, which had been captured in a sea battle early in Rome's history) which were used to decorate it. One of the most famous speeches made from the Rostra was Mark Antony's speech over the body of Julius Caesar in 44 BC. The listening crowds, influenced by Antony's words, became so angry at Caesar's murder that they rioted, seized the body, and cremated it in the Forum. A temple was later built in Caesar's memory at the eastern end of the Forum, on the spot where his body had been burned.

Near the temple of Julius Caesar was a small, round building with a cone-shaped roof. This was the temple of Vesta, where the Vestal Virgins tended the undying sacred flame which symbolized the endurance of Rome.

Through the Forum ran the **Via Sacra** (Sacred Way), which provided an avenue for religious or triumphal processions. When the Romans celebrated a victory in war, the triumphal procession passed through the streets of Rome and along the Via Sacra and ended by traveling up to the Capitoline hill, where the victorious general gave thanks at the temple of Jupiter. The story on pages 153–154 describes a similar procession to dedicate the arch of Titus by the Emperor Domitian in approximately AD 81. This arch, on the rise of a gentle slope at the eastern end of the Via Sacra, commemorated the victory of Titus, Domitian's brother, over the Jewish people.

Not far from the Rostra and the curia was the prison. Prisoners of war, like the seven Jews in the stories of this Stage, were held in this prison before being led in a triumphal procession. Afterwards they would be taken back to the prison and killed.

The Sacred Way leading up to the arch of Titus.

The temple of Vesta.

The prison. Once a cistern for storing water, this cell was entered through a hole in the roof.

Rome and Judea

In about 65 BC, Jerusalem was taken by Pompey the Great, and Judea became a client state of Rome. This was simply the latest invasion in a land with a turbulent history of foreign domination. Both Caesar and Augustus had recognized Judaism as a legitimate religion, allowing the construction of synagogues, the celebration of the Sabbath, and the collection of a Temple tax. However, by the time of our stories, imposition of higher taxes had placed a heavy burden on the population. The latest governors were non-Jews who made every effort to exploit their office financially rather than maintain order and security. Lack of unified Jewish leadership resulted in violent clashes among the various Jewish factions.

Above: *A synagogue at Masada.*
Below: *A room in a Roman-style bathhouse at Masada, showing some of the hypocaust pillars and wall flue bricks.*

Serious rioting in Jerusalem led to a general revolt against Roman rule in AD 66 while Nero was emperor. Vespasian, who was then a commander in the Roman army, was given the job of crushing the rebellion. Civil war in Rome resulted in Vespasian's taking over the throne there. Once he had secured Italy, the Roman army, under the command of his son, Titus, besieged Jerusalem. Jerusalem was conquered and the Temple was destroyed in the spring of AD 70. Titus returned to Rome with prisoners and the Temple treasury to celebrate a triumph with his father.

Unwilling to concede defeat, a band of zealots under Eleazar ben Ya'ir occupied Masada, a nearly impregnable fortress built for King Herod on a 1,300-foot (400-meter) butte near the Dead Sea. There they held out against Flavius Silva's Tenth Legion Fretensis until AD 73. The Jews' last stand at Masada as described in the story on pages 150–151 is based on the account of the first-century AD historian Josephus. The victory over Judea was considered a major military success for the Flavian dynasty (Vespasian, Titus, and Domitian).

A piece of pottery found at Masada with the name "ben Ya'ir" which is thought to refer to Eleazar.

Artist's impression of the hanging palace of Herod at Masada.

Silva's headquarters camp, one of the five Roman camps surrounding the rock.

The rock of Masada seen from the north. The Roman ramp can be clearly seen rising from the right. The western palace on the right of the ramp and the northern palace on the left were built by Herod the Great a century before the Roman siege in AD 72–73.

Vocabulary checklist 29

aliī … aliī	*some … others*
ascendō, ascendere, ascendī	*climb, rise*
audācia, audāciae, f.	*boldness, audacity*
captīvus, captīvī, m.	*prisoner, captive*
circumveniō, circumvenīre, circumvēnī, circumventus	*surround*
dēfendō, dēfendere, dēfendī, dēfēnsus	*defend*
dīrus, dīra, dīrum	*dreadful*
dolor, dolōris, m.	*grief, pain*
incēdō, incēdere, incessī	*march, stride*
līberī, līberōrum, m.pl.	*children*
lūx, lūcis, f.	*light, daylight*
mālō, mālle, māluī	*prefer*
ōdī	*I hate*
perficiō, perficere, perfēcī, perfectus	*finish*
populus, populī, m.	*people*
prius	*earlier*
salūs, salūtis, f.	*safety, health*
scelus, sceleris, n.	*crime*
spernō, spernere, sprēvī, sprētus	*despise, reject*
ubīque	*everywhere*
vester, vestra, vestrum	*your (plural)*
vīvus, vīva, vīvum	*alive, living*

A coin (much enlarged), issued in AD 71, of the Emperor Vespasian celebrating the defeat of the Jews. A victorious Roman stands to the left of the palm. A Jewish captive sits on the right.

HATERIUS

Stage 30

cotīdiē cīvēs ad arcum conveniēbant ut figūrās in eō sculptās īnspicerent.

1   Haterius: quam fēlīx sum!
                   heri arcus meus ab Imperātōre dēdicātus est.
                   heri praemium ingēns mihi ā Salviō prōmissum est.
                   hodiē praemium exspectō …

2   Haterius: anxius sum.
                   arcus meus nūper ab Imperātōre laudātus est.
                   nūllum tamen praemium adhūc mihi ā Salviō
                   missum est.
                   num ego ā Salviō dēceptus sum?
                   minimē! Salvius vir probus est …

dignitās

When you have read this story, answer the questions at the end.

cīvēs Rōmānī, postquam arcus ab Imperātōre dēdicātus est,
quattuor diēs fēstōs celebrāvērunt. cotīdiē ad arcum
conveniēbant ut figūrās in eō sculptās īnspicerent. plūrimī
clientēs domum Salviī veniēbant quī grātulātiōnēs eī facerent.
Salvius ipse summō gaudiō affectus est quod Imperātor arcum
Haterii magnopere laudāverat.

    apud Haterium tamen nūllae grātulantium vōcēs audītae
sunt. neque clientēs neque amīcī admissī sunt. Haterius, īrā
commōtus, sōlus domī manēbat. adeō saeviēbat ut dormīre nōn
posset. quattuor diēs noctēsque vigilābat. quīntō diē uxor,
Vitellia nōmine, quae nesciēbat quārē Haterius adeō īrātus esset,
eum mollīre temptābat. ingressa hortum, ubi Haterius hūc illūc
ambulābat, eum anxia interrogāvit.

Vitellia:	cūr tam vehementer saevīs, mī Haterī? et amīcōs et
	clientēs, quī vēnērunt ut tē salūtārent, domō abēgistī.
	neque ūnum verbum mihi hōs quattuor diēs dīxistī.
	sine dubiō, ut istum arcum cōnficerēs, nimis
	labōrāvistī, neglegēns valētūdinis tuae. nunc necesse
	est tibi quiēscere.
Haterius:	quō modō ego, tantam iniūriam passus, quiēscere
	possum?
Vitellia:	verba tua nōn intellegō. quis tibi iniūriam intulit?
Haterius:	ego ā Salviō, quī mihi favēre solēbat, omnīnō
	dēceptus sum. prō omnibus meīs labōribus ingēns
	praemium mihi ā Salviō prōmissum est. nūllum
	praemium tamen, nē grātiās quidem, accēpī.
Vitellia:	contentus estō, mī Haterī! redēmptor nōtissimus es,
	cuius arcus ab Imperātōre ipsō nūper laudātus est.
	multa aedificia pūblica exstrūxistī, unde magnās
	dīvitiās comparāvistī.
Haterius:	dīvitiās nōn cūrō. in hāc urbe sunt plūrimī
	redēmptōrēs quī opēs maximās comparāvērunt.
	mihi autem nōn dīvitiae sed dignitās est cūrae.
Vitellia:	dignitās tua amplissima est. nam nōn modo
	dītissimus es sed etiam uxōrem nōbilissimā gente
	nātam habēs. Rūfilla, soror mea, uxor est Salviī quī
	tibi semper fāvit et saepe tē Imperātōrī
	commendāvit. quid aliud ā Salviō accipere cupis?
Haterius:	volō ad summōs honōrēs pervenīre. prīmum
	sacerdōs esse cupiō; multī enim virī, sacerdōtēs ab
	Imperātōre creātī, posteā ad cōnsulātum
	pervēnērunt. sed Salvius, quamquam sacerdōtium

clientēs: cliēns *client*
5 **grātulātiōnēs: grātulātiō**
             congratulation
gaudiō: gaudium *joy*
grātulantium: grātulāns
             congratulating
10 **vigilābat: vigilāre** *stay awake*
quīntō: quīntus *fifth*
hūc illūc *here and there, up
        and down*

15 **abēgistī: abigere** *drive away*

valētūdinis: valētūdō *health*

20

nē … quidem *not even*
estō! *be!*

pūblica: pūblicus *public*
30 **dīvitiās: dīvitiae** *riches*

est cūrae *is a matter of concern*
amplissima: amplissimus
              very great
35 **dītissimus: dīves** *rich*

commendāvit: commendāre
             recommend
40 **cōnsulātum: cōnsulātus**
    consulship (rank of consul)
sacerdōtium *priesthood*

	mihi identidem prōmīsit, fidem nōn servāvit.
Vitellia:	nōlī dēspērāre, mī Haterī! cōnsilium optimum
	habeō. invītā Salvium ad āream tuam! ostentā eī
	polyspaston tuum! nihil maius nec mīrābilius
	umquam anteā factum est. deinde Salvium
	admīrātiōne affectum rogā dē sacerdōtiō.

fidem … servāvit: fidem servāre
keep a promise, keep faith
45 **āream: ārea** *construction site*
ostentā: ostentāre *show off, display*
nec *nor*

Questions

1 How long was the holiday which followed the dedication of the arch?
2 Describe the scene at the arch during the holiday (lines 2–3).
3 Why did Salvius' clients come to his house?
4 **Salvius … gaudiō affectus est** (line 5). What was the reason for this?
5 What happened to Haterius' friends and clients (line 8)?
6 Haterius' feelings were very different from those of Salvius. Pick out a Latin phrase or verb that tells you how he was feeling (lines 8–10).
7 How did Vitellia behave towards her husband (lines 10–12)?
8 What did she think was the matter with Haterius (lines 17–18)?
9 What remedy did she suggest?
10 In what way did Haterius think he had been deceived (lines 23–26)?
11 Vitellia urged Haterius to be content with his achievements. Give two that she mentioned.
12 **dīvitiās nōn cūrō** (line 31). What did Haterius really want?
13 **uxōrem nōbilissimā gente nātam habēs** (lines 35–36). Explain how Vitellia's family connections have brought Haterius special benefits.
14 What particular honor did Haterius want to receive first? What did he hope it would lead to (lines 39–42)?
15 What actions did Vitellia suggest to Haterius? How did she think her plan would help Haterius to get what he wanted (lines 45–48)?

About the language 1: perfect passive tense

1 In this Stage, you have met the **perfect passive**. Compare it with the perfect active:

<table>
<tr><td>*perfect active*</td><td>*perfect passive*</td></tr>
<tr><td>senex fūrem **accūsāvit**.</td><td>fūr ā sene **accūsātus est**.</td></tr>
<tr><td>*The old man **has accused** the thief.*</td><td>*The thief **has been accused** by the old man.*</td></tr>
<tr><td>Or,</td><td>Or,</td></tr>
<tr><td>*The old man **accused** the thief.*</td><td>*The thief **was accused** by the old man.*</td></tr>
<tr><td></td><td></td></tr>
<tr><td>Rōmānī hostēs **superāvērunt**.</td><td>hostēs ā Rōmānīs **superātī sunt**.</td></tr>
<tr><td>*The Romans **have overcome** the enemy.*</td><td>*The enemy **have been overcome** by the Romans.*</td></tr>
<tr><td>Or,</td><td>Or,</td></tr>
<tr><td>*The Romans **overcame** the enemy.*</td><td>*The enemy **were overcome** by the Romans.*</td></tr>
</table>

2 The forms of the perfect passive are as follows:

SINGULAR

portātus sum	*I have been carried*, or *I was carried*
portātus es	*you (s.) have been carried*, or *you were carried*
portātus est	*he has been carried*, or *he was carried*

PLURAL

portātī sumus	*we have been carried*, or *we were carried*
portātī estis	*you (pl.) have been carried*, or *you were carried*
portātī sunt	*they have been carried*, or *they were carried*

3 Notice that each form of the perfect passive is made up of two words:

a a perfect passive participle (e.g. **portātus**) in either a singular or a plural form;
b a form of the present tense of **sum**.

4 Further examples:

a arcus ab Imperātōre dēdicātus est.
b multī nūntiī ad urbem missī sunt.
c dux hostium ā mīlitibus captus est.
d cūr ad vīllam nōn invītātī estis?
e ā Salviō dēceptus sum.
f audītus est; monitī sumus; laudātus es; interfectī sunt.

5 If **inventus est** means *he was found*, what do you think **inventa est** means?

polyspaston

I

postrīdiē Haterius Salvium ad āream suam dūxit ut polyspaston
eī ostentāret. ibi sedēbat ōtiōsus Glitus, magister fabrōrum. quī
cum dominum appropinquantem cōnspexisset, celeriter surrēxit
fabrōsque dīligentius labōrāre iussit.

    tōta ārea strepitū labōrantium plēna erat. columnae ex   5
marmore pretiōsissimō secābantur; laterēs saxaque in āream
portābantur; ingentēs marmoris massae in plaustra pōnēbantur.
Haterius, cum fabrōs labōre occupātōs vīdisset, Salvium ad
aliam āreae partem dūxit. ibi stābat ingēns polyspaston quod ā
fabrīs parātum erat. in tignō polyspastī sēdēs fīxa erat. tum   10
Haterius ad Salvium versus,

    "mī Salvī," inquit, "nōnne mīrābile est polyspaston? hoc tibi
tālem urbis prōspectum praebēre potest quālem paucī umquam
vīdērunt. placetne tibi?"

    Salvius, ubi sēdem in tignō fīxam vīdit, palluit. sed, quia fabrī   15
oculōs in eum dēfīxōs habēbant, timōrem dissimulāns in sēdem
cōnsēdit. iuxtā eum Haterius quoque cōnsēdit. tum fabrīs
imperāvit ut fūnēs, quī ad tignum adligātī erant, summīs vīribus
traherent. deinde tignum lentē ad caelum tollēbātur. Salvius,
pavōre paene cōnfectus, clausīs oculīs ad sēdem haerēbat.   20
tandem oculōs aperuit.

dīligentius *more diligently,*
                    harder
laterēs: later *brick*

tignō: tignum *beam*
sēdēs *seat*
fīxa erat: fīgere *fix, fasten*
tālem … quālem *such … as*
prōspectum: prōspectus *view*
quia *because*
dissimulāns: dissimulāre
                 conceal, hide
iuxtā *next to*
fūnēs: fūnis *rope*
adligātī erant: adligāre *tie*
vīribus: vīrēs *strength*

Haterius and his crane.

II

Salvius: (*spectāculō attonitus*) dī immortālēs! tōtam urbem
vidēre possum. ecce templum Iovis! ecce flūmen!
ecce amphitheātrum Flāvium et arcus novus! quam
in sōle fulget! Imperātor, simulatque illum arcum
vīdit, summā admīrātiōne affectus est. mihi   *5*
imperāvit ut grātiās suās tibi agerem.

Haterius: magnopere gaudeō quod opus meum ab Imperātōre
laudātum est. sed praemium illud quod tū mihi
prōmīsistī nōndum accēpī.

Salvius: (*vōce blandā*) dē sacerdōtiō tuō, Imperātōrem iam   *10*
saepe cōnsuluī, et respōnsum eius etiam nunc
exspectō. aliquid tamen tibi intereā offerre possum.
agellum quendam possideō, quī prope sepulcra
Metellōrum et Scīpiōnum situs est. tūne hunc
agellum emere velīs?   *15*

Haterius: (*magnō gaudiō affectus*) ita vērō, in illō agellō, prope
sepulcra gentium nōbilissimārum, ego quoque
sepulcrum splendidum mihi meīsque exstruere
velim, figūrīs operum meōrum ōrnātum; ita enim
nōmen factaque mea posterīs trādere possum. prō   *20*
agellō tuō igitur sēstertium vīciēns tibi offerō.

Salvius: (*rīdēns, quod agellus eī grātīs ab Imperātōre datus erat*)
agellus multō plūris est, sed quia patrōnus sum tuus
tibi faveō. mē iuvat igitur sēstertium tantum trīciēns
ā tē accipere. placetne tibi?   *25*

Haterius: mihi valdē placet.

*Haterius fabrīs imperāvit ut tignum lentē dēmitterent. ambō humum
rediērunt, alter spē immortālitātis dēlectātus, alter praesentī pecūniā
contentus.*

Iovis: Iuppiter *Jupiter (god of the
sky, greatest of Roman gods)*
amphitheātrum Flāvium
  *Flavian amphitheater (now
  known as the Colosseum)*

nōndum *not yet*
agellum: agellus *small plot of land*
quendam: quīdam *one, a certain*
sepulcra: sepulcrum *tomb*
Metellōrum: Metellī *the Metelli
  (famous Roman family)*
Scīpiōnum: Scīpiōnēs
  *the Scipiones (famous Roman
  family)*
meīs: meī *my family*
facta: factum *deed, achievement*
posterīs: posterī
  future generations, posterity
sēstertium vīciēns *two million
  sesterces*
multō plūris est *is worth much
  more*
mē iuvat *it pleases me*
sēstertium ... trīciēns
  three million sesterces
humum *to the ground*
immortālitātis: immortālitās
  immortality
praesentī: praesēns *present, ready*

These two portraits, from the tomb of the Haterii, could represent Haterius and his wife.

About the language 2: pluperfect passive tense

1   You have now met the **pluperfect passive**. Compare it with the pluperfect active:

    pluperfect active   *pluperfect passive*
    servus dominum **vulnerāverat**.   dominus ā servō **vulnerātus erat**.
    *A slave **had wounded** the master.*   *The master **had been wounded** by a slave.*

2   The forms of the pluperfect passive are as follows:

    SINGULAR
    portātus eram   *I had been carried*
    portātus erās   *you* (s.) *had been carried*
    portātus erat   *he had been carried*

    PLURAL
    portātī erāmus   *we had been carried*
    portātī erātis   *you* (pl.) *had been carried*
    portātī erant   *they had been carried*

Each form of the pluperfect passive is made up of a perfect passive participle (e.g. **portātus**) and a form of the imperfect tense of **sum** (e.g. **erat**).

3   Further examples:

    a   Simōn ā mātre servātus erat.
    b   custōdēs circum carcerem positī erant.
    c   dīligenter labōrāre iussī erātis.
    d   ā mīlitibus Rōmānīs superātī erāmus.
    e   fēmina ā fīliō vituperāta erat.
    f   pūnīta erat; pūnītae erant; missus eram; audītae erāmus; victus erās.

Word patterns: adjectives and nouns

1 Study the forms and meanings of the following adjectives and nouns:

adjectives		nouns	
probus	*honest*	probitās	*honesty*
līber	*free*	lībertās	*freedom*
gravis	*heavy, serious*	gravitās	*heaviness, seriousness*

2 Now complete the table below:

benignus	*kind*	benignitās	. . . .
līberālis	. . . .	līberālitās	*generosity*
fēlīx	*lucky, happy*	fēlīcitās	. . . .
celer	. . . .	celeritās	*speed*
immortālis	. . . .	immortālitās	. . . .
suāvis	. . . .	. . . .	. . . .

3 Give the meaning of the following nouns:

   crūdēlitās, tranquillitās, calliditās, paupertās.

4 What is the gender of each noun above? To what declension does it belong?

A Roman architect or contractor, holding a measuring stick. On the right (from top) are a chisel, a plumb line, a set square, and the capital of a column; on the left, a stonemason's hammer.

Practicing the language

1 Translate the following sentences. After each one state whether the verb is present or imperfect and whether it is active or passive.

    a populus Rōmānus Titum maximē dīligēbat.
    b fabrī ab Hateriō tōtam noctem incitābantur.
    c hodiē cēna splendida Imperātōrī parātur.
    d quattuor diēs ingēns multitūdō viās urbis complēbat.
    e magnus strepitus in āreā audiēbātur.
    f pauperēs ā dīvitibus saepe opprimuntur.

2 Complete each sentence with the correct word. Then translate the sentence.

    a mercātor, ē carcere . . . ., magistrātuī grātiās ēgit. (līberātus, līberātī)
    b māter, verbīs Eleazārī . . . ., cum līberīs latēbat. (territus, territa)
    c Salvius epistulam, ab Imperātōre . . . ., legēbat. (scrīpta, scrīptam)
    d nāvēs, tempestāte paene . . . ., tandem ad portum revēnērunt. (dēlētus, dēlēta, dēlētae)
    e centuriō captīvōs, ā mīlitibus . . . ., in castra dūxit. (custōdītī, custōdītōs, custōdītīs)

3 Complete each sentence with the most suitable ending of the pluperfect subjunctive. Then translate the sentence.

    For example: cum hospitēs advēn. . . , coquus cēnam intulit.
    This becomes: cum hospitēs **advēnissent**, coquus cēnam intulit.
                       When the guests had arrived, the cook brought the dinner in.

    The forms of the pluperfect subjunctive are given on page 278.

    a cum servus iānuam aperu. . . , senex intrāvit.
    b cum pompam spectāv. . . , ad arcum festīnāvī.
    c Imperātor nōs rogāvit num arcum īnspex. . . .
    d cum Rōmam vīsitāv. . . , domum rediistis?
    e amīcī nōn intellēxērunt cūr Haterium nōn vīd. . . .

Roman engineering

The various carvings on the family tomb of the Haterii, especially the crane, suggest that at least one member of the family was a prosperous building contractor. One of his contracts was for a magnificent arch to commemorate the popular Emperor Titus, who died after only a short reign (AD 79–81). His personal names are unknown but in the stories we have called him Quintus Haterius Latronianus. In Stage 29, Haterius is imagined as anxiously trying to complete the arch during the night before its dedication by the new emperor, Domitian, and in this Stage he is seeking his reward.

Helped by an architect who provided the design and technical advice, Haterius would have employed subcontractors to supply the materials and engage the workmen. Most of these were slaves and poor free men working as unskilled, occasional labor, but there were also craftsmen such as carpenters and stonemasons. It was the job of the carpenters to put up a timber framework to give shape and temporary support to the arches as they were being built (see right). They also erected the scaffolding and made the timber molds for shaping concrete. The masons were responsible for the quarrying of the stone and its transport, often by barge up the river Tiber, to the building site in the city before carving the elaborate decoration and preparing the blocks to be lifted into position. The richly carved panels on Titus' arch show the triumphal procession with prisoners and treasure captured at the sack of Jerusalem in AD 70.

Many of our modern hand-tools have been inherited almost unchanged from those used by Roman craftsmen (for instance, mallets, chisels, crowbars, trowels, saws, and planes), but with the important difference that the Romans did not have the small electric motor that makes the modern power tool so much quicker and less laborious to use.

Another aid to building was good-quality cement. The main ingredients of this versatile and easily produced material were lime mortar, made by heating pieces of limestone to a high temperature and then crushing them to a powder; fine sand; and clay. These were combined with water to make a smooth paste. In this form the cement mortar was used, as today, for a thin but effective adhesive layer between bricks or stones.

Timber frame supporting the stones of an arch. Once the central keystone was in place, the arch could support itself and the wood was removed.

Haterius' crane

There is a crane carved on the tomb of Haterius' family. It consisted of two wooden uprights, forming the jib, fastened together at the top and splayed apart at the feet. The hoisting rope ran around two pulleys, one at the top of the jib, and one at the point where the load was fastened to the rope. After passing around the pulleys the rope led down to a winding drum, which was turned by a treadmill fixed to the side of the crane and operated by two or three men inside. Smaller cranes had, instead of a treadmill, a capstan with projecting spokes to be turned by hand. This arrangement of pulleys and ropes multiplied the force exerted by human muscles so that a small crew could raise loads weighing up to eight or nine tons/tonnes. To prevent the crane from toppling over, stay ropes were stretched out from the jib, also with the help of pulleys, and firmly anchored to the ground. Blocks of dressed stone were lifted by man-powered cranes like this. These machines were certainly cumbersome, slow, and liable to accidents, but with skilled crews in charge they worked well.

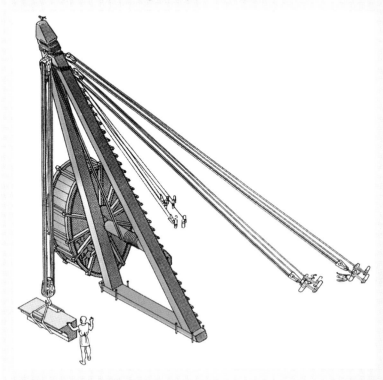

Reconstruction of a crane.

The Romans also mixed cement with rubble, such as stone chips, broken bricks, and pieces of tile, to make **opus caementīcium** (concrete). Concrete became a substitute for stone in the building of arches and vaulted ceilings. For the Romans found that concrete, when shaped into arches, was strong enough to span large spaces without any additional support from pillars, and that it could carry the weight of a heavy superstructure. They used it, for instance, on the aqueducts that supplied Rome with millions of gallons (liters) of fresh water daily, and on the Pantheon, a temple whose domed concrete and brick roof (still in good condition today) has a span of 140 feet (43 meters) and rises to the same height above the floor. They also used it on the huge Flavian amphitheater (known from medieval times as the Colosseum), which could hold up to 50,000 spectators. This is another building depicted on the tomb of the Haterii.

Concrete could also be sandwiched as a core between two faces of more expensive material, such as good-quality stone or brick; these were often then covered with plaster or stucco and painted in bright colors. Marble, too, in thinly cut plates, was used as a facing material where cost was no object.

Not all buildings, of course, were constructed so sturdily. The inhabitants of Rome in the first century AD were housed in a vast number of dwellings, many of them apartment buildings (**īnsulae**) which were built much more cheaply, mainly of brick and timber. They had a reputation for being rickety and liable to catch fire. Augustus fixed a limit of 70 feet (21 meters) in height for these insulae. He also organized fire brigades for their protection.

Nevertheless, serious fires did break out from time to time. The great fire of Rome in AD 64, when Nero was emperor, had a lasting effect on the city. As the historian Tacitus writes:

The flames, which in full fury fell on the level districts first, then shot up to the hills and sank again to burn the lower parts, kept ahead of all remedial measures, traveling fast, the town being an easy prey owing to the narrow, twisting lanes, and formless streets.

Only four of the city's fourteen districts remained intact. Another serious fire in AD 80 compounded the problem. The program of repair was largely the work of the Flavian emperors. Domitian completed the restoration of the temple of Jupiter Optimus Maximus on the Capitoline hill and the construction of the Flavian amphitheater. He built more temples, a stadium, a concert hall, the arch of Titus (see page 159), and a palace on the Palatine, all no doubt to enhance the influence and majesty of the emperor.

Concrete

The Romans were not the first people to make concrete – rubble set in mortar – but they improved its quality and applied it on a grand scale.

The Romans often built walls out of concrete sandwiched between two surfaces of brick or small stones – as we see at the back of a room in the public baths (top left). In the center there is a piece of wall facing us, with the surface stones visible at each side of it. These concrete walls would have been hidden by marble sheets or painted plaster, so that they looked as rich as the colored marble columns and the mosaic floor.

A Roman trowel from Verulamium in Britain.

The boast of Augustus, **urbem latericiam accēpī, marmoream relīquī**, "I found Rome built of brick and left it made of marble," was certainly an exaggeration. For the spaces between the marble-faced public libraries, baths, and temples were crammed with the homes of ordinary people. Many builders must have spent most of their time working on these dwellings, described by the poet Juvenal as "propped up with sticks." But given the opportunity of a large contract and a technical challenge, Roman builders made adventurous use of concrete, cranes, and arches; and Domitian, who was determined to add to the splendors of his capital city, kept architects and builders very busy throughout most of his reign.

Concrete was used to span large spaces. This is the dome of the Pantheon.

*Concrete was used alongside other building materials, as in the Colosseum, above. Top: On the outside the amphitheater appears to be all stone. Bottom: Inside we find a mixture of stone walls (**A** and **B**), walls made of brick-faced concrete (**C**), and concrete vaulting (**D**).*

Vocabulary checklist 30

adhūc	*until now*
afficiō, afficere, affēcī, affectus, affectus, affecta, affectum	*affect affected, overcome*
ambō, ambae, ambō	*both*
cōnsulō, cōnsulere, cōnsuluī, cōnsultus	*consult*
dēmittō, dēmittere, dēmīsī, dēmissus	*let down, lower*
dīves, dīves, dīves, *gen.* dīvitis	*rich*
dīvitiae, dīvitiārum, f. pl.	*riches*
gēns, gentis, f.	*family, tribe*
iniūria, iniūriae, f.	*injustice, injury*
magnopere	*greatly*
nātus, nāta, nātum	*born*
nimis	*too*
nōbilis, nōbile	*noble, of noble birth*
omnīnō	*completely*
opus, operis, n.	*work, construction*
pavor, pavōris, m.	*panic, terror*
quārē?	*why?*
saxum, saxī, n.	*rock*
secō, secāre, secuī, sectus	*cut*
sōl, sōlis, m.	*sun*
soror, sorōris, f.	*sister*
timor, timōris, m.	*fear*

Stamp cut from a Roman brick. Bricks were often stamped with the date and place of manufacture.

IN URBE

Stage 31

1 diēs illūcēscēbat.

2 diē illūcēscente, multī saccāriī in rīpā
flūminis labōrābant.

3 saccāriīs labōrantibus, advēnit nāvis.
nautae nāvem dēligāvērunt.

4 nāve dēligātā, saccāriī frūmentum expōnere
coepērunt.

5 frūmentō expositō, magister nāvis
   pecūniam saccāriīs distribuit.

6 pecūniā distribūtā, saccāriī ad tabernam
   proximam festīnāvērunt.

7 tandem sōl occidere coepit.

8 sōle occidente, saccāriī ā tabernā ēbriī
   discessērunt, omnī pecūniā cōnsūmptā.

Īnsula Tiberīna

adventus

diē illūcēscente, ingēns Rōmānōrum multitūdō viās urbis complēbat. in rīpīs flūminis Tiberis, ubi multa horrea sita erant, frūmentum ē nāvibus ā saccāriīs expōnēbātur. servī, quī ā vēnālīciīs ē Britanniā importātī erant, ē nāvibus dūcēbantur, catēnīs gravibus vīnctī. 5

ex ūnā nāvium, quae modo ā Graeciā advēnerat, puella pulcherrima exiit. epistulam ad Haterium scrīptam manū tenēbat. sarcinae eius ā servō portābantur, virō quadrāgintā annōrum.

sōle ortō, puella ad Subūram advēnit. multitūdine 10 clāmōribusque hominum valdē obstupefacta est. tanta erat multitūdō ut puella cum summā difficultāte prōcēderet. undique pauperēs ex īnsulīs exībant ut aquam ē fontibus traherent. dīvitēs ad forum lectīcīs vehēbantur. mendīcī puellam circumveniēbant, pecūniam postulantēs. nōnnūllī fabrī, puellā 15 vīsā, clāmāre coepērunt; puellam verbīs scurrīlibus appellāvērunt. quae tamen, clāmōribus fabrōrum neglēctīs, vultū serēnō celeriter praeteriit. servum iussit festīnāre nē domum Hateriī tardius pervenīrent.

eōdem tempore multī clientēs per viās contendēbant ut 20 patrōnōs salūtārent. aliī, scissīs togīs ruptīsque calceīs, per lutum lentē ībant. eīs difficile erat festīnāre quia lutum erat altum, viae angustae, multitūdō dēnsa. aliī, quī nōbilī gente nātī sunt, celeriter prōcēdēbant quod servī multitūdinem fūstibus dēmovēbant. clientēs, quī hūc illūc per viās ruēbant, puellae 25 prōcēdentī obstābant.

A bird's-eye view of Rome

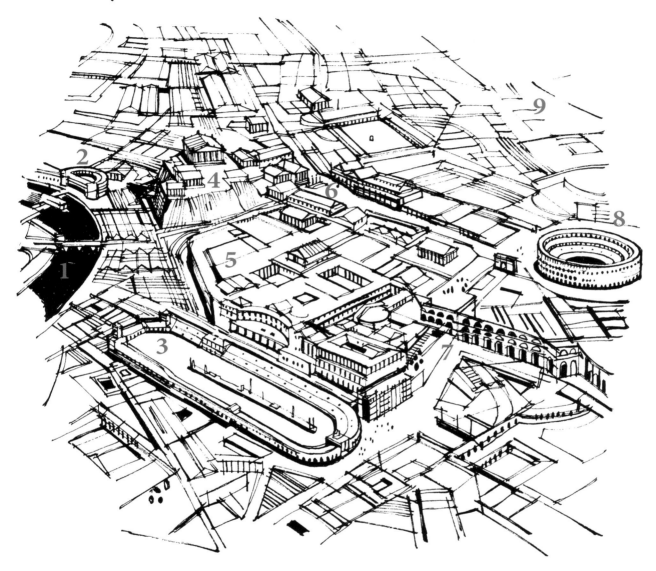

Notice these important features:

1 *River Tiber*
2 *Theater of Marcellus*
3 *Circus Maximus, used for chariot racing*
4 *The Capitol with the temple of Jupiter the Best and Greatest*
5 *Palatine hill with the emperor's palace on it*
6 *Forum Romanum*
7 *An aqueduct*
8 *Colosseum or Flavian amphitheater*
9 *Subura*

The drawing shows Rome as it was in the fourth century AD.

salūtātiō

salūtātiō *the morning visit*
(made by clients to a patron)

I

When you have read this story, answer the questions at the end.

prīmā hōrā clientēs ante domum Hateriī conveniēbant. omnēs,
oculīs in iānuā dēfīxīs, patrōnī favōrem exspectābant. aliī
beneficium, aliī sportulam spērābant. puella, servō adstante, in
extrēmā parte multitūdinis cōnstitit; ignāra mōrum
Rōmānōrum, in animō volvēbat cūr tot hominēs illā hōrā ibi
stārent.

iānuā subitō apertā, in līmine appāruit praecō. corpus eius
erat ingēns et obēsum, vultus superbus, oculī malignī. clientēs,
praecōne vīsō, clāmāre statim coepērunt. eum identidem
ōrāvērunt ut sē ad patrōnum admitteret. ille tamen superbē
circumspectāvit neque quicquam prīmō dīxit.

omnibus tandem silentibus, praecō ita coepit:
"dominus noster, Quīntus Haterius Latrōniānus, ratiōnēs suās
subdūcit. iubet igitur trēs cīvēs ratiōnibus testēs subscrībere.
cēdite C. Iūliō Alexandrō, C. Memmiō Prīmō, L. Venūlēiō
Aprōniānō."

quī igitur, nōminibus suīs audītīs, celeriter prōgressī domum
intrāvērunt. cēterī autem, oculīs in vultū praecōnis dēfīxīs, spē
favōris manēbant.

"ad cēnam," inquit praecō, "Haterius invītat L. Volusium
Maeciānum et M. Licinium Prīvātum. Maeciānus et Prīvātus

ante *before, in front of*

sportulam: sportula *handout*
  (gift of food or money)
5 extrēmā parte: extrēma pars
    edge
mōrum: mōs *custom*
līmine: līmen *threshold,*
    doorway
10 praecō *herald, announcer*
malignī: malignus *spiteful*
superbē *arrogantly*
ratiōnēs ... subdūcit: ratiōnēs
    subdūcere *draw up*
15 *accounts, write up accounts*
subscrībere *sign*
cēdite: cēdere *make way*

20

nōnā hōrā redīre iubentur. nunc autem cēdite aliīs! cēdite
architectō C. Rabīriō Maximō! cēdite T. Claudiō Papīriō!"
    dum illī per iānuam intrant, cēterīs nūntiāvit praecō:
"vōs omnēs iubet Haterius tertiā hōrā sē ad forum dēdūcere."   25   **dēdūcere** *escort*
    hīs verbīs dictīs, paucōs dēnāriōs in turbam sparsit. clientēs,
nē sportulam āmitterent, dēnāriōs rapere temptāvērunt. inter sē
vehementer certābant. intereā puella immōta stābat, hōc
spectāculō attonita.

Questions

1 At what time of day were the clients gathering?

2 **omnēs … patrōnī favōrem exspectābant** (lines 1–2). How is this explained further in the next sentence?

3 Where did the girl stop?

4 What was puzzling her?

5 **in līmine appāruit praecō** (line 7). Describe the herald's appearance.

6 What did the clients do as soon as they saw him (lines 8–9)?

7 What did the clients beg him to do?

8 Why do you think the herald remained silent at first (lines 10–11)?

9 How can we tell that all the clients mentioned in lines 15–16 are Roman citizens? How can we tell that none of them is a freedman of Haterius?

10 When they heard their names why do you think the clients came forward quickly (lines 17–18)?

11 What did the rest of the clients do? Why?

12 **ad cēnam … Haterius invītat … M. Licinium Prīvātum** (lines 20–21). Suggest a reason why the herald used this particular order of words.

13 **paucōs dēnāriōs in turbam sparsit** (line 26). Why do you think the herald chose this way of distributing the money?

14 Reread the last paragraph and write down two Latin adjectives describing the girl's reaction to the clients' behavior.

15 Look back over lines 13–25. Find two examples of tasks that clients have to perform for their patron and one example of a favor done by patrons to their clients.

II

iānuā tandem clausā, abīre clientēs coepērunt, aliī contentī, aliī spē dēiectī. deinde servō puella imperāvit ut iānuam pulsāret. praecōnī regressō servus

"ecce!" inquit. "domina mea, Euphrosynē, adest."

"abī, sceleste! nēmō alius hodiē admittitur," respondit praecō superbā vōce.

"sed domina mea est philosopha Graeca doctissima," inquit servus. "hūc missa est ā Quīntō Hateriō Chrȳsogonō ipsō, Hateriī lībertō, quī Athēnīs habitat."

"īnsānīvit igitur Chrȳsogonus," respondit praecō. "odiō sunt omnēs philosophī Hateriō! redeundum vōbīs est Athēnās unde missī estis."

servus arrogantiā praecōnis īrātus, nihilōminus perstitit.

"sed Eryllus," inquit, "quī est Hateriō arbiter ēlegantiae, epistulam ad Chrȳsogonum scrīpsit in quā eum rogāvit ut philospham hūc mitteret. ergō adsumus!"

hīs verbīs audītīs, praecō, quī Eryllum haudquāquam amābat, magnā vōce

"Eryllus!" inquit. "quis est Eryllus? meus dominus Haterius est, nōn Eryllus! abī!"

haec locūtus servum in lutum dēpulit, iānuamque clausit. Euphrosynē, simulatque servum humī iacentem vīdit, eius īram lēnīre temptāvit.

"nōlī," inquit, "mentem tuam vexāre. rēs adversās aequō animō ferre dēbēmus. nōbīs crās reveniendum est."

spē dēiectī *disappointed in their hope*

Euphrosynē *Euphrosyne (Her* 5 *name means "cheerfulness" or "good thoughts.")*

philosopha *(female) philosopher*

Athēnīs *in Athens*

10 **odiō sunt: odiō esse** *be hateful*

redeundum vōbīs est *you must return*

nihilōminus *nevertheless*

perstitit: perstāre *persist*

15 **arbiter** *expert, judge*

ēlegantiae: ēlegantia *good taste*

ergō *therefore*

20

dēpulit: dēpellere *push down*

mentem: mēns *mind*

aequō animō *calmly, in a calm* 25 *spirit*

About the language 1: ablative absolute

1 Study the following pair of sentences:

> mīlitēs discessērunt.
> *The soldiers departed.*

> **urbe captā**, mīlitēs discessērunt.
> **With the city having been captured**, *the soldiers departed.*

The phrase in **boldface** is made up of a noun, **urbe**, and participle, **captā**, in the *ablative* case. Phrases of this kind are known as ablative absolute phrases, and are very common in Latin.

2 Ablative absolute phrases can be translated in many different ways. For instance, the example in paragraph 1 might be translated:

> *When the city had been captured, the soldiers departed.*

Or,

> *After the city was captured, the soldiers departed.*

3 Further examples:

  a arcū dēdicātō, cīvēs domum rediērunt.
  b pecūniā āmissā, ancilla lacrimāre coepit.
  c victimīs sacrificātīs, haruspex ōmina nūntiāvit.
  d duce interfectō, hostēs dēspērābant.
  e mercātor, clāmōribus audītīs, ē lectō perterritus surrēxit.
  f clientēs, iānuā clausā, invītī discessērunt.

4 In each of the examples above, the participle in the ablative absolute phrase is a perfect passive participle. Ablative absolute phrases can also be formed with present participles. For example:

> **omnibus tacentibus**, lībertus nōmina recitāvit.
> **With everyone being quiet**, *the freedman read out the names.*

Or, in more natural English:

> *When everyone was quiet, the freedman read out the names.*

Further examples:

  a custōdibus dormientibus, captīvī effūgērunt.
  b pompā per viās prōcēdente, spectātōrēs vehementer plausērunt.
  c Imperātor, sacerdōtibus adstantibus, precēs dīvō Titō obtulit.

5 Ablative absolute phrases can also be formed with perfect active participles. For example:

> **dominō ēgressō**, servī garrīre coepērunt.
> ***With the master having gone out***, *the slaves began to chatter.*
> Or, in more natural English:
> *After the master had gone out, the slaves began to chatter.*

Further examples:

a mercātōre profectō, rēs dīra accidit.
b nūntiīs ā Britanniā regressīs, Imperātor senātōrēs arcessīvit.
c cōnsule haec locūtō, omnēs cīvēs attonitī erant.

Word patterns: compound verbs 2

1 Study the following verbs and their translations, and fill in the gaps in the table:

īre	abīre	circumīre	inīre
to go	*to go away*	*to go around*	. . . .
dūcere	abdūcere	. . . .	. . . .
. . . .	. . . .	*to lead around*	*to lead in*
ferre	auferre	circumferre	. . . .
	(*originally* abferre)		
to carry, bring	*to carry away*	. . . .	. . . .

2 Give the meaning of the following compound verbs:

abicere	. . . .	abesse	. . . .	āvertere	. . . .
circumstāre	. . . .	circumvenīre	. . . .	circumspectāre	. . . .
īnfundere	. . . .	immittere	. . . .	irrumpere	. . . .

3 Translate the following sentences, paying particular attention to the compound verbs:

a fabrī puellam circumvēnērunt, verba scurrīlia clāmantēs.
b cēnā parātā, servī vīnum in pōcula īnfūdērunt.
c clientēs, dēnāriīs raptīs, abiērunt ut cibum emerent.

Practicing the language

1 Complete each sentence with the correct form of the verb. Then translate the sentence. Note that the tense of the verb changes after sentence **c**.

   a ōlim multī leōnēs in Āfricā . . . . (captus est, captī sunt)
   b ecce! ille senex ā latrōnibus . . . . (vulnerātus est, vulnerātī sunt)
   c Haterius ā clientibus . . . . (salūtātus est, salūtātī sunt)
   d mīlitēs in ōrdinēs longōs ā centuriōnibus . . . . (īnstrūctus erat, īnstrūctī erant)
   e cīvēs spectāculō . . . . (dēlectātus erat, dēlectātī erant)
   f taurus ā sacerdōte . . . . (ēlēctus erat, ēlēctī erant)

2 Translate each sentence. Then change the words in **boldface** from singular to plural. Use the table of nouns on pages 262–263 to help you.

   a mīles perfidus **amīcum** dēseruit.
   b dux virtūtem **legiōnis** laudāvit.
   c Imperātor multōs honōrēs **lībertō** dedit.
   d iūdex epistulam **testī** trādidit.
   e poēta librum **manū** tenuit.
   f puella, **flōre** dēlectāta, suāviter rīsit.
   g barbarī **vīllam agricolae** incendērunt.
   h rēx pecūniam **mātrī puerī** reddidit.

3 Complete each sentence with the most suitable word from the list below. Then translate the sentence.

portābantur	verbīs	vītārent	adeptī	morbō	abēgisset

   a puerī in fossam dēsiluērunt ut perīculum . . . .
   b Haterius, ... Salviī dēceptus, cōnsēnsit.
   c multae amphorae in triclīnium . . . .
   d senex, ... gravī afflīctus, medicum arcessīvit.
   e praecō, cum Euphrosynēn servumque . . . ., iānuam clausit.
   f clientēs, sportulam . . . ., abiērunt.

1 In Stage 27, you met examples of indirect commands used with **ut**:

> imperāvit nūntiīs ut redīrent.
> *He ordered the messengers that they should return.*
> Or, in more natural English:
> *He ordered the messengers to return.*

2 From Stage 29 onwards, you have met examples of indirect commands used with the word **nē**:

> imperāvit nūntiīs nē redīrent.
> *He ordered the messengers that they should not return.*
> Or, in more natural English:
> *He ordered the messengers not to return.*

Further examples:

a haruspex iuvenem monuit nē nāvigāret.
b fēminae mīlitēs ōrāvērunt nē līberōs interficerent.
c mercātor amīcō persuāsit nē gemmās vēnderet.
d cūr vōbīs imperāvit nē vīllam intrārētis?

Rome's docklands.
Above: *A wharf with arched chambers for storing goods in transit.*
Below: *A Roman rubbish heap that still stands 98 feet (30 meters) high.*

3 You have also met sentences in which **nē** is used with a purpose clause:

> senex pecūniam cēlāvit nē fūrēs eam invenīrent.
> *The old man hid the money so that the thieves would not find it.*
> Or,
> *The old man hid the money in case the thieves should find it.*
> Or,
> *The old man hid the money to prevent the thieves finding it.*

Further examples:

a per viās celeriter contendēbāmus nē ad arcum tardius advenīrēmus.
b in fossā latēbam nē hostēs mē cōnspicerent.
c Imperātor multum frūmentum ab Aegyptō importāvit nē cīvēs famē perīrent.
d servī ē fundō effūgērunt nē poenās darent.

The city of Rome

Rome grew up in a very unplanned and unsystematic way, quite different from the neat gridpattern of other Roman towns. Huge commercial structures and crowded lower-class neighborhoods lay beside great monumental areas with temples, theaters, circuses, baths, basilicas, and promenades. Rome was also an extremely crowded city, as can be seen by comparing its approximate area and population with those of three modern metropolitan districts in North America. First-century Rome, with an approximate area of 8 square miles (21 square kilometers) and a population of 1,000,000, had a population density of 125,000 people per square mile (48,000 per square kilometer).

city	population density	
	people/sq. mile	people/sq. km
Rome	125,000	48,000
Los Angeles	8,200	3,200
Toronto	10,800	4,200
New York City	27,800	10,700
Calcutta	63,000	24,000

Rome's coastal port was Ostia, at the mouth of the river Tiber, where warships docked and Roman cargo boats brought in merchandise from all over the empire. This hub of commercial and maritime activities boasted a man-made harbor begun by Emperor Claudius and its huge warehouses were indispensable to meet the needs of Rome.

From Ostia, ships brought goods up the Tiber to Rome's river port with its docks, riverside markets (**emporia**), and warehouses (**horrea**).

The Tiber, looking north, with the Island (center) *and bridges.*

One of the Tiber riverboats, the Isis Giminiana, loading grain at Ostia to be taken to Rome. Her master, Farnaces, superintends the measuring of the grain from his place at the stern.

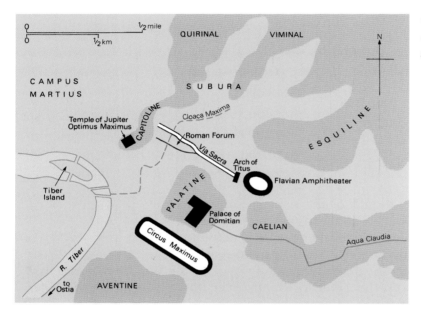

Central features of Rome (first century AD), including the seven hills.

Bottom: In the Subura, Euphrosyne would have passed stalls selling poultry, rabbits, and vegetables (the monkeys were probably pets, not food). There were also blacksmiths' shops (below).

Further upstream, beyond the wharves and warehouses, the river was divided for a short stretch by the Tiber Island (**īnsula Tiberīna**). This elongated island had been built up to look like a ship sailing the river, complete with an ornamental prow (**rōstrum**); it contained a temple of Aesculapius, the god of healing, to which many invalids came in the hope of a cure.

In the story on page 186, Euphrosyne and her slave disembark near the Tiber Island and then move off northeastwards. Their route could have taken them around the lower slopes of the Capitoline hill and through the Forum Romanum (described in Stage 29), passing the Palatine hill where the Emperor Domitian had his palace.

Euphrosyne and her slave would then have continued through the Subura, a densely populated district north of the Forum, full of stores and large, multi-storied, block-long tenement houses or **īnsulae**. Its inhabitants were mostly poor and some very poor indeed; they included barbers, shoemakers, butchers, weavers, blacksmiths, vegetable sellers, prostitutes, and thieves. Several Roman writers refer to the Subura, and give a vivid impression of its noise, its dirt, and its crowds. The following passage from Juvenal describes a street which might easily be in the Subura:

> **We hurry on, but the way is blocked; there is a tidal wave of people in front, and we're pushed and prodded from behind. One man digs me with his elbow, another with the pole of a sedan-chair; somebody catches me on the head with a plank, and somebody else with a wine barrel. My legs are plastered with mud, my feet are stepped on by all and sundry, and a soldier is sticking the nail of his boot in my toe.**

Many rich and aristocratic Romans settled in the district of the Esquiline hill, which lay to the east of the Subura. Here they could enjoy peace and seclusion in huge mansions, surrounded

Two views of prestigious shopping developments in Rome, built by the Emperor Trajan. Most of the Subura streets were much more ramshackle.
Left: *Tenements on the Via Biberatica.*
Right: *Inside a shop, looking across the street towards two more. The one opposite has a window above the shop doorway to light the shop after the shutters were closed; the shopkeeper would probably live there. Above that is the support for a balcony belonging to the apartment above – the apartment block is several stories high. We can see the groove (left) to hold the shutters of the shop on this side, and also two square holes for the bars that held the shutters in place.*

by colonnaded gardens and landscaped parks which contrasted very sharply with the Subura's slums and crowded tenement blocks. In our stories Haterius' house, where Euphrosyne's journey ended, is imagined as being on the Esquiline.

Among the well-known landmarks of Rome were the Circus Maximus, where chariot races were held; the Colosseum; and the Campus Martius, formerly an army training area, which now provided some much-needed open space for the general population.

Above: *Here and there in modern Rome, remains of the ancient aqueduct system can still be seen, dwarfing the houses. Compare the aqueduct on the right-hand side of the picture on page 187.*
Left: *An aqueduct approaching Rome. It carries two water channels, one above the other.*

Crossing the city in various directions were the aqueducts, which brought water into the city at the rate of 200 million gallons (900 million liters) a day. The houses of the rich citizens were usually connected to this supply by means of pipes which brought water directly into their storage tanks; the poorer people had to collect their fresh water from public fountains on street corners. The city also possessed a very advanced system of drains and sewers: a complicated network of underground channels carried sewage and waste water from the larger private houses, public baths, fountains, and lavatories to the central drain (Cloaca Maxima), which emptied into the Tiber.

There were many hazards and discomforts for the inhabitants of Rome. As we have seen in Stage 30, fires were frequent and the insulae in the slums were often cheaply built and liable to collapse. The overcrowding and congestion in the streets have already been mentioned above; wheeled traffic was banned from the city center during the hours of daylight, but blockages were still caused by the wagons of builders like Haterius, which were exempt from the ban. Disease was an ever-present danger in the overcrowded poorer quarters; crime and violence were commonplace in the unlit streets at night. Rome was a city of contrasts, in which splendor and squalor were often found side by side; it could be both an exciting and an unpleasant place to live.

Patronage and Roman society

The story on pages 188–190 shows an aspect of Roman society known as patronage, in which a patron (**patrōnus**) gave help and protection to others less rich or powerful than himself, who performed various services for him in return. Women who had important connections or controlled their own wealth could also act as patronesses not only to women but sometimes even to men. The people waiting outside Haterius' house hoped for various things: money, a meal, a favorable referral for an architect or other craftsman or businessman. In return they might serve as witnesses for documents, pack an audience when the patron gave a recitation of his poems, or swell the importance of their patron by accompanying him through the Forum: the more clients, the more important the patron.

The habit of the morning call (**salūtātiō**) had started in Republican times. In a society where the upper classes had the power, clients needed their patrons' favor and advice for any number of financial or legal transactions. In return, the patrons needed their votes in politics and the addition to their prestige that a large number of clients gave. Freedmen would automatically become the clients of their former owner (male or female), who might help them in setting up a business and then expect part of the profit; soldiers who had served under a particular general would probably become his clients.

By the time of Domitian, however, a more routine set of formalities had been introduced. Most callers were people down on their luck, ready to dress in the cumbersome (and easily soiled) toga that custom required, and, early each morning, make their way (sometimes accompanied by their wives) across the city, for as little, sometimes, as the **sportula** handed out to them. The sportula (little basket) might contain food or money; not much money, according to Martial – not even enough to buy a decent dinner. But Martial, as a poet, needed a patron, and so he put up with the inconvenience and sometimes humiliation of being a client. The humiliations might occur not just at the salutatio itself, but later at dinner when the client might be served food and wine inferior to that given to the higher-ranking friends and clients of the host. Moreover, being a client gave Martial (or Juvenal) opportunities for satire, and in fact, because much of our information about the salutatio comes from satirists, we really do not know how widespread the practice was.

However, we do know that people of considerably higher rank than the miserable crowd Euphrosyne saw were clients themselves. Haterius depended on the good will of his patron, Salvius. Salvius, in turn, like everyone else, and in particular other senators like himself, looked to the emperor for notice and favors.

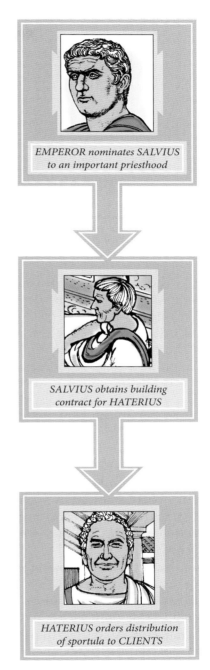

EMPEROR nominates SALVIUS to an important priesthood

SALVIUS obtains building contract for HATERIUS

HATERIUS orders distribution of sportula to CLIENTS

The patronage system.

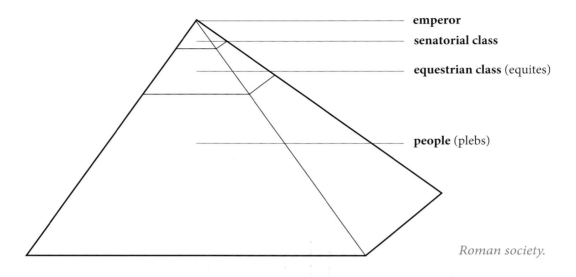

emperor

senatorial class

equestrian class (equites)

people (plebs)

Roman society.

The system of patronage shows how society in Rome was organized along clearly defined ranks. By the time of our stories, the emperor was at the head of all other patrons. He would have his lines of callers waiting for the announcement: **Caesarem iam salūtārī** (The emperor is receiving). Lists of callers would be published and it was a bad sign if someone was refused admission.

Below the emperor were the senators, who formerly had been the leaders of the state and society in the Republic. Salvius and Agricola were men of this class. Men could attain the rank of senator because they were the sons of senators, by election to the financial post of quaestor (in the Republic), or by special gift of the emperor. Senators wore togas with broad purple stripes, sat in special reserved places at public ceremonies, and served as high-ranking priests. They would have been required to have a fortune of at least 1,000,000 sesterces. Magistrates called censors periodically checked the lists of people of the senatorial class to see if they could still be financially ranked as senators.

Haterius was a member of the equestrian class or **equitēs**. Members of this class could be very rich indeed, although their fortune needed to be only 400,000 sesterces, but they did not usually attain the same political or military heights that senators could achieve. Whereas a senator was expected to derive his wealth from property, and could not participate in his own name in trade, the equites could and did. Although many equites might be primarily businessmen, many were active in politics, too, and only a member of the equestrian class might be governor of Egypt. The equestrians were also allowed to wear a gold ring as a status symbol and a toga with a narrow stripe.

The majority of people in Rome, however, were members of the **plebs**, or plebeian class. These might be small businessmen or craftsmen, with reasonably comfortable lives for themselves and their families, or they could be near destitution, as some of the people outside Haterius' door seemed to be. There had been a distribution of free grain for Roman citizens in the city since Republican times, but even with this help, many lived in extreme poverty as day laborers of one kind or another, and really depended on any help they could get from a patron, if they were lucky enough to have one. In theory they could, by hard work and luck, rise to the equestrian class, but on the whole, power and prestige were beyond their reach.

For the plebs, as for everyone else, the emperor was their patron. Vespasian, Domitian's father, had been approached by an engineer who suggested a labor-saving device to haul some columns up to the Capitol. The emperor did not want to hear about it. He did not want to deprive his "little plebs" (**plebicula**) of the opportunity to earn a living.

The curia or senate-house in the Forum Romanum.

Much free grain was distributed to the poor. Here a consignment of grain is being measured.

Vocabulary checklist 31

altus, alta, altum	*high, deep*
ante	*before, in front of*
cōnsistō, cōnsistere, cōnstitī	*halt, stand one's ground*
dux, ducis, m.	*leader*
frūmentum, frūmentī, n.	*grain*
haudquāquam	*not at all*
īdem, eadem, idem	*the same*
identidem	*repeatedly*
nē	*that not, so that . . . not*
neglegō, neglegere, neglēxī,	
neglēctus	*neglect, ignore, disregard*
ōrō, ōrāre, ōrāvī	*beg*
prōgressus, prōgressa,	
prōgressum	*having advanced*
rapiō, rapere, rapuī, raptus	*seize, grab*
scindō, scindere, scidī, scissus	*tear, tear up*
spērō, spērāre, spērāvī	*hope, expect*
superbus, superba, superbum	*arrogant, proud*
tempus, temporis, n.	*time*
undique	*on all sides, from all sides*
vehō, vehere, vexī, vectus	*carry*
vinciō, vincīre, vīnxī, vīnctus	*bind, tie up*
volvō, volvere, volvī, volūtus	*turn*
vultus, vultūs, m.	*expression, face*

This large stone disk is the Bocca della Verità, or Mouth of Truth. It is said that if you put your hand in the mouth and tell a lie, the mouth will close and crush your hand. But originally it was a Roman sewer cover, probably from the Cloaca Maxima.

EUPHROSYNE

Stage 32

1 postrīdiē Euphrosynē domun
regressa est. iterum tamen pra
dūrīs abēgit.

regressa est *returned*

2 servus eam hortātus est ut pra
corrumperet; sed Euphrosynē
ambitiōne abhorruit.

hortātus est *urged*
dōnīs corrumperet: dōnīs corrum
eiusmodī *of that kind*
ambitiōne: ambitiō *bribery, corru*

3 Euphrosynē, septem continuōs diēs ā praecōne abācta, dēnique in Graeciam redīre cōnstituit. hōc cōnsiliō captō, ad flūmen Tiberim ut nāvem cōnscenderet profecta est.

abācta: abigere *drive away*
profecta est *set out*

4 eōdem diē quō Euphrosynē discēdere cōnstituit, celebrābat Haterius diem nātālem. grātulātiōnibus clientium acceptīs, ōtiōsus in hortō sedēbat. subitō Eryllus hortum ingressus est.

ingressus est *entered*

Euphrosynē revocāta

revocāta: revocāre
recall, call back

I

Eryllus, cum hortum intrāvisset, Haterium verbīs blandīs adlocūtus est.

adlocūtus est addressed,
spoke to

Eryllus: domine! omnia quae mandāvistī parāta sunt. centum
amīcī et clientēs ad cēnam invītātī sunt. iussī
coquum cibum sūmptuōsum parāre, cellāriumque   5
vīnum Falernum veterrimum praebēre. nihil
neglēctum est.

vīnum Falernum Falernian
wine (a famous wine from
Campania)

Haterius: nōnne petauristāriōs vel saltātrīcēs condūxistī?
hercle! quam ā petauristāriīs dēlector!

veterrimum: vetus old
petauristāriōs: petauristārius
acrobat

Eryllus: quid dīcis, domine? hominēs eiusmodī cīvibus   10
urbānīs nōn placent. nunc philosophīs favet optimus
quisque.

vel or
optimus quisque
all the best people (literally
each excellent person)

Haterius: īnsānīs, Erylle! nam philosophī sunt senēs sevērī. nec
saltāre nec circulōs trānsilīre possunt.

sevērī: sevērus severe, strict
nec ... nec neither ... nor
circulōs: circulus hoop
trānsilīre jump through
at but

Eryllus: at domine, aliquid melius quam philosophum   15
adeptus sum. mē enim auctōre, philosopha
quaedam, puella pulcherrima, hūc invītāta est. ā
Chrȳsogonō Athēnīs missa est.

adeptus sum I have obtained
mē ... auctōre at my suggestion
quaedam: quīdam a certain, a
iamdūdum for a long time

Haterius: philosopham mīsit Chrȳsogonus? optimē fēcistī,
Erylle! philosopham nē Imperātor quidem habet. sed   20
ubi est haec philosopha quam adeptus es?

Eryllus: iamdūdum eam anxius exspectō. fortasse iste
praecō, homō summae stultitiae, eam nōn admīsit.

Haterius: arcesse hūc praecōnem!

II

ubi praecō ingressus est, Haterius rogāvit utrum philosopham abēgisset necne.

utrum ... necne
whether ... or not

Haterius: philosopham pulchram anxius exspectō. num stultus
eam abēgistī?

praecō: nūllam philosopham pulchram vīdī, domine.   5

Haterius: tibi nōn crēdō. poenās maximās minor nisi vērum loqueris.

praecō: (*pallēscēns*) domine, ignōsce mihi. nesciēbam quantum tū
philosophīs favērēs. illa philosopha, quam ignārus
abēgī, ad flūmen profecta est ut nāvem
cōnscenderet.   10

minor I am threatening
nisi unless, if ... not
loqueris you are telling
ignōsce: ignōscere forgive

Haterius: abī statim, caudex! festīnā ad Tiberim! nōlī
umquam revenīre nisi cum philosophā!

*domō ēgressus, praecō per viās contendit. ad flūmen cum advēnisset,
Euphrosynēn in nāvem cōnscēnsūram cōnspexit. magnā vōce eam
appellāvit. Euphrosynē, nōmine audītō, cōnstitit.*   15

Euphrosynēn
Greek accusative of
Euphrosynē
cōnscēnsūram: cōnscēnsūrus
about to go on board

praecō: ignōsce mihi, Euphrosynē doctissima! nōlī
            discēdere! necesse est tibi domum Hateriī mēcum
            prōcēdere.
Euphrosynē: cūr mē revocās? odiō sunt omnēs philosophī
            Hateriō, ut tū ipse dīxistī. Athēnās igitur nunc   20
            redeō. valē!

deinde praecō, effūsīs lacrimīs, eam identidem ōrāvit nē discēderet.
diū Euphrosynē perstitit; dēnique, precibus lacrimīsque eius
commōta, domum Hateriī regressa est.

effūsīs lacrimīs *with tears*
pouring out, bursting into
tears

cēna Hateriī

nōnā hōrā amīcī clientēsque, quōs Haterius invītāverat ut sēcum
diem nātālem celebrārent, triclīnium ingrediēbantur. inter eōs
aderant fīliī lībertōrum quī humilī locō nātī magnās opēs adeptī
erant. aderant quoque nōnnūllī senātōrēs quī inopiā oppressī
favōrem Hateriī petēbant.   5
      proximus Hateriō recumbēbat T. Flāvius Sabīnus cōnsul, vir
summae auctōritātis. spē favōris, Haterius Sabīnum blandīs et
mollibus verbīs adloquēbātur. ipse ānulōs gerēbat aureōs quī
gemmīs fulgēbant; dentēs spīnā argenteā perfodiēbat.
      intereā duo Aethiopes triclīnium ingrediēbantur. lancem   10
ingentem ferēbant, in quā positus erat aper tōtus. statim coquus,
quī Aethiopas in triclīnium secūtus erat, ad lancem prōgressus
est ut aprum secāret. aprō perītē sectō, multae avēs statim
ēvolāvērunt, suāviter pīpiantēs. hospitēs, cum vīdissent quid
coquus parāvisset, eius artem vehementer laudāvērunt. quā rē   15
dēlectātus, Haterius servīs imperāvit ut amphorās vīnī Falernī
īnferrent. amphorīs inlātīs, cellārius titulōs quī īnfīxī erant

ingrediēbantur *were entering*

inopiā: inopia *poverty*
proximus *next to*
adloquēbātur *was addressing*
dentēs: dēns *tooth*
spīnā: spīna *toothpick*
perfodiēbat: perfodere *pick*
lancem: lānx *dish*
aper *boar*
secāret: secāre *carve, cut open*
avēs: avis *bird*
pīpiantēs: pīpiāre *chirp*
titulōs: titulus *label*
īnfīxī erant: īnfīgere *fasten*
                                    onto

magnā vōce recitāvit, "Falernum Hateriānum, vīnum centum annōrum!" tum vīnum in pōcula servī īnfundere coepērunt.

hospitibus laetissimē bibentibus, poposcit Haterius silentium. 20
rīdēns digitīs concrepuit. signō datō appāruērunt in līmine duo tubicinēs. tubās vehementer īnflāvērunt. tum Eryllus Euphrosynēn in triclīnium dūxit. hospitēs, simulatque eam vīdērunt, fōrmam eius valdē admīrātī sunt.

Haterius rīdēns Euphrosynēn rogāvit ut sēcum in lectō 25
cōnsīderet. deinde hospitēs adlocūtus est.

"haec puella," inquit glōriāns, "est philosopha doctissima, nōmine Euphrosynē. iussū meō hūc vēnit Athēnīs, ubi habitant philosophī nōtissimī. illa nōbīs dīligenter audienda est."

tum ad eam conversus, 30
"nōbīs placet, mea Euphrosynē," inquit, "ā tē aliquid philosophiae discere."

Hateriānum: Hateriānus
    belonging to Haterius
īnfundere *pour into*
digitīs: digitus *finger*
concrepuit: concrepāre *snap,*
        click
fōrmam: fōrma *beauty,*
    appearance
admīrātī sunt *admired*
glōriāns *boasting, boastfully*

philosophiae: philosophia
    philosophy

About the language 1: deponent verbs

1 Study the following examples:

> poenās **minor** nisi vērum **loqueris**.
> *I am threatening punishment if you are not telling the truth.*

> Eryllus hortum **ingressus est**.
> *Eryllus entered the garden.*

> aliquid melius quam philosophum **adeptus sum**.
> *I have obtained something better than a philosopher.*

Notice the forms and meanings of the words in **boldface**. Each verb has a **passive form** but an **active meaning**. Verbs of this kind are known as deponent verbs. (They have "set aside" – **dēpōnere** – their active forms.)

2 Further examples:

   a spectātōrēs dē arcū novō loquēbantur.
   b cūr ex urbe subitō ēgressī estis?
   c uxor hortāta est ut tēcum dīcerem.
   d forum Rōmānum nunc ingredimur.
   e prōgressī sunt; precor; regrediminī; suspicātus erat; passus es; convertēbātur.

3 You have already met the perfect participles of several deponent verbs. For example:

> adeptus   *having obtained*
> hortātus   *having encouraged*
> regressus   *having returned*

Compare them with the perfect participles of some regular verbs (i.e. verbs which are not deponent):

deponent		*regular*	
adeptus	*having obtained*	dēceptus	*having been deceived*
hortātus	*having encouraged*	laudātus	*having been praised*
regressus	*having returned*	missus	*having been sent*

Notice that:
> the deponent perfect participle has an *active* meaning;
> the regular perfect participle has a *passive* meaning.

4 Give the meanings of the following perfect participles from deponent and regular verbs:

deponent	*regular*
cōnspicātus	portātus
ingressus	iussus
profectus	afflīctus
locūtus	audītus
cōnātus	vulnerātus

The Getty Villa in southern California is a reconstruction of a villa in Herculaneum. Haterius would have lived in a similar mansion.

philosophia

Euphrosynē hospitēs, quī avidē spectābant, sīc adlocūta est:

"prīmum, fābula brevis mihi nārranda est. ōlim fuit homō pauper quī fundum parvum, uxōrem optimam, līberōs cārissimōs habēbat. strēnuē in fundō labōrāre solēbat ut sibi suīsque cibum praebēret."

5   **suīs: suī** *his family*

     scīlicet *obviously*

"scīlicet īnsānus erat," exclāmāvit Apollōnius, quī erat homō ignāvissimus. "nēmō nisi īnsānus labōrat."

cui respondit Euphrosynē vōce serēnā,

"omnibus autem labōrandum est. etiam eī quī spē favōris cēnās magistrātibus dant, rē vērā labōrant."

10   **rē vērā** *in fact, truly*

     Euphrosynēs *Greek genitive*

               of **Euphrosynē**

     edēbat: edere *eat*

     temperāns *temperate,*

quō audītō, Haterius ērubuit; cēterī, verbīs Euphrosynēs obstupefactī, tacēbant. deinde Euphrosynē

"pauper," inquit, "nec nimium edēbat nec nimium bibēbat. in omnibus vītae partibus temperāns esse cōnābātur."

L. Baebius Crispus senātor exclāmāvit,

15   *self-controlled*

"scīlicet avārus erat! ille pauper nōn laudandus est nōbīs sed culpandus. Haterius noster tamen maximē laudandus est quod amīcīs sūmptuōsās cēnās semper praebet."

   culpandus: culpāre *blame*

huic Baebiī sententiae omnēs plausērunt. Haterius, plausū audītō, oblītus philosophiae servīs imperāvit ut plūs vīnī hospitibus offerrent. Euphrosynē tamen haec addidit:

   plausū: plausus *applause*

20   **oblītus** *having forgotten*

"at pauper multōs cāsūs passus est. uxōrem enim et līberōs āmīsit, morbō gravissimō afflīctōs; fundum āmīsit, ā mīlitibus dīreptum; postrēmō ipse, inopiā oppressus et in servitūtem abductus, lībertātem āmīsit. nihilōminus, quia Stōicus erat, rēs adversās semper aequō animō patiēbātur. tandem senectūte labōribusque cōnfectus, tranquillē mortuus est. ille pauper, quem hominēs miserrimum exīstimābant, rē vērā fēlīx erat."

   cāsūs: cāsus *misfortune*

25   **abductus: abdūcere** *lead away*

     Stōicus *Stoic (believer in Stoic*

            philosophy)

     patiēbātur *suffered, endured*

     senectūte: senectūs *old age*

Haterius attonitus "num fēlīcem eum exīstimās," inquit, "quī tot cāsūs passus est?"

30   **tranquillē** *peacefully*

     exīstimābant: exīstimāre

               think, consider

     priusquam *before*

sed priusquam Euphrosynē eī respondēret, cōnsul Sabīnus

"satis philosophiae!" inquit. "age, mea Euphrosynē, dā mihi ōsculum, immo ōscula multa."

35   **immo** *or rather*

Rabīrius Maximus tamen, quī cum haec audīvisset ēbrius surrēxit,

"sceleste," inquit, "nōlī eam tangere!"

haec locūtus, pōculum vīnō plēnum in ōs Sabīnī iniēcit.

statim rēs ad pugnam vēnit. pōcula iaciēbantur; mēnsae ēvertēbantur; togae scindēbantur. aliī Sabīnō, aliī Rabīriō subveniēbant. Haterius hūc illūc currēbat; discordiam compōnere frūstrā cōnābātur.

40

   discordiam: discordia *strife*

   compōnere *settle*

Euphrosynē autem, ad iānuam triclīniī vultū serēnō prōgressa, hospitēs pugnantēs ita adlocūta est:

45

"ēn Rōmānī, dominī orbis terrārum, ventris Venerisque servī!"
   quibus verbīs dictīs, ad flūmen Tiberim ut nāvem quaereret
profecta est.

orbis terrārum *world*
Veneris: Venus *Venus (Roman goddess of love)*

Questions for discussion

1 Why was Euphrosyne's philosophy lecture a failure?

2 Look again at Euphrosyne's remark "**ille pauper … rē vērā fēlīx erat**" (lines 28–29). Was Haterius right to suggest that this is a stupid remark? Or does it have some point?

3 **ēn Rōmānī … servī** (line 46). What experiences at Haterius' dinner party led Euphrosyne to make this comment?

About the language 2: more on gerundives

1 In Stage 26, you met the gerundive used in sentences like this:

   mihi currendum est.
   I must run.

2 In Stage 32, you have met more sentences containing gerundives. For example:

   mihi fābula nārranda est.
   I must tell a story.

   Compare this with another way of expressing the same idea:

   necesse est mihi fābulam nārrāre.

3 Further examples:

   a mihi epistula scrībenda est.
   b tibi testāmentum faciendum est.
   c nōbīs Haterius vīsitandus est.
   d coquō cēna paranda est.
   e mihi dignitās servanda est.
   f tibi puella in vīllam admittenda est.

Word patterns: verbs and nouns

1 As you have already seen in Stage 26, some verbs and nouns are closely connected. Here are further examples:

verb		noun	
lūgēre	*to lament*	lūctus	*grief*
metuere	*to fear*	metus	*fear*
currere	*to run*	cursus	*track, course*

2 What do the following nouns mean? Give the associated verbs.

   adventus, cantus, cōnsēnsus, cōnspectus, exitus, gemitus, monitus, mōtus, plausus, reditus, rīsus, sonitus

3 What is the gender of each noun above?
   To what declension does each noun belong?

Practicing the language

1 Complete each sentence by describing the word in **boldface** with the correct form of the adjective in parentheses. Use paragraphs 1 and 2 on page 264 to help you. Then translate the sentence.

   For example: clientēs **patrōnum** . . . . laudāvērunt. (līberālis)
   Answer: clientēs patrōnum līberālem laudāvērunt.
                  The clients praised their generous patron.

   The gender of some of the verbs in **boldface** is given after the word.

   a   nautae **nāvem** (f.) . . . . comparāvērunt. (optimus)
   b   coquus īram **dominī** . . . . timēbat. (crūdēlis)
   c   mercātor, **itinere** (n.) . . . . fessus, in rīpā flūminis cōnsēdit. (longus)
   d   senex testāmentum **amīcō** . . . . mandāvit. (fidēlis)
   e   centuriō verba **uxōris** . . . . neglēxit. (īrātus)
   f   **saxa** (n.) . . . . ad arcum ā fabrīs trahēbantur. (gravis)
   g   subitō vōcēs **mīlitum** . . . . audīvimus. (noster)
   h   Euphrosynē **hospitibus** . . . . statim respondit. (īnsolēns)

2 In each pair of sentences, translate the first sentence; then change it from a direct command to an indirect command by completing the second sentence with an imperfect subjunctive. Then translate the second sentence.

For example: pontem incende!
                centuriō mīlitī imperāvit ut pontem incender . . . .

Translated and completed, this becomes:

pontem incende!
Burn the bridge down!

centuriō mīlitī imperāvit ut pontem incenderet.
The centurion ordered the soldier to burn the bridge down.

The forms of the imperfect subjunctive are given on page 278.

a pecūniam cēlāte!
   mercātor amīcōs monuit ut pecūniam cēlār. . . .
b arcum mihi ostende!
   puer patrem ōrāvit ut arcum sibi ostender. . . .
c iānuam aperīte!
   Imperātor nōbīs imperāvit ut iānuam aperīr. . . .
d nōlīte redīre!
   nūntius barbarīs persuāsit nē redīr. . . .

In sentences **e** and **f**, turn the direct command into an indirect command by adding the necessary words to the second sentence:

e cēnam optimam parāte!
   dominus servīs imperāvit ut . . . .
f epistulam scrībe!
   frāter mihi persuāsit . . . .

About the language 3: future participles

1 Study the following examples:

> nunc ego quoque **moritūrus** sum.
> *Now I, too, am about to die.*

> nēmō sciēbat quid Haterius **factūrus** esset.
> *Nobody knew what Haterius was going to do.*

> praecō puellam vīdit, nāvem **cōnscēnsūram**.
> *The herald saw the girl about to go on board ship.*

The words in **boldface** are **future participles**.

2 Further examples:

    a nunc ego vōbīs cēnam splendidam datūrus sum.
    b mīlitēs in animō volvēbant quid centuriō dictūrus esset.
    c hospitēs Haterium rogāvērunt num Euphrosynē saltātūra esset.
    d custōdēs fūrēs cēpērunt, pecūniam ablātūrōs.

3 Compare the future participle with the perfect passive participle:

perfect passive participle	*future participle*
portātus	portātūrus
(having been) carried	*about to carry*
doctus	doctūrus
(having been) taught	*about to teach*
tractus	tractūrus
(having been) dragged	*about to drag*
audītus	audītūrus
(having been) heard	*about to hear*

Roman beliefs

As Euphrosyne and her slave passed through the Roman Forum, they would have been able to see the great temple to Jupiter Optimus Maximus on the Capitol. If she, as an Athenian, had been told that the temple had been dedicated to the Capitoline triad – Jupiter, Juno, and Minerva – she would have found the deities very similar to the Greek Zeus, Hera, and Athena. She might have been surprised, however, to learn that, in the cella of the temple, was a stone sacred to Terminus, the god of boundaries, whose worship had been established on the Capitoline hill in the days of the Etruscan kings and did not permit relocation to another site.

The diversity present in the beliefs of the Romans reflected not only the layering of the Greek tradition (gods who looked and behaved like humans) on older agricultural gods and ever-present spirits, such as Terminus, but also their acceptance of a great variety of other deities. Frequently they chose to associate these deities with gods who were familiar to them. In Bath, the local deity, Sulis, was associated with Minerva. The story was the same throughout the empire.

"Mystery religions" from the east, which offered hope of life after death and required initiation ceremonies known only to believers, also flourished in the empire. For example, the temple of Isis at Pompeii had been not only repaired after the earthquake in AD 62 or 63, but also enlarged, whereas the repairs to the temples of Apollo and Jupiter in the forum were still incomplete in 79. Domitian rebuilt the temple of Isis in Rome as well as the temple to Jupiter on the Capitol when they had been destroyed by fire.

Roman authorities, however, had not always welcomed religions from elsewhere. Sometimes foreign cults were expelled from Rome. During the Republic, the worship of Bacchus or Liber (Dionysus, god of the vine) had been temporarily banned, and so had the worship of Isis under Augustus.

A religion from the east that found much support in Rome was Mithraism from Persia. Mithras (or Mithra) was the ancient spirit of light (often addressed in Roman dedications as **Sol invictus Mithras**), that became the god of truth and justice, and antagonist of the powers of evil. Mithraism exalted the ideas of loyalty and fraternity, thereby appealing to many soldiers.

Mithras

Temples of Mithras were constructed to look like caves; the one on the left is in Rome. Banqueting couches line the two sides and there is a relief showing the god slaying the bull. Below is an artist's reconstruction of a ceremony in progress.

Initiates into the rites of Mithras went through seven grades of initiation, involving various tests, in Mithraea that were designed to look like caves or were built partially underground. This was to recall the most famous exploit of Mithras which was the slaying of a bull in a Persian cave, and which was always represented in the shrines. He was depicted doing this in Phrygian (Persian) cap and trousers. The central nave of the Mithraeum was lined with raised benches on which the faithful reclined at sacred meals.

There are several Mithraea in Rome, and in many parts of the empire, in cities, in ports in the western Mediterranean, along the frontier provinces of the Rhine and Danube, and at Hadrian's Wall in England. The shrines are usually not large, but some are richly decorated. The religion seems to have appealed to officers in the army and to wealthy businessmen.

Two other religions from the east were Judaism and Christianity. They will be described more fully in Stage 33.

One very popular form of belief was astrology. Astrologers, like the one in Barbillus' household in Unit 2, claimed that the events in a person's life were controlled by the stars and that it was possible to forecast the future by studying the positions and movements of stars and planets. The position of the stars at the time of a person's birth was known as a **hōroscopos** (horoscope) and regarded as particularly important. Astrology was officially disapproved of, especially if people used it to try to determine when their relatives or acquaintances were going to die, and from time to time all astrologers were banished from Rome. It was a particularly serious offense to inquire about the

Atlas holding the globe inscribed with constellations.

A diagram of the heavens, from a villa at Stabiae, near Pompeii.

horoscope of the emperor. Several emperors, however, were themselves firm believers in astrology and, like Barbillus, kept astrologers of their own.

Some Romans became interested in philosophy. Euphrosyne had come to Rome to lecture on Stoicism. Despite the behavior of the people at Haterius' dinner party, there were Romans who studied philosophy, particularly Stoicism. Stoics believed, as Euphrosyne tried to explain in the story on page 210, that a man's aim in life should be Virtue, right behavior, rather than Pleasure.

At the time of the stories in Stage 32, the most important Stoic philosopher in Rome was Epictetus, a Greek and a former slave. He had belonged to Epaphroditus, the emperor's freedman. The following are two quotes from his teachings:

> **Men are disturbed not by the things which happen, but by the opinions about the things; for example, death is nothing terrible, for if it were, it would have seemed so to Socrates; for the opinion about death, that it is terrible, is the terrible thing.**

> **Remember that you are an actor in a play of such a kind as the teacher (author) may choose; if short, of a short one; if long, of a long one: if he wishes you to act the part of a poor man, see that you act the part naturally; if the part of a lame man, of a magistrate, of a private person, (do the same). For this is your duty, to act well the part that is given to you; but to select the part belongs to another.**

Stoics tended to disapprove of one-man rule, and to prefer the idea of a republic. They did not think supreme political power should be passed on by inheritance from one ruler to the next, and they thought a ruler should aim to benefit all his subjects, not just a few. As a result of this, at various times during the first century, a number of Roman Stoics challenged the power of the emperor, opposed him in the senate, or even plotted to kill him. Their efforts were unsuccessful, and they were punished by exile or death.

For the majority of Romans in the first century AD, however, the numerous temples and their precincts in the city served not just as the site of civic religion, but also as meeting places for the senate (who had to meet in an inaugurated templum so that the auspices could be taken), offices for important magistrates (e.g. for quaestors in the temple of Saturn, which was the Roman treasury), or a place for exhibiting significant treaties and works of art or for storing the Sibylline Books.

Ceremonies and festivals (**fēriae**) associated with the gods and their temples occurred throughout the year. Such festivals might honor the changing seasons (the dances of the Salii in March, for instance), or deceased family members (the Parentalia in February). Other festivals included the Matronalia in March, when husbands gave presents to their wives, the Vestalia in June, when asses that turned the millstones for grain were garlanded and hung with loaves of bread, and the Saturnalia in December, when Saturn was celebrated in a carnival atmosphere of gift-giving and parties. Whether people thought deeply about the religious significance of these festivals we do not know. Sometimes they may not even have remembered why certain very old agricultural ceremonies were being held. Whatever their beliefs, it is clear that religion permeated the life of the Romans.

Euphrosyne (left) *is fictional. Most philosophers were male, as Haterius said in our stories. Their portraits show rather forbidding characters, like Chrysippos, one of the early Stoics, right.*

Vocabulary checklist 32

adversus, adversa, adversum	hostile, unfavorable
rēs adversae, f.pl.	misfortune
aequus, aequa, aequum	fair, calm
compōnō, compōnere, composuī, compositus	put together, arrange, settle
cōnātus, cōnāta, cōnātum	having tried
convertō, convertere, convertī, conversus	turn
effundō, effundere, effūdī, effūsus	pour out
ignōscō, ignōscere, ignōvī	forgive
labor, labōris, m.	work
lībertās, lībertātis, f.	freedom
mēnsa, mēnsae, f.	table
nē … quidem	not even
nec	and not, nor
nec … nec	neither … nor
opprimō, opprimere, oppressī, oppressus	crush
ōtiōsus, ōtiōsa, ōtiōsum	at leisure, idle, on holiday, on vacation
pauper, pauper, pauper, *gen.* pauperis	poor
profectus, profecta, profectum	having set out
quīdam, quaedam, quoddam	one, a certain
secūtus, secūta, secūtum	having followed
subveniō, subvenīre, subvēnī	help, come to help

Mithras slaying the bull, framed by the zodiac symbols. A relief from Roman London.

PANTOMIMUS

Stage 33

1   praecō prīmus: fābula! fābula optima!
                                   Paris, pantomīmus nōtissimus, in theātrō crās fābulam aget.
                                   Myropnous, tībīcen perītissimus, tībiīs cantābit.

2   praecō secundus: lūdī! lūdī magnificī!
                                     duodecim aurīgae in Circō Maximō crās certābunt.
                                   Imperātor ipse victōrī praemium dabit.

3   praecō tertius: spectāculum! spectāculum splendidum!
                             quīnquāgintā gladiātōrēs in amphitheātrō Flāviō crās pugnābunt.
                             multus sanguis fluet.

Tychicus

in hortō Hateriī fābula agēbātur. Paris, pantomīmus nōtissimus, mortem rēgīnae Dīdōnis imitābātur. aderant multī spectātōrēs quī ā Vitelliā, uxōre Hateriī, invītātī erant.

    Paris mōtibus ēlegantissimīs aptissimīsque dolōrem rēgīnae morientis imitābātur. cum dēnique quasi mortuus prōcubuisset, omnēs spectātōrēs admīrātiōne affectī identidem plaudēbant. aliī flōrēs iactābant, aliī Paridem deum appellābant. surrēxit Paris ut plausum spectātōrum exciperet.

    sed priusquam ille plūra ageret, vir quīdam statūrā brevī vultūque sevērō prōgressus magnā vōce silentium poposcit. oculīs in eum statim conversīs, spectātōrēs quis esset et quid vellet rogābant. paucī eum agnōvērunt. Iūdaeus erat, Tychicus nōmine, cliēns T. Flāviī Clēmentis. Paris ipse fābulā interruptā adeō obstupefactus est ut stāret immōtus. omnīnō ignōrābat quid Tychicus factūrus esset.

pantomīmus *pantomime actor, dancer*
imitābātur *was imitating, was miming*
5 **mōtibus: mōtus** *movement*
quasi *as if*

statūrā: statūra *height*
10

interruptā: interrumpere *interrupt*
15

"audīte, ō scelestī!" clāmāvit Tychicus. "vōs prāvī hunc hominem tamquam deum adōrātis. sunt tamen nūllī deī praeter ūnum! ūnus Deus sōlus adōrandus est! hunc Deum vērum quem plūrimī ignōrant, nunc vōbīs dēclārō."

mussitāre coepērunt spectātōrēs. aliī rogāvērunt utrum Tychicus iocōs faceret an īnsānīret; aliī servōs arcessīvērunt quī eum ex hortō ēicerent. Tychicus autem perstitit.

"Deus, ut prophētae nostrī nōbīs praedīxērunt, homō factus est et inter nōs habitāvit. aegrōs sānāvit; evangelium prōnūntiāvit; vītam aeternam nōbīs pollicitus est. tum in cruce suffīxus, mortuus est et in sepulcrō positus est. sed tertiō diē resurrēxit et vīvus ā discipulīs suīs vīsus est. deinde in caelum ascendit, ubi et nunc rēgnat et in perpetuum rēgnābit."

dum haec Tychicus dēclārat, servī Vitelliae signō datō eum comprehendērunt. domō eum trahēbant magnā vōce clāmantem:

"mox Dominus noster, rēx glōriae, ad nōs reveniet; ē caelō dēscendet cum sonitū tubārum, magnō numerō angelōrum comitante. et vīvōs et mortuōs iūdicābit. nōs Chrīstiānī, sī vītam pūram vīxerimus et eī crēdiderimus, ad caelum ascendēmus. ibi semper cum Dominō in pāce aeternā erimus. tū autem, Paris, fīlius diabolī, nisi vitiīs tuīs dēstiteris, poenās dabis. nūlla erit fuga. nam flammae, ē caelō missae, tē et omnēs scelestōs dēvorābunt."

quae cum prōnūntiāvisset, Tychicus multīs verberibus acceptīs domō ēiectus est. spectātōrum plūrimī eum vehementer dērīdēbant; paucī tamen, praesertim servī ac lībertī, tacēbant, quia Chrīstiānī erant ipsī.

praeter	*except*
vērum: vērus	*true*
dēclārō: dēclārāre	*declare, proclaim*
mussitāre	*murmur*
prophētae: prophēta	*prophet*
praedīxērunt: praedīcere	*foretell, predict*
evangelium	*good news, gospel*
prōnūntiāvit: prōnūntiāre	*proclaim, preach*
aeternam: aeternus	*eternal*
pollicitus est	*promised*
cruce: crux	*cross*
suffīxus: suffīgere	*nail, fasten*
resurrēxit: resurgere	*rise again*
discipulīs: discipulus	*disciple, follower*
caelum	*sky, heaven*
rēgnat: rēgnāre	*reign*
in perpetuum	*forever*
glōriae: glōria	*glory*
angelōrum: angelus	*angel*
comitante: comitāns	*accompanying*
iūdicābit: iūdicāre	*judge*
pūram: pūrus	*pure*
erimus	*shall be*
diabolī: diabolus	*devil*
nisi	*unless*
vitiīs: vitium	*sin*
verberibus: verber	*blow*

20

25

30

35

40

Judaism and Christianity

Many Jews in Rome lived across the Tiber from the center of the city. Augustus and other emperors had shown a tolerant attitude toward them. However, Tiberius and Claudius had expelled them from the city, apparently for attempting to convert others to Judaism.

At first the Romans tended to confuse Christianity with Judaism: both came from Judea, and both believed in only one god. There is a reference to followers of Chrestus (sic) as early as the time of Claudius (AD 41–54), who expelled them from Rome, classing them as Jews. St Paul came to Rome to appeal to the emperor in about AD 60, and in one of his letters from Rome passed on greetings from Christians living in the city, including some who belonged to "Caesar's house" (the household of the emperor).

Christians at this early period were frequently from the lower classes and could be viewed with suspicion as other foreign religions with secretive rites might be. Nero, casting about for a scapegoat after the great fire in Rome in AD 64, accused the Christians and ordered them killed. Other emperors did not follow his example. The Roman government usually preferred to leave Christians alone, although there certainly were sporadic persecutions, the worst of which occurred, ironically, just before Christianity was tolerated in AD 313.

The early Christians sometimes portrayed Christ as a beardless young man, like some of the Roman gods. The statue above may show him as an adolescent, perhaps debating with the priests in the Temple at Jerusalem. The mosaic below, from Britain, shows the letters X and P behind Christ's head. These are the first two letters of "Christ" in Greek, and were often used as a Christian symbol (as on the previous page).

in aulā Domitiānī

I

When you have read this part of the story, answer the questions on the opposite page.

in scaenā parvā, quae in aulae Domitiānī ātriō exstrūcta erat, Paris fābulam dē amōre Mārtis et Veneris agēbat. simul pūmiliō, Myropnous nōmine, tībīcen atque amīcus Paridis, suāviter tībiīs cantābat. nūllī aderant spectātōrēs nisi Domitia Augusta, uxor Imperātōris Domitiānī, quae Paridem inter familiārissimōs suōs habēbat. oculīs in eō fīxīs fābulam intentē spectābat. tam mīrābilis, tam perīta ars eius erat ut lacrimās retinēre Domitia vix posset.

> simul *at the same time*
> tībīcen *pipe player*
> tībiīs cantābat: tībiīs cantāre
> *play on the pipes*
> familiārissimōs: familiāris
> *close friend*

subitō servus, nōmine Olympus, quem Domitia iānuam ātriī custōdīre iusserat, ingressus est.

"domina," inquit, "ego Epaphrodītum, Augustī lībertum, modo cōnspicātus sum trānseuntem āream, decem mīlitibus comitantibus. mox hūc intrābit."

> Augustī lībertum: Augustī
> lībertus *freedman of*
> *Augustus, freedman of the*
> *emperor*

quibus verbīs audītīs, Paris ad Domitiam conversus rīsit.

Paris:	dēliciae meae! quam fortūnāta es! ab Epaphrodītō ipsō, Augustī lībertō, vīsitāris.
Domitia:	(*adventū Epaphrodītī commōta*) mī Pari, tibi perīculōsum est hīc manēre. odiō es Epaphrodītō! sī tē apud mē ille invēnerit, poenās certē dabis. iubēbit mīlitēs in carcerem tē conicere. fuge!
Paris:	cūr fugiendum est? illum psittacum Domitiānī haudquāquam vereor.
Domitia:	at ego valdē vereor. nam mihi quoque Epaphrodītus est inimīcus. iussū eius conclāvia mea saepe īnspiciuntur; epistulae meae leguntur; ancillae meae cotīdiē interrogantur. potestās eius nōn minor est quam Imperātōris ipsīus.
Paris:	mea columba, dēsine timēre! mē nōn capiet iste homunculus. paulīsper abībō.

> certē *certainly*

> vereor *I fear, I am afraid*

> conclāvia: conclāve *room*
> īnspiciuntur: īnspicere *search*

haec locūtus, columnam proximam celeriter cōnscendit et per compluvium ēgressus in tēctō sē cēlāvit. Myropnous quoque sē cēlāre cōnstituit. post tapēte quod dē longuriō gravī pendēbat sē collocāvit. Domitia contrā, quae quamquam perterrita erat in lectō manēbat vultū compositō, Olympō imperāvit ut aliquōs versūs recitāret.

> compluvium *compluvium*
> *(opening in roof)*
> tapēte *tapestry, wall hanging*
> longuriō: longurius *pole*
> pendēbat: pendēre *hang*
> contrā *on the other hand*
> compositō: compositus
> *composed, steady*

Questions

1 **in scaenā parvā** (line 1). Where had this stage been built?
2 What story was Paris performing?
3 Who was the pipe player supplying the musical accompaniment? Write down three things that we are told about him.
4 How many spectators were watching the performance?
5 From lines 6–8 pick out:

   a One group of four words that show Domitia's attention was focused on Paris.

   b Another group of words that show she was deeply affected by Paris' skill as an actor.

6 What had Olympus been ordered to do?
7 What news did he bring?
8 **sī tē … tē conicere** (lines 18–20). Explain why Domitia thought it was dangerous for Paris to stay.
9 **iussū eius … interrogantur** (lines 24–26). Domitia mentioned three ways in which Epaphroditus was making life unpleasant for her. What were they?
10 Where did **a** Paris and **b** Myropnous hide?
11 While Paris and Myropnous were hiding, where was Domitia? How did she try to pretend that everything was normal (lines 33–35)?
12 Read lines 14–33 again. What picture have you formed of Paris' personality? Make three different points and refer to these lines to support each of them.

II

Olympō recitante, ingressus est Epaphrodītus. decem mīlitēs
eum comitābantur.

Epaphrodītus:	ubi est iste pantomīmus quem impudēns tū	**impudēns** *shameless*
	amās? ubi eum cēlāvistī?	
Domitia:	verba tua nōn intellegō. sōla sum, ut vidēs. hic *5*	
	servus mē versibus dēlectat, nōn Paris.	
Epaphrodītus:	(*conversus ad mīlitēs*) quaerite Paridem! festīnāte!	
	omnia īnspicite conclāvia!	

mīlitēs igitur conclāvia dīligentissimē īnspexērunt, sed frūstrā.
Paridem nusquam invenīre poterant. *10*

Epaphrodītus:	caudicēs! sī Paris effūgerit, vōs poenās dabitis.	
	cūr tēctum nōn īnspexistis? ferte scālās!	**scālās: scālae** *ladders*

quae cum audīvisset Domitia palluit. Myropnous tamen, quī per
tapēte cautē prōspiciēbat, cōnsilium audācissimum cēpit. tapēte
lēniter manū movēre coepit. mox Epaphrodītus, dum ātrium *15*
suspīciōsus circumspectat, mōtum tapētis vīdit. **suspīciōsus** *suspicious*

Epaphrodītus:	ecce! movētur tapēte! latebrās Paridis invēnī!	**latebrās: latebrae** *hiding-place*
	nunc illum capiam.	

quibus dictīs, Epaphrodītus ad tapēte cum magnō clāmōre sē **sē praecipitāvit: sē**
praecipitāvit. Myropnous haudquāquam perturbātus, ubi *20* **praecipitāre** *hurl oneself*
Epaphrodītus appropinquāvit, tapēte magnā vī dētrāxit. dēcidit **perturbātus** *disturbed, alarmed*
tapēte, dēcidit longurius. Epaphrodītus, tapētī convolūtus atque **dētrāxit: dētrahere** *pull down*
simul longuriō percussus, prōcubuit exanimātus. Myropnous **convolūtus: convolvere**
exsultāns tībiīs cantāre coepit. *entangle*
    Domitia, quae sē iam ex pavōre recēperat, ad mīlitēs in *25*
ātrium cum scālīs regressōs conversa est. eōs iussit
Epaphrodītum extrahere. mīlitibus eum extrahentibus
Myropnous assem in labra eius quasi mortuī posuit. dēnique **assem: as** *as (small coin)*
Paris per compluvium dēspiciēns Epaphrodītō ita valēdīxit: **dēspiciēns: dēspicere** *look*
    "hīc iacet Tiberius Claudius Epaphrodītus, Augustī lībertus, *30* *down*
longuriō strātus." **strātus: sternere** *lay low*

About the language 1: future tense

1   Study the following examples:

> nōlī dēspērāre! amīcus meus tē **servābit**.
> *Don't give up! My friend **will save** you.*

> servī ad urbem heri iērunt; crās **revenient**.
> *The slaves went to the city yesterday; they **will come back** tomorrow.*

The words in **boldface** are in the future tense.

2   The first and second conjugations form their future tense in the following way:

first conjugation		*second conjugation*	
portābō	*I shall carry*	docēbō	*I shall teach*
portābis	*you will carry*	docēbis	*you will teach*
portābit	*s/he will carry*	docēbit	*s/he will teach*
portābimus	*we shall carry*	docēbimus	*we shall teach*
portābitis	*you will carry*	docēbitis	*you will teach*
portābunt	*they will carry*	docēbunt	*they will teach*

3   The third and fourth conjugations form their future tense in another way:

third conjugation		*fourth conjugation*	
traham	*I shall drag*	audiam	*I shall hear*
trahēs	*you will drag*	audiēs	*you will hear*
trahet	*s/he will drag*	audiet	*s/he will hear*
trahēmus	*we shall drag*	audiēmus	*we shall hear*
trahētis	*you will drag*	audiētis	*you will hear*
trahent	*they will drag*	audient	*they will hear*

4   Further examples:

    a crās ad Graeciam nāvigābitis.
    b ille mercātor est mendāx; tibi numquam pecūniam reddet.
    c fuge! mīlitēs tē in carcerem conicient!
    d dux noster est vir benignus, quī vōs omnēs līberābit.
    e "quid crās faciēs?" "ad theātrum ībō."
    f laudābō; respondēbit; appropinquābunt; rīdēbitis.
    g veniēmus; trādent; dīcam; dormiet.

5   The future tense of **sum** is as follows:

erō	*I shall be*	erimus	*we shall be*
eris	*you will be*	eritis	*you will be*
erit	*s/he will be*	erunt	*they will be*

Word patterns: diminutives

1 Study the form and meaning of the following nouns:

homō	*man*	homunculus	*little man*
servus	*slave*	servulus	*little slave*
corpus	*body*	corpusculum	*little body*
ager	*field*	agellus	*small plot of land*

2 Using paragraph 1 as a guide, complete the table below:

lapis	*rock*	lapillus	. . . .
fīlia	. . . .	fīliōla	. . . .
versus	. . . .	versiculus	. . . .
liber	. . . .	. . . .	*booklet*

3 The nouns in the right-hand columns above are known as **diminutives**. Suggest a meaning for each of the following diminutives:

cēnula, fābella, gladiōlus, mēnsula, nāvicula, ponticulus, vīllula.

4 Study the following nouns and their diminutives:

calx	*stone*
calculus	*pebble (used as a piece in board games, as a voting "ballot" and as a counter for making calculations)*
capsa	*box (for books)*
capsula	*small container*
cōdex (often spelled caudex)	*a piece of wood; someone with no more sense than a block of wood, i.e. a blockhead*
cōdicillī	*wooden writing tablets; codicil (written instructions added to a will)*
grānum	*grain, seed*
grānulum	*small grain or granule*
mūs	*mouse*
musculus	*little mouse; muscle*
sporta	*basket*
sportula	*little basket; gift for clients from a patron (named after its original container)*

Practicing the language

1 Complete each sentence with the correct participle. Then translate the sentence.

   a hīs verbīs . . . . , Paris aequō animō respondit. (audītīs, portātīs)
   b signō . . . . , servī Tychicum ēiēcērunt. (victō, datō)
   c nāve . . . . , mercātor dēspērābat. (āmissā, refectā)
   d clientibus . . . . , praecō iānuam clausit. (dīmissīs, dēpositīs)
   e equitibus . . . . , hostēs fūgērunt. (cōnspectīs, dēfēnsīs)
   f cēnā . . . . , Haterius amīcōs in triclīnium dūxit. (cōnsūmptā, parātā)

2 Translate the first sentence of each pair. Then complete the second sentence with
   the passive form of the verb to express the same idea. Use the table on page 276
   to help you. Finally, translate the second sentence.

   For example: hospitēs fābulam spectābant.
                   fābula ā hospitibus . . . .

   Translated and completed, this becomes:

                   hospitēs fābulam spectābant.
                   The guests were watching the play.

                   fābula ā hospitibus spectābātur.
                   The play was being watched by the guests.

   In sentences **a–c**, the verbs are in the *imperfect* tense:

   a servī amphorās portābant.
      amphorae ā servīs . . . .
   b Salvius Haterium dēcipiēbat.
      Haterius ā Salviō . . . .
   c barbarī horreum oppugnābant.
      horreum ā barbarīs . . . .

   In sentences **d–f**, the verbs are in the *present* tense:

   d rhētor puerōs docet.
      puerī ā rhētore . . . .
   e aliquis iānuam aperit.
      iānua ab aliquō . . . .
   f centuriō mīlitēs cōnsistere iubet.
      mīlitēs ā centuriōne cōnsistere . . . .

About the language 2: future perfect tense

1 Study the following example:

> sī tē audīverō, respondēbō.
> *If I hear you, I shall reply.*

The replying takes place in the future, so Latin uses the future tense (**respondēbō**). The hearing also takes place in the future, but at a different time: hearing comes before replying. To indicate the difference in time, Latin uses an unusual tense known as the **future perfect** (**audīverō**).

2 Literally **audīverō** means *I shall have heard*, but it is often translated by an English present tense, as in the example above.

3 The forms of the future perfect are as follows:

portāverō	portāverimus
portāveris	portāveritis
portāverit	portāverint

4 Further examples:

  a sī Epaphrodītus nōs cōnspexerit, tē interficiet.
  b sī dīligenter quaesīveris, pecūniam inveniēs.
  c sī servī bene labōrāverint, eīs praemium dabō.
  d sī mīlitēs vīderō, fugiam.

A picture made from pieces of colored marbles, showing the procession at the start of the chariot races. The patron of the games, perhaps an emperor, drives a two-horse chariot. Behind him are riders in the colors of the four teams, red, blue, green, and white.

Roman entertainment

The Roman year was punctuated by days dedicated to the gods as official **lūdī** (games), which usually began with a series of **lūdī scaenicī** (theatrical shows), and followed with some days devoted to **lūdī circensēs** (chariot races). At the end of the Republic, ludi were celebrated on over fifty days each year, and during the empire this number increased. The **Lūdī Rōmānī**, the oldest, had started under the kings. Other games followed: e.g. they might be held after the invasion of Hannibal, or to propitiate various gods, for instance Apollo and the Magna Mater, or to honor military victories. These public celebrations affirmed the conservative Roman ideas on class distinction. The senators and equestrians had seats in the front and sometimes the poor stood at the top. Women sat with men in the Circus but may have sat separately at other performances. Because everyone attended, even ordinary citizens could voice approval and disapproval of both people and performers.

By the time of Domitian, formal plays, both tragedy and comedy, were no longer very popular, although when they had been produced it might have been with more lavishness than good taste. For instance, in one revival of a play during the Republic, 600 mules were brought on stage. Pantomimes

An ivory carving showing a pantomime performer with the masks and props of three characters.

Although this picture may show an actor in tragedy rather than pantomime, it gives a good idea of the flowing robes and the masks Paris wore.

and mimes had taken the place of drama. Paris was a famous pantomime actor in this period and is described on page 223 performing the tragedy of Dido, and then a famous story from myth about Mars and Venus. He would have danced and acted all the parts of the story, without speaking, and would have had a musical accompaniment, whether an orchestra and chorus, or just a single performer, like Myropnous. Mimes, on the other hand, were slapstick farces on themes from everyday life and usually involved several actors.

The final days of the ludi were devoted to the ludi circenses in the Circus Maximus. This could hold 250,000 spectators, an indication of how popular chariot races were in Rome (and in other cities of the empire, too). Fans bet on their favorite teams and also tried to harm their opponents by means of the defixiones

Left: *The interior of the Colosseum. The animal cages and machinery below were originally hidden by a wooden floor spread with sand.*

The Circus Maximus, with Domitian's palace on the Palatine overlooking it on the left. You can see the central **spīna** *of the circus around which the chariots raced.*

described on page 34. Four teams (**factiōnēs**) competed: the whites, reds, blues, and greens. Domitian added purple and gold, which do not seem to have continued after his death. After a procession into the Circus, the presiding magistrate signaled the start of the race by dropping a napkin (**mappa**).

A day's program normally consisted of twenty-four races, each lasting seven laps (about 5 miles or 8 kilometers) and taking about a quarter of an hour to run. Seven huge eggs of marble or wood were hoisted high above the central platform (**spīna**), and every time the lead chariot completed a lap, one egg was lowered. The charioteer had to race at full speed down the length of the circus and then display his greatest skill at the turning point (**mēta**); if he took the bend too slowly he would be overtaken, and if he took it too fast he might crash. He raced with the reins tied tightly around his body, and in his belt he carried a knife: if he crashed, his life might depend on how quickly he could cut himself free from the wreckage.

In addition to the ludi, upper-class Romans in the pre-imperial period sometimes paid for **mūnera** or gladiatorial shows. These munera were originally part of the rites owed to the dead. They became examples, though, of conspicuous consumption when people like Pompey or Julius Caesar staged not only many gladiatorial duels, but also **vēnātiōnēs** using exotic animals. In 55 BC when Pompey dedicated his theater, the first stone theater in Rome, he exhibited hundreds of lions and leopards in the Circus Maximus, but the last day ended anticlimactically when eighteen elephants were brought out to be hunted. The Roman audience pitied them, and the elephants also nearly stampeded into the seats. Later, when Caesar staged his games in his triumph in 46 BC, he used the elephants displayed as transport, not as targets!

In the empire, only the emperor put on these munera, which continued to involve not just animals and professional gladiators, but also condemned criminals. Augustus sponsored numerous venationes in the Circus and in the Forum. In addition, on the bank of the Tiber, he constructed special areas for **naumachiae** (naval battles). Domitian's father, Vespasian, started the **amphitheātrum Flāvium** (the Colosseum), which was opened by his brother, Titus, in AD 80. Rome now had a permanent arena for the gladiatorial combats, one which could hold 50,000 people.

Not least among the entertainments offered free to all Romans were the numerous processions and ceremonies throughout the city, held at the beginning of most events, including the ludi. But the parade of all parades was the triumphal procession after a military victory. In the Republic, the highest honor the state could bestow was the right to

A "Thracian" gladiator. His helmet is decorated with feathers and a griffin's head.

march through the city as a **triumphātor**. In the empire, only the emperor could enjoy such an honor, and Josephus, the historian of *The Jewish War*, has left an account of the joint triumph of Vespasian and Titus, commemorated on the arch of Titus in the Forum. The day began in the Campus Martius. Vespasian and Titus, dressed in triumphal robes, offered prayers to the gods and entered the city through the **Porta Triumphālis**. In front of the parade came all the splendors of the spoils of war; then huge traveling stages, some three or four stories high, exhibiting scenes from the conquest; groups of captives elaborately dressed; more spoils carried by more soldiers; and then Vespasian and Titus in chariots, with Domitian on a horse alongside. The procession finished at the temple of Jupiter on the Capitol, where they waited until the announcement came that the leader of the enemy had just been killed, before beginning the concluding sacrifices and prayers.

Such parades, along with the spectacles of the ludi and munera and the numerous festivals throughout the year, offered everyone the chance to see and be seen with the political and social leaders of the day. However dubiously we may view some of these occasions, as bloodthirsty, garish, or simply puzzling, they permitted all people in the city, Romans and non-Romans, rich and poor, a share in the splendor of the city's gods, its history, and its power.

Not all entertainment was public. Rich Romans enjoyed presenting private shows of various kinds, as in the story on pages 223–224, where Paris performs in Haterius' garden for Vitellia and her friends. One elderly lady, Ummidia Quadratilla, kept her own private troupe of pantomimi. Often entertainment would be presented at a dinner party. This might consist of dancing girls, freaks, actors, jugglers, acrobats, a band of musicians, a novelty like the philosopher Euphrosyne, or a trained slave reciting a poem or other literary work – possibly written by the host, which might sometimes be rather embarrassing for the guests. The more serious types of entertainment were often put on by highly educated hosts for equally cultivated and appreciative guests; but they might sometimes, like Euphrosyne's philosophy lecture, be presented by ignorant and uninterested hosts who merely wanted to be fashionable or were trying to pass themselves off as persons of good taste and culture.

An acrobat doing a handstand on a crocodile.

Two scenes at the Circus Maximus

Study these two pictures of chariot racing.

In the top picture:

1 The charioteer on the left has fallen from his chariot. Why might this accident have happened?

2 What urgent action must he take now?

3 What is the purpose of the row of dolphins in the background?

In the bottom picture:

4 It has been suggested that the charioteer on the left is reining in the inside horse. Why would he do this?

5 The horseman on the right seems to be whipping his horse. What might be his purpose in the race?

Two terracotta plaques showing chariot racing at the Circus Maximus.

Vocabulary checklist 33

appellō, appellāre, appellāvī, appellātus	call, call out to
at	but
brevis, brevis, breve	short, brief
coniciō, conicere, coniēcī, coniectus	hurl, throw
contrā	against, on the other hand
crās	tomorrow
dēcidō, dēcidere, dēcidī	fall down
dēscendō, dēscendere, dēscendī	come down, go down
ēiciō, ēicere, ēiēcī, ēiectus	throw out
et … et	both … and
excipiō, excipere, excēpī, exceptus	receive
fuga, fugae, f.	escape
hīc	here
lūdus, lūdī, m.	game
moveō, movēre, mōvī, mōtus	move
nisi	except, unless
numerus, numerī, m.	number
potestās, potestātis, f.	power
quia	because
reficiō, reficere, refēcī, refectus	repair
rēgīna, rēgīnae, f.	queen
utrum	whether
vērus, vēra, vērum	true, real
rē vērā	in fact, truly, really

Coin of the Emperor Titus, celebrating the opening of the Colosseum.

LIBERTUS

Stage 34

ultiō Epaphrodītī

Epaphrodītus, ā Paride atque Domitiā ēlūsus, eōs ulcīscī
vehementissimē cupiēbat. Imperātor quoque, īrā et suspīciōne
commōtus, Epaphrodītum saepe hortābātur ut Paridem
Domitiamque pūnīret. Epaphrodītō tamen difficile erat
Domitiam, uxōrem Imperātōris, et Paridem, pantomīmum   5
nōtissimum, apertē accūsāre. auxilium igitur ab amīcō Salviō
petīvit.

    Epaphrodītus "nōn modo ego," inquit, "sed etiam Imperātor
Paridem Domitiamque pūnīre cupit. sī mē in hāc rē adiūveris,
magnum praemium tibi dabitur."   10

    Salvius, rē paulīsper cōgitātā, tranquillē respondit:

    "cōnfīde mihi, amīce; ego tibi rem tōtam administrābō.
īnsidiae parābuntur; Domitia et Paris in īnsidiās ēlicientur; ambō
capientur et pūnientur."

    "quid Domitiae accidet?" rogāvit Epaphrodītus.   15

    "Domitia accūsābitur; damnābitur; fortasse relēgābitur."

    "et Paris?"

    Salvius rīsit.

    "ēmovēbitur."

ēlūsus: ēlūdere *trick, outwit*
ulcīscī *to take revenge on*
suspīciōne: suspīciō *suspicion*

ēlicientur: ēlicere *lure, entice*

relēgābitur: relēgāre *exile*

Epaphroditus

Epaphroditus was a former slave of the Emperor Nero. Under Domitian, Epaphroditus' official title was secretary **ā libellīs** (in charge of petitions – the word **ā** has a special meaning in this phrase), which means that he helped the emperor to deal with the various petitions or requests submitted to him by groups and individuals. The opportunities for bribery are obvious, and imperial freedmen like him were widely unpopular.

The large block of marble below is part of an inscription honoring him. The top line tells us he is the emperor's freedman: [A]VGL stands for **Augustī lībertus**. The bottom line boasts of gold crowns (**corōnīs aureīs**) he has been awarded, possibly as a reward for the part he played in unmasking a conspiracy against Nero.

When he eventually fell out of favor with Domitian, he was executed on the grounds that he helped Nero commit suicide twenty-seven years before.

Epaphroditus wearing the toga, the mark of a citizen. When he was freed he gained the right to wear it. On the table is his pilleus, *the cap of liberty he was given to mark his manumission.*

īnsidiae

I

When you have read this part of the story, answer the questions at the end.

paucīs post diēbus Domitia ancillam, nōmine Chionēn, ad sē vocāvit.

"epistulam," inquit, "ā Vitelliā, uxōre Hateriī, missam modo accēpī. ēheu! Vitellia in morbum gravem incidit. statim mihi vīsitanda est. tē volō omnia parāre." 5

tum Chionē, ē cubiculō dominae ēgressa, iussit lectīcam parārī et servōs arcessī. medicum quoque quaesīvit quī medicāmenta quaedam Vitelliae parāret. inde Domitia lectīcā vecta, comitantibus servīs ancillāque, domum Hateriī profecta est. difficile erat eīs per viās prōgredī, quod nox obscūra erat 10 multumque pluēbat.

cum domum Hateriī pervēnissent, iānuam apertam invēnērunt. servīs extrā iānuam relictīs, Domitia cum Chionē ingressa est. spectāculum mīrābile eīs ingredientibus obiectum est. ātrium magnificē ōrnātum erat: ubīque lūcēbant lucernae, 15 corōnae rosārum dē omnibus columnīs pendēbant. sed omnīnō dēsertum erat ātrium. inde fēminae, triclīnium ingressae, id quoque dēsertum vīdērunt. in mediō tamen cēna sūmptuōsa posita erat: mēnsae epulīs exquīsītissimīs cumulātae erant,

Chionēn *Greek accusative of* **Chionē**

parārī *to be prepared*
arcessī *to be summoned, to be sent for*
medicāmenta: medicāmentum *medicine, drug*

eīs ... obiectum est *met them, was presented to them*

epulīs: epulae *dishes*
cumulātae erant: cumulāre *heap*

pōcula vīnō optimō plēna erant. quibus vīsīs, ancilla timidā   20
vōce,

    "cavendum est nōbīs," inquit. "aliquid mīrī hīc agitur."

    "fortasse Vitellia morbō affecta est cum cēnāret. sine dubiō
iam in cubiculō iacet," respondit Domitia, ignāra īnsidiārum
quās Salvius parāverat.   25

cavendum est: cavēre *beware*
mīrī: mīrus *extraordinary*

Questions

1 What did Domitia tell Chione (lines 3–4)?

2 What was said to have happened to Vitellia?

3 What did Domitia decide must be done at once?

4 What preparations did Chione make (lines 6–8)?

5 Where were Domitia and her party going?

6 Why was the journey difficult?

7 What did Domitia and Chione discover at the entrance?

8 What happened to the slaves (line 13)?

9 **ātrium magnificē ōrnātum erat** (line 15). In what ways did the atrium look particularly splendid?

10 What was odd about the atrium and the dining room?

11 Why is the dinner described as **sūmptuōsa** (line 18)?

12 What did Chione say about the situation (line 22)?

13 What explanation did Domitia give? What did she think Vitellia was now doing?

14 Which two Latin words show that Domitia was unaware of what was going on?

15 What do you think will happen next?

II

itaque per domum dēsertam, ancillā timidē sequente, Domitia
prōgredī coepit. cum ad cubiculum ubi Vitellia dormīre solēbat
pervēnisset, in līmine cōnstitit. cubiculum erat obscūrum.
Chionēn ad triclīnium remīsit quae lucernam ferret. in silentiō
noctis diū exspectābat dum redīret ancilla. haec tamen nōn   5
rediit. tandem Domitia morae impatiēns in cubiculum irrūpit.
vacuum erat. tum dēmum pavōre magnō perturbāta est.
tenebrae, silentium, ancillae absentia, haec omnia perīculī
indicia esse vidēbantur. scīlicet falsa erat epistula!

    Domitia ad aulam quam celerrimē regredī cōnstituit   10
priusquam aliquid malī sibi accideret. dum per ātrium vacuum
fugit, vōce hominis subitō perterrita est.

remīsit: remittere *send back*
dum *until, while*
morae impatiēns *impatient at the delay*
vacuum: vacuus *empty*
tum dēmum *then at last, only then*
absentia *absence*
vidēbantur: vidērī *seem*

"dēliciae meae, salvē! tūne quoque ad cēnam invītāta es?"
tum vōcem agnōvit.

"mī Pari," inquit, "īnsidiae, nōn cēna, nōbīs parātae sunt.   15
effugiendum nōbīs est, dum possumus."

exitium

exitium *ruin, destruction*

I

Domitiā haec dīcente, Myropnous, quī dominum comitātus erat,
ad iānuam contendit. cautē prōspexit. ecce! via tōta mīlitibus
praetōriānīs plēna erat. neque lectīca, neque ancilla, neque servī
usquam vidērī poterant.

    ad ātrium reversus Myropnous "āctum est dē nōbīs!"   5
exclāmāvit. "appropinquant praetōriānī! mox hūc ingredientur!"

    hōc tamen cognitō, Paris "nōlī dēspērāre," inquit. "cōnsilium
habeō. Myropnū, tibi iānua custōdienda est. prohibē mīlitēs
ingredī. sī mē vel Domitiam in hōc locō cēperint, certē nōs
interficient. cōnābimur per postīcum ēlābī."   10

    Myropnous igitur iānuam claudere contendit. quō factō,
sellās ex ātriō, lectōs ē cubiculīs proximīs raptim in faucēs
trahere coepit. brevī ingēns pyra exstrūcta est.

    mīlitēs praetōriānī, cum iānuam clausam cōnspexissent,
haesitantēs cōnstitērunt. sed tribūnus, nē Paris et Domitia   15
effugerent, iānuam effringī iussit.

    "iānuam secūribus pulsāte!" inquit. "sī prōditōrēs effūgerint,
vōs omnēs pūniēminī."

    Myropnous ubi strepitum pulsantium audīvit pyram incendit.
amphoram oleī ē culīnā portāvit quā flammās augēret. tum pyrā   20
flagrante, amīcōs sequī contendit.

praetōriānīs: praetōriānus *praetorian (member of emperor's bodyguard)*
usquam *anywhere*
reversus: revertī *return*
āctum est dē nōbīs *it's all over for us*
postīcum *back gate*
ēlābī *escape*
faucēs *passage, entranceway*
pyra *pyre*

secūribus: secūris *axe*
prōditōrēs: prōditor *traitor*

oleī: oleum *oil*
flagrante: flagrāre *blaze*

II

Paris et Domitia, ubi ad postīcum pervēnērunt, duōs mīlitēs ibi
positōs invēnērunt. quōs cum vīdissent, quamquam Domitia
omnīnō dē salūte dēspērābat, Paris in hōc discrīmine
audācissimum atque callidissimum sē praestitit. nam cēlātā
haud procul Domitiā, ipse per postīcum audācter prōgressus sē   5
mīlitibus ostendit. tum quasi fugiēns, retrō in hortum cucurrit.

    statim clāmāvērunt mīlitēs: "ecce Paris! Paris effugere
cōnātur!"

    mīlitibus sequentibus, Paris per hortum modo hūc modo illūc
ruēbat. post statuās sē cēlābat mīlitēsque vōce blandā dērīdēbat.   10
illī incertī ubi esset pantomīmus, vōcem Paridis circā hortum
sequēbantur.

retrō *back*

modo … modo *now … now*

circā *around*

tandem audīvit Paris strepitum cēterōrum mīlitum domum irrumpentium. iussū tribūnī flammae celeriter exstīnctae sunt. brevī tōta domus mīlitibus plēna erat. dēnique Paris intellēxit quantō in perīculō esset sed etiam tum haudquāquam dēspērāvit.

medīo in hortō stābat arbor veterrima, quae tēctō domūs imminēbat. simulatque intrāvērunt mīlitēs hortum, arborem Paris cōnscendit. hinc prōsilīre in tēctum cōnātus est. prōsiluit, sed tēgulae tēctī lūbricae erant. paulīsper in margine tēctī stetit; deinde praeceps humum lāpsus est.

intereā Domitia, quae per postīcum nūllō vidente ēgressa erat, prope vīllam manēbat dum Paris ad sē venīret. lāpsō tamen corpore eius, tantus erat fragor ut etiam ad aurēs Domitiae advenīret. quae metū āmēns vītaeque suae neglegēns in hortum reversa est. ubi corpus Paridis humī iacēns vīdit, dolōre cōnfecta sē in eum coniēcit eīque ōscula multa dedit.

"valē, dēliciae meae, valē!"

adiit tribūnus. Domitiam ad aulam dēdūcī iussit. ipse caput pantomīmī amputātum ad Epaphrodītum rettulit.

15

20

25

30

exstīnctae sunt: exstinguere
                 put out

arbor *tree*

prōsilīre *jump*
tēgulae: tēgula *tile*
lūbricae: lūbricus *slippery*
margine: margō *edge*
nūllō (*used as ablative of*
    nēmō) *no one*
fragor *crash*
āmēns *out of her mind, in a*
    frenzy
cōnfecta: cōnfectus *overcome*

amputātum: amputāre *cut off*

About the language 1: present passive infinitive

1 In Stage 13, you met sentences containing infinitives:

currere volō.   servī **labōrāre** nōn possunt.
*I want **to run**.*   *The slaves are not able **to work**.*
                            Or, *The slaves cannot work.*

This kind of infinitive is known in full as the **present active infinitive**.

2 In Stage 34, you have met another kind of infinitive:

volō epistulam **recitārī**.   Paris **invenīrī** nōn poterat.
*I want the letter **to be read out**.*   *Paris was unable **to be found**.*
                            Or, *Paris could not be found.*

This infinitive is known as the **present passive infinitive**.

3 Compare the following examples of present active and present passive infinitives:

	present active		*present passive*	
first conjugation	portāre	*to carry*	portārī	*to be carried*
second conjugation	docēre	*to teach*	docērī	*to be taught*
third conjugation	trahere	*to drag*	trahī	*to be dragged*
fourth conjugation	audīre	*to hear*	audīrī	*to be heard*

4 Further examples of the present passive infinitive:

  a volō iānuam aperīrī.
  b dux iussit captīvum līberārī.
  c fūr capī nōlēbat.
  d neque Vitellia neque ancilla vidērī poterat.
  e Haterius vīnum statim effundī iussit.

5 Deponent verbs form their infinitive in the following way:

first conjugation	cōnārī	*to try*
second conjugation	pollicērī	*to promise*
third conjugation	sequī	*to follow*
fourth conjugation	orīrī	*to rise*

Note that the infinitive has a passive ending, but an active meaning.

Further examples:

  a tribūnus iussit mīlitēs pantomīmum sequī.
  b aegrōtī deam precārī volēbant.
  c mercātor tandem proficīscī cōnstituit.
  d puerī tam perterritī erant ut loquī nōn possent.
  e hostēs ē castrīs ēgredī nōlēbant.

honōrēs

Salviō aulam intrantī obviam iit Epaphrodītus. cōmiter excēpit.

Epaphrodītus: mī Salvī, quālis artifex es! tuā arte iste
pantomīmus occīsus est. tuā arte Domitia ex
Ītaliā relēgāta est. Imperātor, summō gaudiō
affectus, spectāculum splendidissimum in   5
amphitheātrō Flāviō darī iussit. crās diēs fēstus
ab omnibus cīvibus celebrābitur; puerī
puellaeque deōrum effigiēs corōnīs flōrum
ōrnābunt; sacerdōtēs sacrificia offerent; ingēns
cīvium multitūdō Imperātōrem ad templum   10
Iovis comitābitur, ubi ille dīs immortālibus
grātiās aget. mox senātōrēs ad cūriam fēstīs
vestīmentīs prōgredientur et Domitiānō
grātulābuntur. venī mēcum! nōn morandum est
nōbīs. Imperātor enim nōs exspectat. mihi   15
ōrnāmenta praetōria, tibi cōnsulātum prōmīsit.

Salvius: cōnsulātum adipīscar? quam fortūnātus
sum!

Epaphrodītus: venī! Imperātōrī grātiās agere dēbēmus.

Epaphrodītō et Salviō ēgressīs ut Domitiānum salūtārent, ē   20
latebrīs rēpsit Myropnous. nunc dēnique intellēxit quis esset
auctor exitiī Paridis. lacrimīs effūsīs, indignam amīcī mortem
lūgēbat. manibus ad caelum sublātīs nōmen Salviī dētestātus est.
tum tībiās āmēns frēgit, haec verba locūtus:
    "ego numquam iterum tībiīs cantābō priusquam perierit   25
Salvius."

dīs = deīs: deus *god*
cūriam: cūria *senate-house*

morandum est: morārī *delay*

ōrnāmenta praetōria
    honorary praetorship,
    honorary rank of praetor
    (judicial magistrate)

auctor *person responsible,*
    originator
indignam: indignus
    unworthy, undeserved
sublātīs (past participle):
    tollere *raise, lift up*
priusquam perierit
    until … perishes

*Tombstone of a dwarf pipe
player called Myropnous.*

Domitia

Domitia was the wife of Emperor Domitian. However, in AD 83, Domitian divorced and exiled her for a period. Suetonius says that this was because she had an affair with the pantomime actor Paris. Or the cause may have been Domitia's failure to produce a healthy son and heir. Whatever the reason, she was soon back at court to continue in her activities as the emperor's consort.

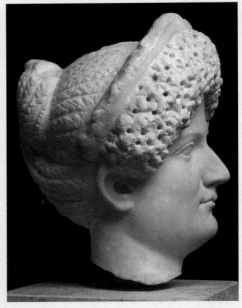

Domitia

A sestertius showing Domitia and her son.

About the language 2: future passive tense

1 Study the following examples:

cēna sūmptuōsa **parābitur**.
*An expensive dinner **will be prepared**.*

crās nūntiī ad rēgem **mittentur**.
*Tomorrow messengers **will be sent** to the king.*

ab Imperātōre **honōrābor**.
*I **shall be honored** by the emperor.*

vōs omnēs **pūniēminī**.
*You **will** all **be punished**.*

The verbs in **boldface** are passive forms of the future tense.

2 First and second conjugation verbs form the passive of their future tense in the following way:

first conjugation		*second conjugation*	
portābor	*I shall be carried*	docēbor	*I shall be taught*
portāberis	*you will be carried*	docēberis	*you will be taught*
portābitur	*s/he will be carried*	docēbitur	*s/he will be taught*
portābimur	*we shall be carried*	docēbimur	*we shall be taught*
portābiminī	*you will be carried*	docēbiminī	*you will be taught*
portābuntur	*they will be carried*	docēbuntur	*they will be taught*

3 Third and fourth conjugation verbs form the passive of their future tense in the following way:

third conjugation		*fourth conjugation*	
trahar	*I shall be dragged*	audiar	*I shall be heard*
trahēris	*you will be dragged*	audiēris	*you will be heard*
trahētur	*s/he will be dragged*	audiētur	*s/he will be heard*
trahēmur	*we shall be dragged*	audiēmur	*we shall be heard*
trahēminī	*you will be dragged*	audiēminī	*you will be heard*
trahentur	*they will be dragged*	audientur	*they will be heard*

4 Further examples:

a ingēns praemium victōrī dabitur. omnēs vīllae dēlēbuntur.
b nisi effūgerimus, capiēmur. in carcerem iaciēris.
c damnābiminī; condūcentur; ēiciētur; cogēris; accūsābor.

5 Notice how the future tense of deponent verbs is formed:

cōnābor	*I shall try*	loquar	*I shall speak*
cōnāberis	*you will try*	loquēris	*you will speak*
cōnābitur	*s/he will try*	loquētur	*s/he will speak*
cōnābimur	*we shall try*	loquēmur	*we shall speak*
cōnābiminī	*you will try*	loquēminī	*you will speak*
cōnābuntur	*they will try*	loquentur	*they will speak*

6 Further examples:

a mīlitēs crās proficīscentur. dux hostium nihil suspicābitur.
b sī hoc venēnum cōnsūmpseris, moriēris.
c revertentur; prōgrediar; ēgrediēminī; amplectēris; hortābitur.

Word patterns: verbs and nouns

1 Study the form and meaning of the following verbs and nouns:

verb		noun	
haesitāre	*to hesitate*	haesitātiō	*hesitation*
nāvigāre	*to sail*	nāvigātiō	*voyage*
mūtāre	*to change, alter*	mūtātiō	*change, alteration*

2 Using paragraph 1 as a guide, complete the table below:

verb		noun	
coniūrāre	*to conspire*	coniūrātiō	. . . .
salūtāre	. . . .	. . . .	*greeting*
cōgitāre	. . . .	cōgitātiō	. . . .

3 Match the correct translation to the following nouns:

a	dubitātiō	**i**	encouragement
b	festīnātiō	**ii**	refusal
c	hortātiō	**iii**	public reading
d	recitātiō	**iv**	uncertainty
e	recūsātiō	**v**	haste
f	rogātiō	**vi**	request

4 What is the gender of each noun above?
To what declension does each noun belong?

Left: *The consular chair and fasces which were the symbol of the consulship as promised to Salvius in the story* **honōrēs**. *The fasces were bundles of rods and axes, to symbolize the consul's power to order beatings and executions. They were carried for him by a procession of twelve lictors; the statuette on the right shows one of them.*

Practicing the language

1 Complete each sentence with the correct form of the verb. Then translate the sentence.

   a ego vōbīs rem tōtam . . . . (nārrābō, nārrābimus)
   b amīcī meī cibum vestīmentaque nōbīs . . . . (praebēbit, praebēbunt)
   c Imperātor spectāculum splendidum in amphitheātrō crās . . . . (dabunt, dabit)
   d vōs estis fortiōrēs quam illī barbarī; eōs facile . . . . (superābitis, superābis)
   e tū in vīllā manē; nōs per postīcum . . . . (effugiam, effugiēmus)
   f caudex! mē numquam . . . . (capiēs, capiētis)
   g ego sum probus; tibi pecūniam . . . . (reddēmus, reddam)
   h fugite! hostēs mox . . . . (aderunt, aderit)

2 Translate each English sentence into Latin by selecting correctly from the list of Latin words.

   a *Many flowers were being thrown by the spectators.*

multa	flōris	ā spectātōribus	iactābant
multī	flōrēs	inter spectātōrēs	iactābantur

   b *They warned my friend not to cross the bridge.*

amīcum	meīs	monuerant	nē	pōns	trānsīret
amīcōs	meum	monuērunt	ut	pontem	trānsībat

   c *Having been ordered by the leader, we carried out the body.*

ad ducem	iussus	corpus	extulī
ā duce	iussī	corporum	extulimus

   d *We saw the man whose brother you (singular) had arrested.*

hominem	quī	frāter	comprehenderātis	vidēmus
hominum	cuius	frātrem	comprehenderās	vīdimus

   e *When the soldiers had been drawn up, I gave the centurion a sign.*

mīlitibus	īnstrūctīs	centuriōnem	signum	dedī
mīlitēs	īnstrūctōs	centuriōnī	signō	dedit

3 Translate the first sentence of each pair. Then complete the second sentence with the passive form of the verb. Use the table on page 277 to help you. Finally, translate the second sentence.

For example: centuriō fūrēs vulnerāverat.
                      fūrēs ā centuriōne . . . .

Translated and completed, this becomes:

> centuriō fūrēs vulnerāverat.
> *The centurion had wounded the thieves.*
>
> fūrēs ā centuriōne vulnerātī erant.
> *The thieves had been wounded by the centurion.*

The perfect and pluperfect tenses are both used in this exercise. The verbs in sentences **a–e** are all first conjugation like **portō.**

a coquus cibum parāverat.
       cibus ā coquō . . . .
b mercātor latrōnēs superāverat.
       latrōnēs ā mercātōre . . . .
c dominī servōs laudāvērunt.
       servī ā dominīs . . . .
d clientēs patrōnum salūtāvērunt.
       patrōnus ā clientibus . . . .
e rēx mē ipsum accūsāvit.
       ego ipse ā rēge . . . .
f custōs magnum clāmōrem audīvit.
       magnus clāmor ā custōde . . . .

Freedmen and freedwomen

The legal status granted to ex-slaves was noticeably more generous in ancient Rome than in other slave-owning societies. When slaves were manumitted, they ceased to be the property of their masters or mistresses and became **lībertī** or **lībertae**. The freedmen of a Roman citizen often became Roman citizens themselves. This practice seems to have been unique to Rome. Although citizenship was also attainable for freedwomen, it may have been less accessible than for freedmen.

As a Roman citizen, the freedman now had three names, of which the first two came from the name of his ex-master or his ex-mistress's father. For example, Tiro, the freedman of Marcus Tullius Cicero, became Marcus Tullius Tiro, and, in our stories, we have imagined that Clemens became Quintus Caecilius Clemens. A freedwoman was called by the feminine form of her ex-master's name or by her ex-mistress's name followed by her slave name. As a male citizen, a libertus now had the right to vote in elections and to make a will or business agreements which would be valid in the eyes of the law. Freedmen and freedwomen could also get married. If they had been living in an unofficial marriage with a fellow-slave, one of their first acts after manumission might have been to save up enough money to buy them out of slavery and marry them legally.

There were, however, some limits to the rights and privileges of ex-slaves, compared with other Roman citizens. A libertus could not become a senator or an eques, except by special favor of the emperor, and a liberta could not become a senator's wife. A libertus could not serve in the legions or stand as a candidate in elections. But the limitations were relatively few, and any children might be wholly exempt from them.

A freedman or freedwoman retained legal obligations to their former master or mistress, becoming a cliens or clienta, while their former owner was now their patronus or patrona. Some freedmen and freedwomen were supposed to leave money to their patrons in their wills, although ex-masters and -mistresses did not often insist on this. They were forbidden to do anything that would bring harm to their patron; and they had to do a certain number of days' work for their patron every year or pay a sum of money instead. Freedmen and freedwomen were bound to show deference and respect to their patrons. For example, a freedman was expected to attend his former master on public occasions, and assist him in misfortune.

Relief showing two freedmen being manumitted. Although they both wear the cap of freedom, one kneels to his master, implying that he still has obligations to him.

In return, a patron would help a needy client with the sportula distributed at the salutatio. If a freedman or freedwoman died first, the patron often paid for a decent funeral and had the ashes buried near the place where his own ashes would rest. He might also be the guardian of certain freedwomen. Patrons often helped their former slaves with funds to make a start in their new lives, just as, in our stories, Quintus established Clemens in a glass shop; or a patron might introduce and recommend his client to potential customers. Sometimes freedmen and freedwomen even continued to live in their ex-masters' and -mistresses' households, doing the same work that they had done as slaves. One such man was Pliny's talented freedman, Zosimus, who was equally skilled at reciting, lyre playing, and comedy acting. Pliny treated Zosimus with kindness and affection, and when Zosimus fell ill with tuberculosis, Pliny arranged a holiday abroad for him. In short, the patron–client relationship tended to be one of mutual helpfulness.

Further evidence of friendly relationships between ex-masters and -mistresses and their freedmen and freedwomen comes from the large number of inscriptions, particularly on tombstones, that refer to freedmen and freedwomen. Sometimes, for example, freedmen set up tombstones in honor of their ex-masters:

> D M
> T. FLAVIO HOMERO T.
> FLAVIVS HYACINTHVS
> PATRONO BENE MERENTI

DM = dīs manibus *to the spirits of the departed*
bene merentī: bene merēns *well deserving, deserving kindness*

Publius Varius Ampelus and Varia Ennuchis set up a tomb for their former mistress and themselves:

> P. VARIVS AMPELVS
> ET VARIA ENNVCHIS
> FECERVNT SIBI ET
> VARIAE P. F SERVANDAE PATRONAE

P. F = Publiī filiae

Sometimes ex-masters set up tombstones to their favorite freedmen:

> D M
> IVLIO VITALI
> PATRONVS LIBERTO
> BENE MERENTI

Some ex-masters allowed freedmen and freedwomen to be buried with them in their tombs:

D M
TITVS FLAVIVS EV
MOLPVS ET FLAVIA
QVINTA SIBI FECE
RVNT ET LIBERTIS LI
BERTABVSQVE POS
TERISQVE EORVM

libertābus: līberta *freedwoman*
posterīs: posterī *future*
generations

Although it was generally thought inappropriate for a patrona to marry her ex-slave, an ex-master might marry his freedwoman:

D M
T. FLAVIVS CERIALIS
FLAVIAE PHILAENIDI
LIBERTAE IDEM
ET COIVGI
B M F

idem here = *also*
coiugī = coniugī: coniūnx *wife*
BMF = bene merentī fēcit

Some slaves might be manumitted as a reward for long service or for some exceptional action, such as Felix's rescue of baby Quintus in our stories. But it is clear from the legal obligations of a client that it would often be financially worthwhile for a master to manumit a slave; the patron would still be able to make some use of the ex-slave's services, but would no longer have to provide for his food, clothing, and shelter.

Many highly skilled or educated freedmen were quickly able to earn a good living because they already possessed some special ability or experience; for example, a freedman might already be a skilled craftsman, teacher, musician, or secretary, or be experienced in accountancy, trade, or banking. The most competent freedmen found lucrative careers, even important managerial posts in small businesses and industry. Freedwomen might achieve financial security by working in shops, laundries, or the textile industry. Freedmen and freedwomen who had previously used these skills in their masters' and mistresses' service could now use them for their own benefit. There was plenty of demand for such services and not much competition from freeborn Romans, who often lacked the necessary skills or regarded such work as beneath their dignity.

It is not surprising, therefore, that many freedmen, and perhaps some freedwomen, became rich and successful, and a few freedmen became very rich indeed. The Vettii brothers, who set up their own business in Pompeii and eventually owned one of the most splendid houses in the town, are good examples of such successful freedmen. But perhaps the most famous example of a wealthy freedman is a fictitious one: Trimalchio, the vulgar and ostentatious millionaire in Petronius' novel *Satyrica*. The story **cēna Hateriī** in Stage 32 is partly based on Petronius' account of Trimalchio's dinner party.

After manumission, freedmen and freedwomen had to put up with a certain amount of prejudice from those who despised them for having been slaves. Even the next generation, which often enjoyed full privileges of citizenship, continued to be viewed by the citizens of freeborn ancestry as social inferiors. The poet Juvenal writes that at a banquet the patron gets "a delicate loaf white as snow, kneaded of the finest flour" while his clients are served "a bit of hard bread that you can scarce break in two or bits of solid dough that have turned moldy." This custom of having different food for different guests was disapproved of by the more discerning Romans. Pliny wrote, "I invite my guests to dine and not to be humiliated." The poet Horace was the object of suspicion and envy because of his friendship with Maecenas, a famous patron of the arts. Horace's father was a freedman whom Horace proudly praised for giving him the intellectual and moral training which won him a place in Maecenas' circle. Horace also praised Maecenas for his social fairness: "You, Maecenas, do not, like most of the world, curl up your nose at men of unknown birth, men like myself, a freedman's son."

One privilege, however, was available to freedmen and to no one else. A freedman could become one of the six priests (**sevirī Augustālēs**) who were appointed in many Italian towns and some provincial ones to oversee the cult of Rome and the worship of the deified Emperor Augustus. Like all priesthoods, the priesthood of Augustus was a position of honor and prestige, but this one was open to freedmen only.

A small but very important group of freedmen worked as personal assistants to the emperor. As slaves, they had been known as **servī Caesaris** and as freedmen they were known as **libertī Augustī**. (Caesar and Augustus were both used as titles of the emperor.) One of these men was Epaphroditus (full name Tiberius Claudius Neronis Augusti libertus Epaphroditus), Domitian's secretary **ā libellīs** (see page 241).

Other freedmen of the emperor were in charge of correspondence (**ab epistulīs**) and accounts (**ā ratiōnibus**). They all worked closely with the emperor in the day-to-day running of government business.

Under some emperors, especially Claudius and Nero, these freedmen became immensely rich and powerful. They were often bitterly resented by the Roman nobles and senators. This

The Emperor Domitian's vast palace on the Palatine hill overlooking the Circus Maximus. This picture shows part of the emperor's personal quarters, centered on a garden with the remains of a large fountain.

Augustales

To be chosen as an Augustalis, or priest of the emperor, was the greatest honor open to many freedmen.

Top left: *The hall in Herculaneum where the Augustales would meet for worship and for ceremonial dinners.* Below left: *Part of the inscription from a tomb at Pompeii, put up by a freedman for himself and his patroness, Vesonia. Notice how he must have been made an Augustalis after he had had the tomb built, because the word has been awkwardly squeezed in by a different letter-cutter. The honor, when it came, was too important to leave out of Vesonius Phileros' tomb inscription.*

resentment can be seen very plainly in two letters which Pliny wrote about Pallas, the secretary a rationibus of the Emperor Claudius. Pallas had been awarded the **ōrnāmenta praetōria** (honorary praetorship), like Epaphroditus in our stories. This means he was given the various privileges normally possessed by a praetor – special dress, special seat at public ceremonies, special funeral after death, and so on – without having any of the responsibilities. Pliny, when he came across the inscription commemorating these honors, was indignant and furious, even though the whole incident had happened fifty years previously. He described Pallas as a "furcifer," and much else besides. He was particularly angry that the inscription praised Pallas for refusing a further gift of 15 million sesterces. In Pliny's opinion, Pallas was insulting the praetorian rank by refusing the money as excessive while accepting the privileges as if they meant less; besides, he already had 300 million sesterces of his own. Pliny's outburst shows very clearly how much ill feeling could be caused by an emperor's use of ex-slaves as important and powerful assistants in running the empire.

Vocabulary checklist 34

accūsō, accūsāre, accūsāvī,
   accūsātus   *accuse*
auctor, auctōris, m.   *creator, originator*
   mē auctōre   *at my suggestion*
dum   *while, until*
frangō, frangere, frēgī, frāctus   *break*
gaudium, gaudiī, n.   *joy*
haud   *not*
modo   *just*
priusquam   *before, until*
procul   *far*
quasi   *as if*
sine   *without*
sonitus, sonitūs, m.   *sound*
vel   *or*
vestīmenta, vestīmentōrum, n. pl.   *clothes*

Deponent verbs

adipīscor, adipīscī, adeptus sum   *obtain*
comitor, comitārī, comitātus sum   *accompany*
cōnor, cōnārī, cōnātus sum   *try*
cōnspicor, cōnspicārī,
   cōnspicātus sum   *catch sight of*
ēgredior, ēgredī, ēgressus sum   *go out*
hortor, hortārī, hortātus sum   *encourage, urge*
ingredior, ingredī, ingressus sum   *enter*
loquor, loquī, locūtus sum   *speak*
morior, morī, mortuus sum   *die*
nāscor, nāscī, nātus sum   *be born*
patior, patī, passus sum   *suffer*
precor, precārī, precātus sum   *pray (to)*
proficīscor, proficīscī,
   profectus sum   *set out*
prōgredior, prōgredī,
   prōgressus sum   *advance*
regredior, regredī, regressus sum   *go back, return*
sequor, sequī, secūtus sum   *follow*
suspicor, suspicārī,
   suspicātus sum   *suspect*

*An aureus of the Emperor
Domitian.*

LANGUAGE INFORMATION

Contents

Part One: About the language
Nouns

1

	first declension	*second declension*			*third declension*
GENDER	f.	m.	m.	n.	m.
SINGULAR					
nominative and *vocative*	puella	servus (*voc.* serve)	faber	templum	mercātor
genitive (of)	puellae	servī	fabrī	templī	mercātōris
dative (to, for)	puellae	servō	fabrō	templō	mercātōrī
accusative	puellam	servum	fabrum	templum	mercātōrem
ablative (by, with)	puellā	servō	fabrō	templō	mercātōre
PLURAL					
nominative and *vocative*	puellae	servī	fabrī	templa	mercātōrēs
genitive (of)	puellārum	servōrum	fabrōrum	templōrum	mercātōrum
dative (to, for)	puellīs	servīs	fabrīs	templīs	mercātōribus
accusative	puellās	servōs	fabrōs	templa	mercātōrēs
ablative (by, with)	puellīs	servīs	fabrīs	templīs	mercātōribus

	fourth declension		*fifth declension*	
GENDER	m.	n.	m.	f.
SINGULAR				
nominative and *vocative*	portus	genū	diēs	rēs
genitive (of)	portūs	genūs	diēī	reī
dative (to, for)	portuī	genū	diēī	reī
accusative	portum	genū	diem	rem
ablative (by, with)	portū	genū	diē	rē
PLURAL				
nominative and *vocative*	portūs	genua	diēs	rēs
genitive (of)	portuum	genuum	diērum	rērum
dative (to, for)	portibus	genibus	diēbus	rēbus
accusative	portūs	genua	diēs	rēs
ablative (by, with)	portibus	genibus	diēbus	rēbus

m.	m.	f.	f.	n.	n.	GENDER
						SINGULAR
leō	cīvis	vōx	urbs	nōmen	tempus	*nominative* and *vocative*
leōnis	cīvis	vōcis	urbis	nōminis	temporis	*genitive (of)*
leōnī	cīvī	vōcī	urbī	nōminī	temporī	*dative (to, for)*
leōnem	cīvem	vōcem	urbem	nōmen	tempus	*accusative*
leōne	cīve	vōce	urbe	nōmine	tempore	*ablative (by, with)*
						PLURAL
leōnēs	cīvēs	vōcēs	urbēs	nōmina	tempora	*nominative* and *vocative*
leōnum	cīvium	vōcum	urbium	nōminum	temporum	*genitive (of)*
leōnibus	cīvibus	vōcibus	urbibus	nōminibus	temporibus	*dative (to, for)*
leōnēs	cīvēs	vōcēs	urbēs	nōmina	tempora	*accusative*
leōnibus	cīvibus	vōcibus	urbibus	nōminibus	temporibus	*ablative (by, with)*

2 For the ways in which the different cases are used, see p. 285.

3 Notice again the way in which the cases of third declension nouns are formed. In particular, compare the nominative singular of **leō**, **vōx**, and **nōmen** with the genitive singular. Which of these cases is a better guide to the way the other cases are formed?

Use the Vocabulary on pp. 293–323 to find the genitive singular of the following nouns; then use the tables here to find their ablative singular and plural:

dux; homō; pēs; difficultās; nox; iter.

4 Translate the following pairs of sentences. State the case, number (i.e. singular or plural), and declension of each noun in **boldface**. Use the table of nouns to help you.

a servī **nōmina** Graeca habēbant.
fēmina pauper erat, sed vītam contentam agēbat.

b magnus numerus **leōnum** in arēnam ruit.
lībertus **coquum** iussit cēnam magnificam parāre.

c **captīvī**, ē carcere ēductī, in pompā incēdēbant.
Imperātor arcum **frātrī** dēdicāre cōnstituit.

d **multitūdō** hominum viās urbis complēbat.
puella, **ānulō** dēlectāta, iuvenī grātiās ēgit.

Adjectives

1 first and second declension

SINGULAR	masculine	feminine	neuter	masculine	feminine	neuter
nominative and *vocative*	bonus (voc. bone)	bona	bonum	pulcher	pulchra	pulchrum
genitive	bonī	bonae	bonī	pulchrī	pulchrae	pulchrī
dative	bonō	bonae	bonō	pulchrō	pulchrae	pulchrō
accusative	bonum	bonam	bonum	pulchrum	pulchram	pulchrum
ablative	bonō	bonā	bonō	pulchrō	pulchrā	pulchrō
PLURAL						
nominative and *vocative*	bonī	bonae	bona	pulchrī	pulchrae	pulchra
genitive	bonōrum	bonārum	bonōrum	pulchrōrum	pulchrārum	pulchrōrum
dative	bonīs	bonīs	bonīs	pulchrīs	pulchrīs	pulchrīs
accusative	bonōs	bonās	bona	pulchrōs	pulchrās	pulchra
ablative	bonīs	bonīs	bonīs	pulchrīs	pulchrīs	pulchrīs

2 third declension

SINGULAR	masculine and feminine	neuter	masculine and feminine	neuter
nominative and *vocative*	fortis	forte	ingēns	ingēns
genitive	fortis	fortis	ingentis	ingentis
dative	fortī	fortī	ingentī	ingentī
accusative	fortem	forte	ingentem	ingēns
ablative	fortī	fortī	ingent-ī/-e	ingent-ī/-e
PLURAL				
nominative and *vocative*	fortēs	fortia	ingentēs	ingentia
genitive	fortium	fortium	ingentium	ingentium
dative	fortibus	fortibus	ingentibus	ingentibus
accusative	fortēs	fortia	ingentēs	ingentia
ablative	fortibus	fortibus	ingentibus	ingentibus

3 Compare the third declension adjectives in paragraph 2 with the third declension nouns on pp. 262-263. Notice in particular the different form of the ablative singular.

4 With the help of paragraphs 1 and 2 opposite and the table of nouns on pp. 262-263, find the Latin for the words in *italic type* in the following sentences:

    a   I took the *brave girl* to the centurion.
    b   He was the son of a *good king*.
    c   They were attacked by a *huge slave*.
    d   We visited many *beautiful cities*.
    e   The walls of the *huge temples* were built slowly and carefully.
    f   The dancing girl had *beautiful hands*.

5 Translate the following sentences. Then change the words in **boldface** into the plural. You may have to refer to the Vocabulary at the end of the book.

    a   pater **parvum fīlium** ad arcum Titī dūxit.
    b   senātor **fēminae trīstī** auxilium dedit.
    c   hostēs, **mūrō ingentī** dēfēnsī, diū resistēbant.
    d   omnēs audāciam **mīlitis Rōmānī** laudāvērunt.
    e   cīvēs **iuvenī callidō** praemium obtulērunt.
    f   **senex sapiēns** regī nōn **crēdidit**.

Comparison of adjectives

1

	comparative	*superlative*
longus *long*	longior *longer*	longissimus *longest, very long*
pulcher *beautiful*	pulchrior *more beautiful*	pulcherrimus *most beautiful, very beautiful*
fortis *brave*	fortior *braver*	fortissimus *bravest, very brave*
fēlīx *lucky*	fēlīcior *luckier*	fēlīcissimus *luckiest, very lucky*
prūdēns *shrewd*	prūdentior *shrewder*	prūdentissimus *shrewdest, very shrewd*
facilis *easy*	facilior *easier*	facillimus *easiest, very easy*

2 Irregular forms:

bonus *good*	melior *better*	optimus *best, very good*
malus *bad*	peior *worse*	pessimus *worst, very bad*
magnus *big*	maior *bigger*	maximus *biggest, very big*
parvus *small*	minor *smaller*	minimus *smallest, very small*
multus *much*	plūs *more*	plūrimus *most, very much*
multī *many*	plūrēs *more*	plūrimī *most, very many*

3 Study the forms of the comparative adjective **longior** (*longer*) and the superlative adjective **longissimus** (*longest, very long*):

SINGULAR	masculine and feminine	neuter	masculine	feminine	neuter
nominative and vocative	longior	longius	longissimus (voc. longissime)	longissima	longissimum
genitive	longiōris	longiōris	longissimī	longissimae	longissimī
dative	longiōrī	longiōrī	longissimō	longissimae	longissimō
accusative	longiōrem	longius	longissimum	longissimam	longissimum
ablative	longiōre	longiōre	longissimō	longissimā	longissimō
PLURAL					
nominative and vocative	longiōrēs	longiōra	longissimī	longissimae	longissima
genitive	longiōrum	longiōrum	longissimōrum	longissimārum	longissimōrum
dative	longiōribus	longiōribus	longissimīs	longissimīs	longissimīs
accusative	longiōrēs	longiōra	longissimōs	longissimās	longissima
ablative	longiōribus	longiōribus	longissimīs	longissimīs	longissimīs

4 Compare the endings of **longior** with those of the third declension nouns **mercātor** and **tempus** on pp. 262 and 263. Notice in particular the nominative and accusative forms of the neuter singular.

5 With the help of paragraphs 1–3 and the table of nouns on pp. 262–263, find the Latin for the words in *italic type* in the following sentences:

   a   I have never known a *longer day*.
   b   She sent the *worst slaves* back to the slave dealer.
   c   *Better times* will come.
   d   The *bravest citizens* were fighting the front line.
   e   We did not visit the *biggest temple*, as we had seen a *more beautiful* temple next to it.
   f   *Most girls* did not believe the soldiers' stories.

Adverbs

1 Adverbs ending in **-ē** are connected with 1st and 2nd declension adjectives.

ADVERB	ADJECTIVE
laetē *happily*	laetus, laeta, laetum *happy*
pulchrē *beautifully*	pulcher, pulchra, pulchrum *beautiful*

2 Adverbs ending in **-ter** are connected with 3rd declension adjectives.

ADVERB	ADJECTIVE
fortiter *bravely*	fortis, fortis, forte *brave*
audācter *boldly*	audāx, audāx, audāx *bold*

3 The comparative form of adverbs is the same as the neuter nominative singular of comparative adjectives.

ADVERB	ADJECTIVE
laetius *more happily*	laetior, laetior, laetius *happier*
fortius *more bravely*	fortior, fortior, fortius *braver*

4 The superlative form of adverbs ends in **-ē**, since superlative adjectives are all 1st and 2nd declension.

ADVERB	ADJECTIVE
laetissimē *very happily*	laetissimus, laetissima, laetissimum *very happy*
fortissimē *very bravely*	fortissimus, fortissima, fortissimum *very brave*

5 Irregular forms. Compare these adverbial forms with the adjectives on page 266.

bene *well*	melius *better*	optimē *best, very well*
male *badly*	peius *worse*	pessimē *worst, very badly*
magnopere *greatly*	magis *more*	maximē *most, very greatly*
paulum *little*	minus *less*	minimē *least, very little*
multum *much*	plūs *more*	plūrimum *most, very much*

6 Comparative forms (of both adjectives and adverbs) are sometimes used with the meaning "too."

> medicus **tardius** advēnit.
> *The doctor arrived **too late**. (i.e. later than he should have)*

7 Superlative forms (of both adjectives and adverbs) are sometimes used with **quam**, meaning "as … as possible."

> **quam celerrimē** advēnit.
> *He arrived **as quickly as possible**.*

8 Translate the following examples.

   a nēmō rēs meās prūdentius cūrat quam tū.
   b servus dominō breviter respondit.
   c rēx tōtam īnsulam occupāre perfidē cupit.
   d Belimicus maiōra praemia audācius postulābat.
   e quis hanc prōvinciam administrāre melius scit quam Imperātor?
   f captīvī ad carcerem reductī sunt, custōdem maximē vituperantēs.
   g hīs iuvenibus quam minimē crēdere dēbēmus.
   h fūrēs in cubiculum tacitē intrāvērunt, ē cubiculō timidē fūgērunt.

Pronouns I: ego, tū, nōs, vōs, sē

1 **ego** and **tū** (*I, you,* etc.)

	SINGULAR		PLURAL	
nominative	ego	tū	nōs	vōs
genitive	meī	tuī	nostrum	vestrum
dative	mihi	tibi	nōbīs	vōbīs
accusative	mē	tē	nōs	vōs
ablative	mē	tē	nōbīs	vōbīs

2 **sē** (*herself, himself, itself, themselves,* etc.)

	SINGULAR	PLURAL
nominative	(*no forms*)	
genitive	suī	suī
dative	sibi	sibi
accusative	sē	sē
ablative	sē	sē

3 Translate the following sentences:

  a nōs, ā tē monitī, perīculum vītāvimus.
  b captīvī, quod nūlla spēs salūtis erat, sē occīdērunt.
  c vīsne mēcum īre?
  d amīcī, quod diūtius manēre nōlēbant, domum sine vōbīs rediērunt.
  e Salvius, cum ad aulam prōcēderet, multōs servōs sēcum habēbat.
  f sorōrem rogāvī num stolās novās sibi comparāvisset.

Pick out the pronoun in each sentence and state its case.

Pronouns II: **hic, ille, ipse, is, īdem**

1 hic (*this, these*, etc.)

	SINGULAR			PLURAL		
	masculine	*feminine*	*neuter*	*masculine*	*feminine*	*neuter*
nominative	hic	haec	hoc	hī	hae	haec
genitive	huius	huius	huius	hōrum	hārum	hōrum
dative	huic	huic	huic	hīs	hīs	hīs
accusative	hunc	hanc	hoc	hōs	hās	haec
ablative	hōc	hāc	hōc	hīs	hīs	hīs

The various forms of **hic** can also be used to mean *he, she, they*, etc.:

hic tamen nihil dīcere poterat.
He, however, could say nothing.

2 ille (*that, those*, etc.; sometimes used with the meaning *he, she, it*, etc.)

	SINGULAR			PLURAL		
	masculine	*feminine*	*neuter*	*masculine*	*feminine*	*neuter*
nominative	ille	illa	illud	illī	illae	illa
genitive	illīus	illīus	illīus	illōrum	illārum	illōrum
dative	illī	illī	illī	illīs	illīs	illīs
accusative	illum	illam	illud	illōs	illās	illa
ablative	illō	illā	illō	illīs	illīs	illīs

3 ipse (*myself, yourself, himself*, etc.)

	SINGULAR			PLURAL		
	masculine	*feminine*	*neuter*	*masculine*	*feminine*	*neuter*
nominative	ipse	ipsa	ipsum	ipsī	ipsae	ipsa
genitive	ipsīus	ipsīus	ipsīus	ipsōrum	ipsārum	ipsōrum
dative	ipsī	ipsī	ipsī	ipsīs	ipsīs	ipsīs
accusative	ipsum	ipsam	ipsum	ipsōs	ipsās	ipsa
ablative	ipsō	ipsā	ipsō	ipsīs	ipsīs	ipsīs

..., *she*, *it*, etc.)

	SINGULAR			PLURAL		
	masculine	*feminine*	*neuter*	*masculine*	*feminine*	*neuter*
nominative	is	ea	id	eī	eae	ea
genitive	eius	eius	eius	eōrum	eārum	eōrum
dative	eī	eī	eī	eīs	eīs	eīs
accusative	eum	eam	id	eōs	eās	ea
ablative	eō	eā	eō	eīs	eīs	eīs

The forms of **is** can also be used to mean *that*, *those*, etc.:

> eā nocte rediit dominus.
> *That night, the master returned.*

5 From Stage 23 on, you have met various forms of the word **īdem**, meaning *the same*:

	SINGULAR			PLURAL		
	masculine	*feminine*	*neuter*	*masculine*	*feminine*	*neuter*
nominative	īdem	eadem	idem	eīdem	eaedem	eadem
genitive	eiusdem	eiusdem	eiusdem	eōrundem	eārundem	eōrundem
dative	eīdem	eīdem	eīdem	eīsdem	eīsdem	eīsdem
accusative	eundem	eandem	idem	eōsdem	eāsdem	eadem
ablative	eōdem	eādem	eōdem	eīsdem	eīsdem	eīsdem

Compare the forms of **īdem** with **is** in paragraph 4.

With the help of the table above, find the Latin for the words in *italic type* in the following sentences:

a I heard *the same* boy again.
b *The same* women were there.
c This is *the same* man's house.
d He saw *the same* girl.
e They were seized by *the same* soldiers.
f They always visited *the same* temple.

Pronouns III: **quī**

1 Notice the genitive, dative, and ablative plural of the relative pronoun **quī**:

	SINGULAR			PLURAL		
	masculine	*feminine*	*neuter*	*masculine*	*feminine*	*neuter*
nominative	quī	quae	quod	quī	quae	quae
genitive	cuius	cuius	cuius	quōrum	quārum	quōrum
dative	cui	cui	cui	quibus	quibus	quibus
accusative	quem	quam	quod	quōs	quās	quae
ablative	quō	quā	quō	quibus	quibus	quibus

> duōs servōs ēmī, **quōrum** alter Graecus, alter Aegyptius erat.
> *I bought two slaves, one of whom was a Greek, the other an Egyptian.*
> nūntiī, **quibus** mandāta dedimus, heri discessērunt.
> *The messengers to whom we gave the instructions departed yesterday.*
> mīlitēs aedificia, **ē quibus** hostēs fūgerant, celeriter incendērunt.
> *The soldiers quickly set fire to the buildings, from which the enemy had fled.*

2 Notice again the use of **quī** as a *connecting relative* to begin a sentence:

> lībertus pecūniam custōdiēbat. **quem** cum cōnspexissent, fūrēs fūgērunt.
> *A freedman was guarding the money. When they had caught sight of him the
> thieves ran away.*

> centuriō "ad carnificēs dūcite!" inquit. **quibus** verbīs perterritī, captīvī
> clāmāre ac lacrimāre coepērunt.
> *"Take them to the executioners!" said the centurion. Terrified by these words,
> the prisoners began to shout and weep.*

3 Sometimes the relative pronoun is used with forms of the pronoun **is**:

> fēcī **id quod** iussistī.
> *I have done that which you ordered.*

Or, in more natural English, using the word *what* to translate both Latin words:

> fēcī **id quod** iussistī.
> *I have done what you ordered.*

Further examples:
a id quod Salvius in epistulā scrīpsit falsum est.
b id quod mihi dīxistī vix intellegere possum.
c nūntius ea patefēcit quae apud Britannōs audīverat.
d servus tamen, homō ignāvissimus, id quod dominus iusserat omnīnō neglēxit.
e ea quae fēcistī ab omnibus laudantur.

Verbs

Indicative active

1

	first conjugation	*second conjugation*	*third conjugation*	*fourth conjugation*
PRESENT	*I carry, you carry, etc.*	*I teach, you teach, etc.*	*I drag, you drag, etc.*	*I hear, you hear, etc.*
	portō	doceō	trahō	audiō
	portās	docēs	trahis	audīs
	portat	docet	trahit	audit
	portāmus	docēmus	trahimus	audīmus
	portātis	docētis	trahitis	audītis
	portant	docent	trahunt	audiunt
IMPERFECT	*I was carrying*	*I was teaching*	*I was dragging*	*I was hearing*
	portābam	docēbam	trahēbam	audiēbam
	portābās	docēbās	trahēbās	audiēbās
	portābat	docēbat	trahēbat	audiēbat
	portābāmus	docēbāmus	trahēbāmus	audiēbāmus
	portābātis	docēbātis	trahēbātis	audiēbātis
	portābant	docēbant	trahēbant	audiēbant

2 In Stage 33, you met the *future tense*:

I shall carry	*I shall teach*	*I shall drag*	*I shall hear*
portābō	docēbō	traham	audiam
portābis	docēbis	trahēs	audiēs
portābit	docēbit	trahet	audiet
portābimus	docēbimus	trahēmus	audiēmus
portābitis	docēbitis	trahētis	audiētis
portābunt	docēbunt	trahent	audient

Notice again how the first and second conjugations form their future tense in one way, the third and fourth conjugations in another.

3 In paragraph 2, find the Latin for:

they will carry; we shall drag; you (s.) will teach; I shall hear; you (pl.) will drag; he will carry.

4 Translate the following examples:

audiēmus; portābit; mittent; aedificābitis; veniam; manēbis.

5 Translate each verb in the list below. Then with the help of paragraph 2 change it into the future tense, keeping the same person and number (i.e. 1st person singular, etc.). Then translate again.

For example: **portāmus** (*we carry*) would become **portābimus** (*we shall carry*).

portātis; docēbam; docēbāmus; trahō; audīs; audiēbat.

6

	first conjugation	*second conjugation*	*third conjugation*	*fourth conjugation*
PERFECT	*I (have) carried*	*I (have) taught*	*I (have) dragged*	*I (have) heard*
	portāvī	docuī	trāxī	audīvī
	portāvistī	docuistī	trāxistī	audīvistī
	portāvit	docuit	trāxit	audīvit
	portāvimus	docuimus	trāximus	audīvimus
	portāvistis	docuistis	trāxistis	audīvistis
	portāvērunt	docuērunt	trāxērunt	audīvērunt
PLUPERFECT	*I had carried*	*I had taught*	*I had dragged*	*I had heard*
	portāveram	docueram	trāxeram	audīveram
	portāverās	docuerās	trāxerās	audīverās
	portāverat	docuerat	trāxerat	audīverat
	portāverāmus	docuerāmus	trāxerāmus	audīverāmus
	portāverātis	docuerātis	trāxerātis	audīverātis
	portāverant	docuerant	trāxerant	audīverant

7 In Stage 33, you met the *future perfect tense*:

	I shall have carried	*I shall have taught*	*I shall have dragged*	*I shall have heard*
	portāverō	docuerō	trāxerō	audīverō
	portāveris	docueris	trāxeris	audīveris
	portāverit	docuerit	trāxerit	audīverit
	portāverimus	docuerimus	trāxerimus	audīverimus
	portāveritis	docueritis	trāxeritis	audīveritis
	portāverint	docuerint	trāxerint	audīverint

The future perfect is often translated by an English present tense:

sī effūgerō, iter ad vōs faciam.
If I escape, I shall make my way to you.

Indicative passive

1 In Stage 29, you met the following forms of the *passive*:

	first conjugation	*second conjugation*	*third conjugation*	*fourth conjugation*
PRESENT	*I am (being) carried* portor portāris portātur portāmur portāminī portantur	*I am (being) taught* doceor docēris docētur docēmur docēminī docentur	*I am (being) dragged* trahor traheris trahitur trahimur trahiminī trahuntur	*I am (being) heard* audior audīris audītur audīmur audīminī audiuntur
IMPERFECT	*I was being carried* portābar portābāris portābātur portābāmur portābāminī portābantur	*I was being taught* docēbar docēbāris docēbātur docēbāmur docēbāminī docēbantur	*I was being dragged* trahēbar trahēbāris trahēbātur trahēbāmur trahēbāminī trahēbantur	*I was being heard* audiēbar audiēbāris audiēbātur audiēbāmur audiēbāminī audiēbantur

2 Translate each verb, then change it from a singular to plural, so that it means *they …* instead of *s/he* or *it …* Then translate again.

     audītur; trahēbātur; dūcēbātur; laudātur; custōdiēbātur; dēlētur

3 In Stage 34, you met the *future tense* of the *passive*:

I shall be carried portābor portāberis portābitur portābimur portābiminī portābuntur	*I shall be taught* docēbor docēberis docēbitur docēbimur docēbiminī docēbuntur	*I shall be dragged* trahar trahēris trahētur trahēmur trahēminī trahentur	*I shall be heard* audiar audiēris audiētur audiēmur audiēminī audientur

4 In Stage 30, you met the *perfect* and *pluperfect tenses* of the passive:

	first conjugation	*second conjugation*	*third conjugation*	*fourth conjugation*
PERFECT	*I have been carried, I was carried*	*I have been taught, I was taught*	*I have been dragged, I was dragged*	*I have been heard, I was heard*
	portātus sum	doctus sum	tractus sum	audītus sum
	portātus es	doctus es	tractus es	audītus es
	portātus est	doctus est	tractus est	audītus est
	portātī sumus	doctī sumus	tractī sumus	audītī sumus
	portātī estis	doctī estis	tractī estis	audītī estis
	portātī sunt	doctī sunt	tractī sunt	audītī sunt
PLUPERFECT	*I had been carried*	*I had been taught*	*I had been dragged*	*I had been heard*
	portātus eram	doctus eram	tractus eram	audītus eram
	portātus erās	doctus erās	tractus erās	audītus erās
	portātus erat	doctus erat	tractus erat	audītus erat
	portātī erāmus	doctī erāmus	tractī erāmus	audītī erāmus
	portātī erātis	doctī erātis	tractī erātis	audītī erātis
	portātī erant	doctī erant	tractī erant	audītī erant

5 Give the meaning of:

audītus eram; portātus erat; portātī sunt; doctus sum; tractus es; portātī erāmus.

6 In paragraph 4, find the Latin for:

they had been carried; I have been dragged; you (s.) have been taught; he was carried.

7 Notice again that the two tenses in paragraph 4 are formed with perfect passive participles, which change their endings to indicate *gender* (masculine, feminine, and neuter) and *number* (singular and plural). For example:

masculine singular	puer ā mīlitibus **captus** est.
neuter singular	templum ā mīlitibus **captum** est.
feminine singular	urbs ā mīlitibus **capta** est.
feminine plural	multae urbēs ā mīlitibus **captae** sunt.

8 Translate the following examples:

docta est; tractum erat; vocātus sum; custōdītae sunt; missī erāmus; monita erās; ductī sunt; dēlēta sunt.

Subjunctive

1

	first conjugation	*second conjugation*	*third conjugation*	*fourth conjugation*
IMPERFECT SUBJUNCTIVE	portārem	docērem	traherem	audīrem
	portārēs	docērēs	traherēs	audīrēs
	portāret	docēret	traheret	audīret
	portārēmus	docērēmus	traherēmus	audīrēmus
	portārētis	docērētis	traherētis	audīrētis
	portārent	docērent	traherent	audīrent
PLUPERFECT SUBJUNCTIVE	portāvissem	docuissem	trāxissem	audīvissem
	portāvissēs	docuissēs	trāxissēs	audīvissēs
	portāvisset	docuisset	trāxisset	audīvisset
	portāvissēmus	docuissēmus	trāxissēmus	audīvissēmus
	portāvissētis	docuissētis	trāxissētis	audīvissētis
	portāvissent	docuissent	trāxissent	audīvissent

2 For ways in which the subjunctive is used, see pp. 288-289.

Other forms of the verb

1

	to carry	*to teach*	*to drag*	*to hear*
PRESENT ACTIVE INFINITIVE	portāre	docēre	trahere	audīre

2

	to be carried	*to be taught*	*to be dragged*	*to be heard*
PRESENT PASSIVE INFINITIVE	portārī	docērī	trahī	audīrī

3

	carry!	*teach!*	*drag!*	*hear!*
IMPERATIVE SINGULAR	portā	docē	trahe	audī
PLURAL	portāte	docēte	trahite	audīte

4

PRESENT PARTICIPLE	*carrying* portāns	*teaching* docēns	*dragging* trahēns	*hearing* audiēns

Study the forms of the present participle **portāns**:

	SINGULAR *masculine and feminine*	*neuter*	PLURAL *masculine and feminine*	*neuter*
nominative and *vocative*	portāns	portāns	portantēs	portantia
genitive	portantis	portantis	portantium	portantium
dative	portantī	portantī	portantibus	portantibus
accusative	portantem	portāns	portantēs	portantia
ablative	portantī	portantī	portantibus	portantibus

The ablative singular of present participles sometimes ends in -**e**, e.g. **portante**, **docente**.

5

PERFECT PASSIVE PARTICIPLE	(*having been*) *carried* portātus	(*having been*) *taught* doctus	(*having been*) *dragged* tractus	(*having been*) *heard* audītus

Perfect passive participles change their endings in the same way as **bonus** (shown on p. 264).

For examples of perfect *active* participles, see **Deponent verbs**, p. 280.

6

FUTURE PARTICIPLE	*about to carry* portātūrus	*about to teach* doctūrus	*about to drag* tractūrus	*about to hear* audītūrus

Future participles change their endings in the same way as **bonus**.

For examples of ways in which participles are used, see pp. 286-287.

7

GERUNDIVE	portandus	docendus	trahendus	audiendus

Gerundives change their endings in the same way as **bonus**.
Notice again the way in which the gerundive is used:

nōbīs audiendum est.   mihi amphora portanda est.
We must listen.   *I must carry the wine jar.*

Deponent verbs

1 From Stage 32 on, you have met *deponent verbs*:

PRESENT	cōnor	*I try*	loquor	*I speak*
	cōnāris	*you try*	loqueris	*you speak*
	cōnātur	*s/he tries*	loquitur	*s/he speaks*
	cōnāmur	*we try*	loquimur	*we speak*
	cōnāminī	*you try*	loquiminī	*you speak*
	cōnantur	*they try*	loquuntur	*they speak*
IMPERFECT	cōnābar	*I was trying*	loquēbar	*I was speaking*
	cōnābāris	*you were trying*	loquēbāris	*you were speaking*
	cōnābātur	*s/he was trying*	loquēbātur	*s/he was speaking*
	cōnābāmur	*we were trying*	loquēbāmur	*we were speaking*
	cōnābāminī	*you were trying*	loquēbāminī	*you were speaking*
	cōnābantur	*they were trying*	loquēbantur	*they were speaking*
PERFECT	cōnātus sum	*I (have) tried*	locūtus sum	*I spoke, I have spoken*
	cōnātus es	*you (have) tried*	locūtus es	*you spoke, you have spoken*
	cōnātus est	*he (has) tried*	locūtus est	*he spoke, he has spoken*
	cōnātī sumus	*we (have) tried*	locūtī sumus	*we spoke, we have spoken*
	cōnātī estis	*you (have) tried*	locūtī estis	*you spoke, you have spoken*
	cōnātī sunt	*they (have) tried*	locūtī sunt	*they spoke, they have spoken*
PLUPERFECT	cōnātus eram	*I had tried*	locūtus eram	*I had spoken*
	cōnātus erās	*you had tried*	locūtus erās	*you had spoken*
	cōnātus erat	*he had tried*	locūtus erat	*he had spoken*
	cōnātī erāmus	*we had tried*	locūtī erāmus	*we had spoken*
	cōnātī erātis	*you had tried*	locūtī erātis	*you had spoken*
	cōnātī erant	*they had tried*	locūtī erant	*they had spoken*
PERFECT ACTIVE PARTICIPLE	cōnātus	*having tried*	locūtus	*having spoken*

Perfect active participles change their endings in the same way as **bonus** (shown on p. 264).

PRESENT INFINITIVE	cōnārī	*to try*	loquī	*to speak*

2 In Stage 34, you met the *future tense* of deponent verbs:

cōnābor	*I shall try*	loquar	*I shall speak*
cōnāberis	*you will try*	loquēris	*you will speak*
cōnābitur	*s/he will try*	loquētur	*s/he will speak*
cōnābimur	*we shall try*	loquēmur	*we shall speak*
cōnābiminī	*you will try*	loquēminī	*you will speak*
cōnābuntur	*they will try*	loquentur	*they will speak*

3 Give the meaning of:

cōnātus eram; locūtī sumus; ingressī sumus; ingressus erās; profectus es; profectī erāmus; secūtī sunt; hortātī erātis.

4 Translate each word (or pair of words), then change it from plural to singular, so that it means *he …* instead of *they …* . Then translate again.

loquuntur; cōnātī sunt; profectī sunt; hortantur; sequēbantur; ēgressī erant; precābuntur; loquentur.

5 Compare the two verbs in paragraphs 1 and 2 with the passive forms of **portō** and **trahō** listed on pp. 276–277 above.

6 For further practice of deponent verbs, see paragraphs 6–8 on p. 286.

Irregular verbs

Indicative

1

PRESENT	*I am*	*I am able*	*I go*	*I want*	*I bring*	*I take*
	sum	possum	eō	volō	ferō	capiō
	es	potes	īs	vīs	fers	capis
	est	potest	it	vult	fert	capit
	sumus	possumus	īmus	volumus	ferimus	capimus
	estis	potestis	ītis	vultis	fertis	capitis
	sunt	possunt	eunt	volunt	ferunt	capiunt

IMPERFECT	*I was*	*I was able*	*I was going*	*I was wanting*	*I was bringing*	*I was taking*
	eram	poteram	ībam	volēbam	ferēbam	capiēbam
	erās	poterās	ībās	volēbās	ferēbās	capiēbās
	erat	poterat	ībat	volēbat	ferēbat	capiēbat
	erāmus	poterāmus	ībāmus	volēbāmus	ferēbāmus	capiēbāmus
	erātis	poterātis	ībātis	volēbātis	ferēbātis	capiēbātis
	erant	poterant	ībant	volēbant	ferēbant	capiēbant

2 Study the forms of the *future tense*:

I shall be	*I shall be able*	*I shall go*	*I shall want*	*I shall bring*	*I shall take*
erō	poterō	ībō	volam	feram	capiam
eris	poteris	ībis	volēs	ferēs	capiēs
erit	poterit	ībit	volet	feret	capiet
erimus	poterimus	ībimus	volēmus	ferēmus	capiēmus
eritis	poteritis	ībitis	volētis	ferētis	capiētis
erunt	poterunt	ībunt	volent	ferent	capient

3 Translate each verb, then change it into the future tense, keeping the same person and number (i.e. 1st person singular, etc.). Then translate again.

   est; potestis; ībam; vīs; ferunt; capiēbāmus.

4

PERFECT	I have been, I was	I have been able, I was able	I have gone, I went	I (have) wanted	I (have) brought	I have taken, I took
	fuī	potuī	iī	voluī	tulī	cēpī
	fuistī	potuistī	iistī	voluistī	tulistī	cēpistī
	fuit	potuit	iit	voluit	tulit	cēpit
	fuimus	potuimus	iimus	voluimus	tulimus	cēpimus
	fuistis	potuistis	iistis	voluistis	tulistis	cēpistis
	fuērunt	potuērunt	iērunt	voluērunt	tulērunt	cēpērunt

PLUPERFECT	I had been	I had been able	I had gone	I had wanted	I had brought	I had taken
	fueram	potueram	ieram	volueram	tuleram	cēperam
	fuerās	potuerās	ierās	voluerās	tulerās	cēperās
	fuerat	potuerat	ierat	voluerat	tulerat	cēperat
	fuerāmus	potuerāmus	ierāmus	voluerāmus	tulerāmus	cēperāmus
	fuerātis	potuerātis	ierātis	voluerātis	tulerātis	cēperātis
	fuerant	potuerant	ierant	voluerant	tulerant	cēperant

5 Study the following *passive* forms of **ferō** and **capiō**:

PRESENT	fertur	s/he is brought	capitur	s/he is taken
	feruntur	they are brought	capiuntur	they are taken

IMPERFECT	ferēbātur	s/he was being brought	capiēbātur	s/he was being taken
	ferēbantur	they were being brought	capiēbantur	they were being taken

FUTURE	ferētur	s/he will be brought	capiētur	s/he will be taken
	feruntur	they will be brought	capientur	they will be taken

PERFECT	lātus sum	I have been brought, I was brought	captus sum	I have been taken, I was taken
	lātus es	you have been brought, you were brought	captus es	you have been taken, you were taken
	etc.		etc.	

PLUPERFECT	lātus eram	I had been brought	captus eram	I had been taken
	lātus erās	you had been brought	captus erās	you had been taken
	etc.		etc.	

PERFECT PASSIVE PARTICIPLE	lātus	having been brought	captus	having been taken

6 Give the meaning of:

captus erat; lātī erant; lātī sunt; captī sumus.

What would be the Latin for the following?

he had been brought; he has been taken; we have been brought; they were taken

Subjunctive

IMPERFECT SUBJUNCTIVE						
essem	possem	īrem	vellem	ferrem	caperem
essēs	possēs	īrēs	vellēs	ferrēs	caperēs
esset	posset	īret	vellet	ferret	caperet
essēmus	possēmus	īrēmus	vellēmus	ferrēmus	caperēmus
essētis	possētis	īrētis	vellētis	ferrētis	caperētis
essent	possent	īrent	vellent	ferrent	caperent

PLUPERFECT SUBJUNCTIVE						
fuissem	potuissem	iissem	voluissem	tulissem	cēpissem
fuissēs	potuissēs	iissēs	voluissēs	tulissēs	cēpissēs
fuisset	potuisset	iisset	voluisset	tulisset	cēpisset
fuissēmus	potuissēmus	iissēmus	voluissēmus	tulissēmus	cēpissēmus
fuissētis	potuissētis	iissētis	voluissētis	tulissētis	cēpissētis
fuissent	potuissent	iissent	voluissent	tulissent	cēpissent

Other forms of the verb

PRESENT INFINITIVE					
esse *to be*	posse *to be able*	īre *to go*	velle *to want*	ferre *to bring*	capere *to take*

Uses of the cases

1 *nominative*
captīvus clāmābat.   *The prisoner was shouting.*

2 *vocative*
vale, **domine!**   *Good-bye, master!*

3 *genitive*
  a māter **puerōrum**   *the mother of the boys*
  b plūs **pecūniae**   *more money*
  c vir **maximae virtūtis**   *a man of very great courage*

4 *dative*
  a **mīlitibus** cibum dedimus.   *We gave food to the soldiers.*
  b **vestrō candidātō** nōn faveō.   *I do not support your candidate.*

5 *accusative*
  a **pontem** trānsiimus.   *We crossed the bridge.*
  b **trēs hōrās** labōrābam.   *I was working for three hours.*
  c per **agrōs**; ad **vīllam**   *through the fields; to the house*
  d in **forum**   *into the forum*

6 *ablative*
  a **spectāculō** attonitus   *astonished by the sight*
  b senex **longā barbā**   *an old man with a long beard*
  c **nōbilī gente** nātus   *born from a noble family*
  d **quārtō diē** revēnit.   *He came back on the fourth day.*
  e cum **amīcīs**; ab **urbe**; in **forō**   *with friends; away from the city; in the forum*

For examples of ablative absolute phrases, see paragraph 4 on p. 286.

7 Further examples of some of the uses listed above:

  a Salvius erat vir summae callid.itātis.
  b decimā hōrā ex oppidō contendimus.
  c uxor Imperātōris, in ātrium ingressa, ancillīs fidēlibus grātiās ēgit.
  d fabrī, spē praemiī incitātī, arcum ante prīmam lūcem perfēcērunt.
  e multōs diēs Haterius ē vīllā discēdere recūsāvit.
  f Salvī, cūr cōnsiliīs meīs obstās?
  g senātor in lectō manēbat quod nimium cibī cōnsūmpserat.
  h lēgātus mīlitibus imperāvit ut hostēs hastīs gladiīsque oppugnārent.

Uses of the participle

1 In Unit 3, you saw how a participle changes its endings to agree with the noun it describes.

2 Notice again some of the various ways in which a participle can be translated:

> fūrēs, canem cōnspicātī, fūgērunt.
> *The thieves, having caught sight of the dog, ran away.*
> *When the thieves caught sight of the dog, they ran away.*
> *On catching sight of the dog, the thieves ran away.*
> *The thieves ran away because they had caught sight of the dog.*

3 Translate the following examples:

   a ingēns multitūdō pompam per Viam Sacram prōcēdentem spectābat.
   b custōdēs puerō lacrimantī nihil dīxērunt.
   c mīlitēs, ā centuriōnibus iussī, in longīs ōrdinibus stābant.
   d mercātor amīcōs, ā Graeciā regressōs, ad cēnam sūmptuōsam invītāvit.

Pick out the noun and participle pair in each sentence, and say whether it is nominative, accusative, or dative, singular or plural.

4 In Stage 31, you met examples of *ablative absolute* phrases, consisting of a noun and participle in the ablative case:

> bellō cōnfectō, Agricola ad Ītaliam rediit.
> **With the war having been finished, Agricola returned to Italy.**

Or, in more natural English:

> *When the war had been finished, Agricola returned to Italy,* or,
> *After finishing the war, Agricola returned to Italy.*

Further examples:

   a ponte dēlētō, nēmō flūmen trānsīre poterat.
   b hīs verbīs audītīs, cīvēs plausērunt.
   c nāve refectā, mercātor ā Britanniā discessit.
   d iuvenēs, togīs dēpositīs, balneum intrāvērunt.
   e latrōnēs, omnibus dormientibus, tabernam incendērunt.
   f cōnsule ingressō, omnēs senātōrēs surrēxērunt.
   g fēle absente, mūrēs lūdere solent.

5 From Stage 31 on, you have met examples in which a noun and participle in the *dative* case are placed at the beginning of the sentence:

> **amīcō** auxilium **petentī** multam pecūniam obtulī.
> ***To a friend asking for** help I offered a lot of money.*

Or, in more natural English:

> *When my friend asked for help I offered him a lot of money.*

Further examples:

a servō haesitantī Vitellia "intrā!" inquit.
b Hateriō haec rogantī Salvius nihil respondit.
c praecōnī regressō senex epistulam trādidit.
d puellae prōcēdentī obstābat ingēns multitūdō clientium.

Uses of the subjunctive

1 with **cum** (meaning *when*)

Iūdaeī, cum cōnsilium Eleazārī audīvissent, libenter cōnsēnsērunt.
When the Jews had heard Eleazar's plan, they willingly agreed.

2 *indirect question*

cōnsul nesciēbat quis arcum novum aedificāvisset.
The consul did not know who had built the new arch.

mē rogāvērunt num satis pecūniae habērem.
They asked me whether I had enough money.

From Stage 28 on, you have met the words **utrum** and **an** in indirect questions:

incertī erant utrum dux mortuus an vīvus esset.
They were unsure whether their leader was dead or alive.

3 *purpose clause*

ad urbem iter fēcimus ut amphitheātrum vīsitārēmus.
We traveled to the city in order to visit the amphitheater.

In Stage 29, you met purpose clauses used with the relative pronoun **quī**:

nūntiōs ēmīsit quī prīncipēs ad aulam arcesserent.
He sent out messengers who were to summon the chieftains to the palace.
Or, in more natural English:
He sent out messengers to summon the chieftains to the palace.

From Stage 29 on, you have met purpose clauses used with **nē**:

centuriō omnēs portās clausit nē captīvī effugerent.
The centurion shut all the gates so that the prisoners would not escape.

4 *indirect command*

Domitiānus Salviō imperāverat ut rēgnum Cogidubnī occupāret.
Domitian had ordered Salvius to seize Cogidubnus' kingdom.

From Stage 29 on, you have met indirect commands introduced by **nē**:

puella agricolam ōrāvit nē equum occīderet.
The girl begged the farmer not to kill the horse.

Haterius ab amīcīs monitus est nē Salviō cōnfīderet.
Haterius was warned by friends not to trust Salvius.

5 *result clause*

> tam perītus erat faber ut omnēs eum laudārent.
> *The craftsman was so skillful that everyone praised him.*

6 Translate the following examples:

    a cīvēs Rōmānī templa vīsitābant ut dīs grātiās agerent.
    b cum servī vīnum intulissent, Haterius silentium poposcit.
    c tanta erat fortitūdō Iūdaeōrum ut perīre potius quam cēdere māllent.
    d nēmō sciēbat utrum Haterius an Salvius rem administrāvisset.
    e uxor mihi persuāsit nē hoc susciperem.
    f extrā carcerem stābant decem mīlitēs quī captīvōs custōdīrent.

In each sentence, give the reason why a subjunctive is being used.

7 From Stage 33 on, you have met the subjunctive used with **priusquam** (meaning *before*) and **dum** (meaning *until*):

> Myropnous iānuam clausit priusquam mīlitēs intrārent.
> *Myropnous shut the door before the soldiers could enter.*

> exspectābam dum amīcus advenīret.
> *I was waiting until my friend should arrive.*
> Or, in more natural English:
> *I was waiting for my friend to arrive.*

Word order

1 In Unit 1, you met the following word order:

   dēspērābat senex.   *The old man was in despair.*

   Further examples:

   a fugit Modestus.   **b** revēnērunt mercātōrēs.

2 From Stage 21 on, you have met the following word order:

   dedit signum haruspex.   *The soothsayer gave the signal.*

   Further examples:

   a rapuērunt pecūniam fūrēs.   **b** īnspiciēbat mīlitēs Agricola.

3 From Stage 23 on, you have met the following word order:

   ēmīsit Salvius equitēs.   *Salvius sent out horsemen.*

   Further examples:

   a tenēbat Cephalus pōculum.   **b** posuērunt cīvēs statuam.

4 Further examples of all three types of word order:

   a discessit nūntius.   **d** poposcit captīvus lībertātem.
   b fēcērunt hostēs impetum.   **e** vexābant mē puerī.
   c reficiēbat mūrum faber.   **f** periērunt īnfantēs.

5 Study the word order in the following examples:

   in hāc prōvinciā   ad nostrum patrem
   in this province   *to our father*

   You have also met a different word order:

   mediīs in undīs   hanc ad tabernam
   in the middle of the waves *to this shop*

   Further examples:

   a hāc in urbe   **d** omnibus cum legiōnibus
   b multīs cum mīlitibus   **e** tōtam per noctem
   c parvum ad oppidum   **f** mediō in flūmine

Longer sentences

1   Study each sentence and answer the questions that follow it:

   a postquam Haterius fabrōs, quī labōrābant in āreā, dīmīsit, Salvius
      negōtium agere coepit.
      Where were the craftsmen working? What did Haterius do to them? What did
      Salvius then do?
      Now translate the sentence.

   b spectātōrēs, cum candēlābrum aureum ē templō Iūdaeōrum raptum
      cōnspexissent, iterum iterumque plausērunt.
      What did the spectators catch sight of? From where had it been seized? What
      was the reaction of the spectators?
      Now translate the sentence.

   c fūr, cum verba centuriōnis audīvisset, tantō metū poenārum affectus
      est ut pecūniam quam ē tabernā abstulerat, statim abicere cōnstitueret.
      What did the thief hear? How was he affected? What did he decide to do?
      Where had the money come from?
      Now translate the sentence.

2   Further examples for study and translation:

   a ancillae, quod dominam vehementer clāmantem audīvērunt,
      cubiculum eius quam celerrimē petīvērunt.
   b equitēs adeō pugnāre cupiēbant ut, simulac dux signum dedit, ē portīs
      castrōrum ērumperent.
   c postquam cōnsul hanc sententiam dīxit, Domitiānus servō adstantī
      imperāvit ut epistulam ab Agricolā nūper missam recitāret.
   d cum Haterius sōlus domī manēret, Vitellia eum anxia rogāvit cūr
      amīcōs clientēsque admittere nōllet.
   e quamquam fēminae Simōnem frātrēsque cēlāvērunt nē perīrent,
      Rōmānī eōs comprehēnsōs ad Ītaliam mīsērunt.

Numerals

I	ūnus	1	XVI	sēdecim	16
II	duo	2	XVII	septendecim	17
III	trēs	3	XVIII	duodēvīgintī	18
IV	quattuor	4	XIX	ūndēvīgintī	19
V	quīnque	5	XX	vīgintī	20
VI	sex	6	XXX	trīgintā	30
VII	septem	7	XL	quadrāgintā	40
VIII	octō	8	L	quīnquāgintā	50
IX	novem	9	LX	sexāgintā	60
X	decem	10	LXX	septuāgintā	70
XI	ūndecim	11	LXXX	octōgintā	80
XII	duodecim	12	XC	nōnāgintā	90
XIII	tredecim	13	C	centum	100
XIV	quattuordecim	14	M	mīlle	1000
XV	quīndecim	15	MM	duo mīlia	2000

Part Two: Vocabulary

1 Nouns and adjectives are listed as in the Unit 2 Language information section.

2 Prepositions used with the ablative, such as **ex**, are marked (+ ABL); those used with the accusative, such as **per**, are marked (+ ACC).

3 Most verbs are usually listed in the following way:

- the 1st person singular of the present tense, e.g. **pōnō** (*I place*);
- the infinitive, e.g. **pōnere** (*to place*);
- the 1st person singular of the perfect tense, e.g. **posuī** (*I placed*);
- the perfect passive participle, e.g. **positus** (*having been placed*);
- the meaning(s), e.g. *place*.

4 Study the following examples, listed in the way described in paragraph 3. Notice particularly the patterns in which the different conjugations form their principal parts:

1st conjugation
amō, amāre, amāvī, amātus *love, like*
laudō, laudāre, laudāvī, laudātus *praise*

2nd conjugation
moneō, monēre, monuī, monitus *warn*
praebeō, praebēre, praebuī, praebitus *provide*

3rd conjugation
Verbs of the 3rd conjugation form their perfect tense and perfect passive participle in several different ways. Here are some of the ways:

claudō, claudere, clausī, clausus *shut, close*
dūcō, dūcere, dūxī, ductus *lead*
frangō, frangere, frēgī, frāctus *break*

3rd conjugation ("-iō")
faciō, facere, fēcī, factus *do, make*
rapiō, rapere, rapuī, raptus *seize*

4th conjugation
custōdiō, custōdīre, custōdīvī, custōdītus *guard*
impediō, impedīre, impedīvī, impedītus *hinder*

5 Use paragraph 4 to find the meaning of:

amāvī; laudātus; monēre; praebitus; dūxī; frēgī; frāctus; facere; rapiō; custōdīre; impedītus.

6 Deponent verbs (met and explained in Stage 32) are listed in the following way:

- the 1st person singular of the present indicative. This always ends in **-or**, e.g. **cōnor** (*I try*);
- the present infinitive. This always ends in **-ī**, e.g. **cōnārī** (*to try*);
- the 1st person singular of the perfect indicative, e.g. **cōnātus sum** (*I tried*);
- the meaning, e.g. *try*.

So, if the following principal parts are given:
loquor, loquī, locūtus sum *speak*
loquor means *I speak*, **loquī** means *to speak*, **locūtus sum** means *I spoke*.

7 Study the following deponent verbs, listed in the way described in paragraph 6:

cōnspicor, cōnspicārī, cōnspicātus sum *catch sight of*
ingredior, ingredī, ingressus sum *enter*
lābor, lābī, lāpsus sum *fall*

Give the meaning of:
cōnspicor, ingredī, lāpsus sum, ingredior, cōnspicātus sum, lābī.

8 Use pages 295–323 to find the meaning of:

ēgredior, hortātus sum, pollicērī, sequor, minārī, adeptus sum.

9 All words which are given in the Vocabulary checklists for Stages 1–34 are marked with the number of the relevant stage, e.g. 16.

a

17, 21	ā, ab (+ ABL)	*from; by*
	abdūcō, abdūcere, abdūxī, abductus	*lead away*
10	abeō, abīre, abiī	*go away*
	abhinc	*ago*
	abhorreō, abhorrēre, abhorruī	*shrink (from)*
	abigō, abigere, abēgī, abāctus	*drive away*
	ablātus *see* auferre	
	absēns, absēns, absēns, *gen.* absentis	*absent*
	absentia, absentiae, f.	*absence*
26	abstulī *see* auferō	
6	absum, abesse, āfuī	*be out, be absent, be away*
	absurdus, absurda, absurdum	*absurd*
28	ac	*and*
25	accidō, accidere, accidī	*happen*
10	accipiō, accipere, accēpī, acceptus	*accept, take in, receive*
34	accūsō, accūsāre, accūsāvī, accūsātus	*accuse*
	āctor, āctōris, m.	*actor*
4	āctus *see* agō	
3	ad (+ ACC)	*to, at*
	addō, addere, addidī, additus	*add*
	addūcō, addūcere, addūxī, adductus	*lead, lead on, encourage*
20	adeō, adīre, adiī	*approach, go up to*
27	adeō	*so much, so greatly*
22	adeptus, adepta, adeptum	*having obtained, having received*
5	adest *see* adsum	
	adhibeō, adhibēre, adhibuī, adhibitus	*use, apply*
30	adhūc	*until now*
34	adipīscor, adipīscī, adeptus sum	*receive, obtain*
	aditus, aditūs, m.	*entrance*
21	adiuvō, adiuvāre, adiūvī	*help*

	adligō, adligāre, adligāvī, adligātus	*tie*
	adloquor, adloquī, adlocūtus sum	*speak to, address*
	administrō, administrāre, administrāvī, administrātus	*look after, manage*
	admīrātiō, admīrātiōnis, f.	*admiration*
	admīror, admīrārī, admīrātus sum	*admire*
	admittō, admittere, admīsī, admissus	*admit, let in*
	adōrō, adōrāre, adōrāvī, adōrātus	*worship*
	adstō, adstāre, adstitī	*stand by*
5	adsum, adesse, adfuī	*be here, be present*
13	adveniō, advenīre, advēnī	*arrive*
	adventus, adventūs, m.	*arrival*
32	adversus, adversa, adversum	*hostile, unfavorable*
32	rēs adversae	*misfortune*
	advesperāscit, advesperāscere, advesperāvit	*get dark, become dark*
	aedificium, aedificiī, n.	*building*
16	aedificō, aedificāre, aedificāvī, aedificātus	*build*
13	aeger, aegra, aegrum	*sick, ill*
	aegrōtus, aegrōtī, m.	*invalid*
	Aegyptius, Aegyptia, Aegyptium	*Egyptian*
	Aegyptus, Aegyptī, f.	*Egypt*
32	aequus, aequa, aequum	*fair, calm*
	aequō animō	*calmly, in a calm spirit*
	aeternus, aeterna, aeternum	*eternal*
	Aethiopes, Aethiopum, m.f.pl.	*Ethiopians*
	afferō, afferre, attulī, adlātus	*bring*
30	afficiō, afficere, affēcī, affectus	*affect*
30	affectus, affecta, affectum	*affected, overcome*
	afflīgō, afflīgere, afflīxī, afflīctus	*afflict, hurt*
	agellus, agellī, m.	*small plot of land*
	ager, agrī, m.	*field*
	agger, aggeris, m.	*ramp, mound of earth*

8	agitō, agitāre, agitāvī, agitātus	chase, hunt	
	agna, agnae, f.	lamb	
9	agnōscō, agnōscere, agnōvī, agnitus	recognize	
4	agō, agere, ēgī, āctus	do, act	
	āctum est dē nōbīs	it's all over for us	
	age!	come on!	
	fābulam agere	act in a play	
19	grātiās agere	thank, give thanks	
	negōtium agere	do business, work	
	persōnam agere	play a part	
	vītam agere	lead a life	
5	agricola, agricolae, m.	farmer	
	ālea, āleae, f.	dice	
	aliquandō	sometimes	
14, 25	aliquis, aliquid	someone, something	
	aliquid mīrī	something extraordinary	
15	alius, alia, aliud	other, another, else	
	alius ... alius	one ... another	
29	aliī ... aliī	some ... others	
13	alter, altera, alterum	the other, another, a second, the second	
	alter ... alter	one ... the other	
31	altus, alta, altum	high, deep	
	amārus, amāra, amārum	bitter	
	ambitiō, ambitiōnis, f.	bribery	
30	ambō, ambae, ambō	both	
5	ambulō, ambulāre, ambulāvī	walk	
	āmēns, āmēns, āmēns, gen. āmentis	out of one's mind, in a frenzy	
	amīcitia, amīcitiae, f.	friendship	
2	amīcus, amīcī, m.	friend	
12	āmittō, āmittere, āmīsī, āmissus	lose	
19	amō, amāre, amāvī, amātus	love, like	
22	amor, amōris, m.	love	
	amphitheātrum, amphitheātrī, n.	amphitheater	
	Amphitheātrum Flāvium	Flavian Amphitheater	

	amphora, amphorae, f.	wine jar	
	amplector, amplectī, amplexus sum	embrace	
	amplexus, amplexa, amplexum	having embraced	
	amplissimus, amplissima, amplissimum	very great	
	amputō, amputāre, amputāvī, amputātus	cut off	
	amulētum, amulētī, n.	amulet, lucky charm	
	an	or	
	utrum ... an	whether ... or	
2	ancilla, ancillae, f.	slave girl, slave woman	
	angelus, angelī, m.	angel	
	angulus, angulī, m.	corner	
	angustus, angusta, angustum	narrow	
17	animus, animī, m.	spirit, soul, mind	
	aequō animō	calmly, in a calm spirit	
	in animō habēre	have in mind, intend	
	in animō volvere	wonder, turn over in the mind	
21	annus, annī, m.	year	
31	ante (+ ACC)	before, in front of	
27	anteā	before	
4	ānulus, ānulī, m.	ring	
	anus, anūs, f.	old woman	
	anxius, anxia, anxium	anxious	
	aper, aprī, m.	boar	
25	aperiō, aperīre, aperuī, apertus	open	
	apertē	openly	
	apodytērium, apodytēriī, n.	changing room	
27	appāreō, appārēre, appāruī	appear	
33	appellō, appellāre, appellāvī, appellātus	call, call out to	
17	appropinquō, appropinquāre, appropinquāvī (+ DAT)	approach, come near to	
	aptus, apta, aptum	suitable	
14	apud (+ ACC)	among, at the house of	
15	aqua, aquae, f.	water	
	Aquae Sūlis, Aquārum Sūlis, f.pl.	Aquae Sulis (modern Bath)	

17	āra, ārae, f.	altar
	arānea, arāneae, f.	spider, spider's web
	arbiter, arbitrī, m.	expert, judge
	arbor, arboris, f.	tree
	arca, arcae, f.	strongbox, chest
20	arcessō, arcessere, arcessīvī, arcessītus	summon, send for
	architectus, architectī, m.	builder, architect
	arcus, arcūs, m.	arch
27	ardeō, ardēre, arsī	burn, be on fire
	ardor, ardōris, m.	spirit, enthusiasm
	ārea, āreae, f.	courtyard, construction site
	argenteus, argentea, argenteum	made of silver
	arma, armōrum, n.pl.	arms, weapons
	armārium, armāriī, n.	chest, cupboard
	armō, armāre, armāvī, armātus	arm
	armātī, armātōrum, m.pl.	armed men
	arrogantia, arrogantiae, f.	arrogance, gall
20	ars, artis, f.	art, skill
	artifex, artificis, m.f.	artist, craftsman
	as, assis, m.	as (small coin)
29	ascendō, ascendere, ascendī	climb, rise
	asinus, asinī, m.	ass, donkey
	aspiciō, aspicere, aspexī	look towards
	astrologus, astrologī, m.	astrologer
33	at	but
	Athēnae, Athēnārum, f.pl.	Athens
	Athēnīs	at Athens
	āthlēta, āthlētae, m.	athlete
28	atque	and
	ātrium, ātriī, n.	atrium, reception hall
14	attonitus, attonita, attonitum	astonished
34	auctor, auctōris, m.	creator, originator, person responsible
34	mē auctōre	at my suggestion
24	auctōritās, auctōritātis, f.	authority
	auctus see augeō	
29	audācia, audāciae, f.	boldness, audacity
	audācter	boldly
24	audāx, audāx, audāx, gen. audācis	bold, daring

18	audeō, audēre	dare
5	audiō, audīre, audīvī, audītus	hear, listen to
26	auferō, auferre, abstulī, ablātus	take away, steal
	augeō, augēre, auxī, auctus	increase
14	aula, aulae, f.	palace
	aureus, aurea, aureum	golden, made of gold
	aureus, aureī, m.	gold coin
	aurīga, aurīgae, m.	charioteer
	auris, auris, f.	ear
25	autem	but
16	auxilium, auxiliī, n.	help
	avāritia, avāritiae, f.	greed
	avārus, avārī, m.	miser
	avē atque valē	hail and farewell
	avia, aviae, f.	grandmother
	avidē	eagerly
	avis, avis, f.	bird

b

	balneum, balneī, n.	bath
	barba, barbae, f.	beard
	barbarus, barbara, barbarum	barbarian
	barbarus, barbarī, m.	barbarian
	Beelzebub, m.	Beelzebub, the Devil
26	bellum, bellī, n.	war
26	bellum gerere	wage war, campaign
17	bene	well
	bene merēns	well deserving, deserving kindness
	optimē	very well
	beneficium, beneficiī, n.	act of kindness, favor
	benignē	kindly
17	benignus, benigna, benignum	kind
	bēstia, bēstiae, f.	wild animal, beast
3	bibō, bibere, bibī	drink
	blanditiae, blanditiārum, f.pl.	flatteries
	blandus, blanda, blandum	flattering, charming, enticing
16	bonus, bona, bonum	good

16	melior, melius	*better*
	melius est	*it would be better*
5	optimus, optima, optimum	*very good, excellent, best*
	optimus quisque	*all the best people*
	bracchium, bracchiī, n.	*arm*
	brevī	*in a short time*
33	brevis, brevis, breve	*short, brief*
	breviter	*briefly*
	Britannī, Britannōrum, m.pl.	*Britons*
	Britannia, Britanniae, f.	*Britain*
	Britannicus, Britannica, Britannicum	*British*

C

	C. = Gāius	
	cachinnō, cachinnāre, cachinnāvī	*laugh, cackle*
	cadō, cadere, cecidī	*fall*
	caecus, caeca, caecum	*blind*
22	caelum, caelī, n.	*sky, heaven*
	calceus, calceī, m.	*shoe*
	Calēdonia, Calēdoniae, f.	*Scotland*
	calliditās, calliditātis, f.	*cleverness, shrewdness*
10	callidus, callida, callidum	*clever, smart*
	candēlābrum, candēlābrī, n.	*lampstand, candelabrum*
	candidātus, candidātī, m.	*candidate*
1	canis, canis, m.	*dog; the lowest throw at dice*
13	cantō, cantāre, cantāvī	*sing, chant*
	tībiīs cantāre	*play on the pipes*
	capillī, capillōrum, m.pl.	*hair*
11	capiō, capere, cēpī, captus	*take, catch, capture*
	cōnsilium capere	*make a plan, have an idea*
	Capitōlium, Capitōliī, n.	*Capitol*
	captīva, captīvae, f.	*(female) prisoner, captive*
29	captīvus, captīvī, m.	*prisoner, captive*
18	caput, capitis, n.	*head*
24	carcer, carceris, m.	*prison*
	carmen, carminis, n.	*song*

	carnifex, carnificis, m.	*executioner*
19	cārus, cāra, cārum	*dear*
	casa, casae, f.	*small house, cottage*
	castellum, castellī, n.	*fort*
25	castra, castrōrum, n.pl.	*military camp*
	cāsus, cāsūs, m.	*misfortune*
	catēna, catēnae, f.	*chain*
	caudex, caudicis, m.	*blockhead, idiot*
	caupō, caupōnis, m.	*innkeeper*
	causa, causae, f.	*reason, cause*
	cautē	*cautiously*
	caveō, cavēre, cāvī	*beware*
	cecidī *see* cadō	
23	cēdō, cēdere, cessī	*give in, yield*
	celebrō, celebrāre, celebrāvī, celebrātus	*celebrate*
	celer, celeris, celere	*quick, fast*
9	celeriter	*quickly, fast*
	celerrimē	*very quickly, very fast*
	quam celerrimē	*as quickly as possible*
	celerrimus, celerrima, celerrimum	*very fast*
	cella, cellae, f.	*cell, sanctuary*
	cellārius, cellāriī, m.	*(house) steward*
21	cēlō, cēlāre, cēlāvī, cēlātus	*hide*
2	cēna, cēnae, f.	*dinner*
7	cēnō, cēnāre, cēnāvī	*eat dinner, dine*
28	centum	*a hundred*
	centuriō, centuriōnis, m.	*centurion*
	cēpī *see* capiō	
	cēra, cērae, f.	*wax, wax tablet*
	certāmen, certāminis, n.	*struggle, contest, fight*
	certē	*certainly*
	certō, certāre, certāvī	*compete*
	certus, certa, certum	*certain, infallible*
	prō certō habēre	*know for certain*
	cessī *see* cēdō	
13	cēterī, cēterae, cētera	*the others, the rest*
	Chrīstiānī, Chrīstiānōrum, m.pl.	*Christians*
2	cibus, cibī, m.	*food*
	circā (+ ACC)	*around*
	circiter (+ ACC)	*about*

circulus, circulī, m.	hoop
21 circum (+ ACC)	around
3 circumspectō, circumspectāre, circumspectāvī	look around
29 circumveniō, circumvenīre, circumvēnī, circumventus	surround
circus, circī, m.	circus, stadium
Circus Maximus	Circus Maximus
citharoedus, citharoedī, m.	cithara player
11 cīvis, cīvis, m.f.	citizen
clādēs, clādis, f.	disaster
clām	secretly, in private
3 clāmō, clāmāre, clāmāvī	shout
5 clāmor, clāmōris, m.	shout, uproar, racket
23 clārus, clāra, clārum	famous, distinguished
15 claudō, claudere, clausī, clausus	shut, close, block, conclude, complete
clēmēns, clēmēns, clēmēns, gen. clēmentis	merciful
cliēns, clientis, m.	client
Cn. = Gnaeus	
18 coepī	I began
19 cōgitō, cōgitāre, cōgitāvī	think, consider
rem cōgitāre	consider the problem
sēcum cōgitāre	consider to oneself
18 cognōscō, cognōscere, cognōvī, cognitus	find out, get to know
25 cōgō, cōgere, coēgī, coāctus	force, compel
cohors, cohortis, f.	cohort
colligō, colligere, collēgī, collēctus	gather, collect, assemble
collocō, collocāre, collocāvī, collocātus	place, put
colloquium, colloquiī, n.	talk, chat
colō, colere, coluī, cultus	seek favor of, make friends with
columba, columbae, f.	dove, pigeon
columna, columnae, f.	pillar
27 comes, comitis, m.f.	comrade, companion
cōmiter	politely, courteously
34 comitor, comitārī,	

comitātus sum	accompany
comitāns, comitāns, comitāns, gen. comitantis	accompanying
commeātus, commeātūs, m.	(military) leave
commemorō, commemorāre, commemorāvī, commemorātus	talk about, mention, recall
commendō, commendāre, commendāvī, commendātus	recommend
committō, committere, commīsī, commissus	commit, begin
26 commōtus, commōta, commōtum	moved, upset, affected, alarmed, excited, distressed, overcome
19 comparō, comparāre, comparāvī, comparātus	obtain
12 compleō, complēre, complēvī, complētus	fill
compluvium, compluviī, n.	compluvium (opening in roof of atrium)
32 compōnō, compōnere, composuī, compositus	put together, arrange, settle, mix, make up
compositus, composita, compositum	composed, steady
24 comprehendō, comprehendere, comprehendī, comprehēnsus	arrest, seize
32 cōnātus, cōnāta, cōnātum	having tried
conclāve, conclāvis, n.	room
concrepō, concrepāre, concrepuī	snap
condūcō, condūcere, condūxī, conductus	hire
19 cōnficiō, cōnficere, cōnfēcī, cōnfectus	finish
cōnfectus, cōnfecta, cōnfectum	worn out, exhausted, overcome

	rem cōnficere	*finish the job*
25	cōnfīdō, cōnfīdere (+ DAT)	*trust, put trust in*
	cōnfīsus, cōnfīsa, cōnfīsum (+ DAT)	*having trusted, having put trust in*
33	coniciō, conicere, coniēcī, coniectus	*hurl, throw*
	coniūrātiō, coniūrātiōnis, f.	*plot, conspiracy*
	coniūrō, coniūrāre, coniūrāvī	*plot, conspire*
34	cōnor, cōnārī, cōnātus sum	*try*
	cōnscendō, cōnscendere, cōnscendī	*climb on, embark on, go on board, mount*
16	cōnsentiō, cōnsentīre, cōnsēnsī	*agree*
	cōnsīdō, cōnsīdere, cōnsēdī	*sit down*
16	cōnsilium, cōnsiliī, n.	*plan, idea, advice*
	cōnsilium capere	*make a plan, have an idea*
31	cōnsistō, cōnsistere, cōnstitī	*stand one's ground, stand firm, halt, stop*
	cōnspectus, cōnspectūs, m.	*sight*
23	cōnspicātus, cōnspicāta, cōnspicātum	*having caught sight of*
7	cōnspiciō, cōnspicere, cōnspexī, cōnspectus	*catch sight of*
34	cōnspicor, cōnspicārī, cōnspicātus sum	*catch sight of*
	cōnspicuus, cōnspicua, cōnspicuum	*conspicuous, easily seen*
28	cōnstituō, cōnstituere, cōnstituī, cōnstitūtus	*decide*
	cōnsul, cōnsulis, m.	*consul (highest elected official of Roman government)*
	cōnsulātus, cōnsulātūs, m.	*the office of consul, consulship*
30	cōnsulō, cōnsulere, cōnsuluī, cōnsultus	*consult*
8	cōnsūmō, cōnsūmere, cōnsūmpsī, cōnsūmptus	*eat*
	contemnō, contemnere, contempsī, contemptus	*reject, despise*
5	contendō, contendere, contendī	*hurry*

	contentiō, contentiōnis, f.	*argument*
10	contentus, contenta, contentum	*satisfied*
	contineō, continēre, continuī	*contain*
	continuus, continua, continuum	*continuous, on end*
33	contrā (+ ACC)	*(1) against*
33	contrā	*(2) on the other hand*
	contrārius, contrāria, contrārium	*opposite*
	rēs contrāria	*the opposite*
	contumēlia, contumēliae, f.	*insult, abuse*
	convalēscō, convalēscere, convaluī	*get better, recover*
11	conveniō, convenīre, convēnī	*come together, gather, meet*
	conversus *see* convertor	
32	convertō, convertere, convertī, conversus	*turn*
	convertor, convertī, conversus sum	*turn*
	convolvō, convolvere, convolvī, convolūtus	*entangle*
4	coquō, coquere, coxī, coctus	*cook*
1	coquus, coquī, m.	*cook*
	corōna, corōnae, f.	*garland, wreath*
28	corpus, corporis, n.	*body*
	corrumpō, corrumpere, corrūpī, corruptus	*corrupt*
	dōnīs corrumpere	*bribe*
14	cotīdiē	*every day*
33	crās	*tomorrow*
11	crēdō, crēdere, crēdidī (+ DAT)	*trust, believe, have faith in*
	creō, creāre, creāvī, creātus	*make, create*
20	crūdēlis, crūdēlis, crūdēle	*cruel*
	cruentus, cruenta, cruentum	*bloody, blood-stained*
	crux, crucis, f.	*cross*
6	cubiculum, cubiculī, n.	*bedroom*
	cucurrī *see* currō	
	cui, cuius *see* quī	

	culīna, culīnae, f.	kitchen	
	culpō, culpāre, culpāvī	blame	
	culter, cultrī, m.	knife	
24	cum (1)	when	
7	cum (2) (+ ABL)	with	
	cumulō, cumulāre, cumulāvī, cumulātus	heap	
9	cupiō, cupere, cupīvī	want	
4	cūr?	why?	
23	cūra, cūrae, f.	care	
	cūrae esse	be a matter of concern	
	cūria, cūriae, f.	senate-house	
19	cūrō, cūrāre, cūrāvī	take care of, supervise	
5	currō, currere, cucurrī	run	
	currus, currūs, m.	chariot	
	cursus, cursūs, m.	course, flight	
12	custōdiō, custōdīre, custōdīvī, custōdītus	guard	
13	custōs, custōdis, m.	guard	

d

	damnō, damnāre, damnāvī, damnātus	condemn
	dare see dō	
11	dē (+ ABL)	from, down from; about
18	dea, deae, f.	goddess
15	dēbeō, dēbēre, dēbuī, dēbitus	owe; ought, should, must
	Deceanglī, Deceanglōrum, m.pl.	Deceangli (a British tribe)
20, 28	decem	ten
	decet, decēre, decuit	be proper
	mē decet	I ought
33	dēcidō, dēcidere, dēcidī	fall down
	decimus, decima, decimum	tenth
22	dēcipiō, dēcipere, dēcēpī, dēceptus	deceive, trick
	dēclārō, dēclārāre, dēclārāvī, dēclārātus	declare, proclaim
14	decōrus, decōra, decōrum	right, proper
	dedī see dō	
	dēdicō, dēdicāre, dēdicāvī,	

		dēdicātus	dedicate
	dēdūcō, dēdūcere, dēdūxī, dēductus	escort	
29	dēfendō, dēfendere, dēfendī, dēfēnsus	defend	
	dēfessus, dēfessa, dēfessum	exhausted, tired out	
	dēfigō, dēfigere, dēfixī, dēfixus	fix	
	dēfixiō, dēfixiōnis, f.	curse	
	dēiciō, dēicere, dēiēcī, dēiectus	throw down, throw	
	dēiectus, dēiecta, dēiectum	disappointed, downcast	
16	deinde	then	
16	dēlectō, dēlectāre, dēlectāvī, dēlectātus	delight, please	
14	dēleō, dēlēre, dēlēvī, dēlētus	destroy	
	dēliciae, dēliciārum, f.pl.	darling	
	dēligō, dēligāre, dēligāvī, dēligātus	bind, tie, tie up, moor	
30	dēmittō, dēmittere, dēmīsī, dēmissus	let down, lower	
	dēmoveō, dēmovēre, dēmōvī, dēmōtus	dismiss, move out of	
	dēmum	at last	
	tum dēmum	then at last, only then	
	dēnārius, dēnāriī, m.	denarius (a small coin worth four sesterces)	
20	dēnique	at last, finally	
	dēns, dentis, m.	tooth, tusk	
	dēnsus, dēnsa, dēnsum	thick	
	dēnūntiō, dēnūntiāre, dēnūntiāvī, dēnūntiātus	denounce, reveal	
	dēpellō, dēpellere, dēpulī, dēpulsus	drive off, push down	
	dēpōnō, dēpōnere, dēposuī, dēpositus	put down, take off	
	dērīdeō, dērīdēre, dērīsī, dērīsus	mock, make fun of	
33	dēscendō, dēscendere, dēscendī	go down, come down	
24	dēserō, dēserere, dēseruī, dēsertus	desert	
	dēsiliō, dēsilīre, dēsiluī	jump down	
	dēsinō, dēsinere	end, cease	

dēsistō, dēsistere, dēstitī — *stop*

20 dēspērō, dēspērāre,
dēspērāvī — *despair, give up*

dēspiciō, dēspicere, dēspexī — *look down*

dēstinō, dēstināre,
dēstināvī, dēstinātus — *intend*

dēstringō, dēstringere,
dēstrīnxī, dēstrictus — *draw out, draw (a sword), pull out*

dētestātus *see* dētestor

dētestor, dētestārī,
dētestātus sum — *curse*

dētrahō, dētrahere,
dētrāxī, dētractus — *pull down*

14 deus, deī, m. — *god*

dī immortālēs! — *heavens above!*

Deva, Devae, f. — *Deva (modern Chester)*

Devae — *at Deva*

Devam — *to Deva*

dēvorō, dēvorāre,
dēvorāvī, dēvorātus — *devour, eat up*

dī *see* deus

diabolus, diabolī, m. — *devil*

13 dīcō, dīcere, dīxī, dictus — *say*

dictō, dictāre, dictāvī,
dictātus — *dictate*

9 diēs, diēī, m. — *day*

diēs fēstus, diēī fēstī, m. — *festival, holiday*

diēs nātālis,
diēī nātālis, m. — *birthday*

14 difficilis, difficilis, difficile — *difficult*

difficillimus, difficillima,
difficillimum — *very difficult*

difficultās, difficultātis, f. — *difficulty*

diffīsus, diffīsa, diffīsum
(+ DAT) — *having distrusted*

digitus, digitī, m. — *finger*

25 dignitās, dignitātis, f. — *dignity, importance, honor, prestige*

dignus, digna, dignum — *worthy, appropriate*

14 dīligenter — *carefully*

dīligentia, dīligentiae, f. — *industry, hard work*

dīligō, dīligere, dīlēxī — *be fond of*

dīmittō, dīmittere, dīmīsī,
dīmissus — *send away, dismiss*

dīripiō, dīripere, dīripuī,
dīreptus — *tear apart, ransack*

29 dīrus, dīra, dīrum — *dreadful, awful*

dīs *see* deus

18 discēdō, discēdere,
discessī — *depart, leave*

disciplīna, disciplīnae, f. — *discipline, orderliness*

discipulus, discipulī, m. — *disciple, follower*

discō, discere, didicī — *learn*

discordia, discordiae, f. — *strife*

discrīmen, discrīminis, n. — *crisis*

dissentiō, dissentīre,
dissēnsī — *disagree, argue*

dissimulō, dissimulāre,
dissimulāvī, dissimulātus — *conceal, hide*

distribuō, distribuere,
distribuī, distribūtus — *distribute*

17 diū — *for a long time*

diūtius — *for a longer time*

30 dīves, dīves, dīves, *gen.*
dīvitis — *rich*

dītissimus, dītissima,
dītissimum — *very rich*

30 dīvitiae, dīvitiārum, f.pl. — *riches*

dīvus, dīva, dīvum — *divine*

dīxī *see* dīcō

9 dō, dare, dedī, datus — *give*

25 poenās dare — *pay the penalty, be punished*

26 doceō, docēre, docuī,
doctus — *teach*

20 doctus, docta, doctum — *educated, learned, skillful*

28 doleō, dolēre, doluī — *hurt, be in pain*

graviter dolēre — *be extremely painful*

29 dolor, dolōris, m. — *grief, pain*

dolus, dolī, m. — *trickery*

14 domina, dominae, f. — *lady (of the house), mistress*

2 dominus, dominī, m. — *master (of the house)*

20 domus, domūs, f. — *home*

domī — *at home*

domum redīre — *return home*

14 dōnum, dōnī, n. — *present, gift*

	dōnīs corrumpere	*bribe*
2	dormiō, dormīre, dormīvī	*sleep*
	dubium, dubiī, n.	*doubt*
8	dūcō, dūcere, dūxī, ductus	*lead*
	sorte ductus	*chosen by lot*
34	dum	*while, until*
12, 20, 28	duo, duae, duo	*two*
	duodecim	*twelve*
21	dūrus, dūra, dūrum	*harsh, hard*
31	dux, ducis, m.	*leader*
	dūxī *see* dūcō	

e

4	ē, ex (+ ABL)	*from, out of*
	ea, eā, eam *see* is	
	eādem, eandem *see* īdem	
	eās *see* is	
	ēbrius, ēbria, ēbrium	*drunk*
3	ecce!	*see! look!*
	edō, edere, ēdī, ēsus	*eat*
	efferō, efferre, extulī, ēlātus	*bring out, carry out*
21	efficiō, efficere, effēcī, effectus	*carry out, accomplish*
	effigiēs, effigiēī, f.	*image, statue*
	effringō, effringere, effrēgī, effrāctus	*break down*
16	effugiō, effugere, effūgī	*escape*
32	effundō, effundere, effūdī, effūsus	*pour out*
	effūsīs lacrimīs	*bursting into tears*
	ēgī *see* agō	
4	ego, meī	*I, me*
	mēcum	*with me*
34	ēgredior, ēgredī, ēgressus sum	*go out*
24	ēgressus, ēgressa, ēgressum	*having left*
4	ēheu!	*alas! oh dear!*
	eī *see* is	
33	ēiciō, ēicere, ēiēcī, ēiectus	*throw out*
	eīs, eius *see* is	
	eiusmodī	*of that kind*
	ēlābor, ēlābī, ēlāpsus sum	*escape*

	ēlāpsus, ēlāpsa, ēlāpsum	*having escaped*
	ēlegāns, ēlegāns, ēlegāns, gen. ēlegantis	*tasteful, elegant*
	ēlegantia, ēlegantiae, f.	*good taste, elegance*
	ēliciō, ēlicere, ēlicuī, ēlicitus	*lure, entice*
22	ēligō, ēligere, ēlēgī, ēlēctus	*choose*
	ēlūdō, ēlūdere, ēlūdī, ēlūsus	*slip past, trick, outwit*
9	ēmittō, ēmittere, ēmīsī, ēmissus	*throw, send out*
6	emō, emere, ēmī, ēmptus	*buy*
	ēmoveō, ēmovēre, ēmōvī, ēmōtus	*move, clear away, remove*
	ēn!	*look!*
	ēn iūstitia!	*so this is justice!*
	ēn Rōmānī!	*so these are the Romans!*
23	enim	*for*
11	eō, īre, iī	*go*
	obviam īre (+ DAT)	*meet, go to meet*
	eō *see* is	
	eōdem *see* īdem	
	eōrum, eōs *see* is	
12	epistula, epistulae, f.	*letter*
	ab epistulīs	*in charge of correspondence*
	epulae, epulārum, f.pl.	*dishes, banquet*
24	eques, equitis, m.	*horseman; man of equestrian rank*
	equitō, equitāre, equitāvī	*ride a horse*
15	equus, equī, m.	*horse*
	eram *see* sum	
	ergō	*therefore*
	ēripiō, ēripere, ēripuī, ēreptus	*snatch, tear*
	errō, errāre, errāvī	*make a mistake*
	longē errāre	*make a big mistake*
	ērubēscō, ērubēscere, ērubuī	*blush*
	ērumpō, ērumpere, ērūpī	*break away, break out*
1	est, estō *see* sum	
	ēsuriō, ēsurīre	*be hungry*
3	et	*and*

33	et ... et	both ... and	

33	et ... et	*both ... and*
15	etiam	*even, also*
	nōn modo ... sed etiam	*not only ... but also*
	euge!	*hurrah!, hurray!*
8	eum *see* is	
	evangelium, evangeliī, n.	*good news, gospel*
	ēvertō, ēvertere, ēvertī, ēversus	*overturn*
	ēvolō, ēvolāre, ēvolāvī	*fly out*
4	ex, ē (+ ABL)	*from, out of*
	exanimātus, exanimāta, exanimātum	*unconscious*
33	excipiō, excipere, excēpī, exceptus	*receive*
13	excitō, excitāre, excitāvī, excitātus	*arouse, wake up, awaken*
10	exclāmō, exclāmāre, exclāmāvī	*exclaim, shout*
	excruciō, excruciāre, excruciāvī, excruciātus	*torture, torment*
	exemplum, exemplī, n.	*example*
3	exeō, exīre, exiī	*go out*
	exerceō, exercēre, exercuī, exercitus	*exercise*
	exīstimō, exīstimāre, exīstimāvī, exīstimātus	*think, consider*
	exitium, exitiī, n.	*ruin, destruction*
	expellō, expellere, expulī, expulsus	*drive out*
25	explicō, explicāre, explicāvī, explicātus	*explain*
	explōrātor, explōrātōris, m.	*scout, spy*
	expōnō, expōnere, exposuī, expositus	*unload*
	expugnō, expugnāre, expugnāvī, expugnātus	*storm, take by storm*
	exquīsītus, exquīsīta, exquīsītum	*special*
3	exspectō, exspectāre, exspectāvī, exspectātus	*wait for*
	exstinguō, exstinguere, exstīnxī, exstīnctus	*extinguish, put out, destroy*

	exstruō, exstruere, exstrūxī, exstrūctus	*build*
	exsultō, exsultāre, exsultāvī	*exult, be triumphant*
	exta, extōrum, n.pl.	*entrails*
	extorqueō, extorquēre, extorsī, extortus	*take by force, extort*
25	extrā (+ ACC)	*outside*
	extrahō, extrahere, extrāxī, extractus	*drag out, pull out, take out*
	extrēmus, extrēma, extrēmum	*furthest*
	extrēma pars	*edge*
	extulī *see* efferō	
	exuō, exuere, exuī, exūtus	*take off*

f

17	faber, fabrī, m.	*craftsman, carpenter, workman*
5	fābula, fābulae, f.	*play, story*
	fābulam agere	*act in a play*
	facēs *see* fax	
8	facile	*easily*
17	facilis, facilis, facile	*easy*
	facinus, facinoris, n.	*crime*
7	faciō, facere, fēcī, factus	*make, do*
	impetum facere	*charge, make an attack*
	sēditiōnem facere	*revolt*
	factum, factī, n.	*deed, achievement*
	Falernus, Falerna, Falernum	*Falernian*
	fallō, fallere, fefellī, falsus	*deceive*
	falsum, falsī, n.	*lie*
26	falsus, falsa, falsum	*false, untrue, dishonest*
	famēs, famis, f.	*hunger*
	faucēs, faucium, f.pl.	*passage, entranceway*
11	faveō, favēre, fāvī	*favor, support*
	favor, favōris, m.	*favor*
	fax, facis, f.	*torch*
	fēcī *see* faciō	
	fefellī *see* fallō	
	fēlīx, fēlīx, fēlīx, *gen.* fēlīcis	*lucky, happy*

5	fēmina, fēminae, f.	*woman*	10	frāter, frātris, m.	*brother*
	fenestra, fenestrae, f.	*window*		fraus, fraudis, f.	*trick*
9	ferō, ferre, tulī, lātus	*bring, carry*		frōns, frontis, f.	*front*
	graviter ferre	*take badly*	31	frūmentum, frūmentī, n.	*grain*
6	ferōciter	*fiercely*	12	frūstrā	*in vain*
8	ferōx, ferōx, ferōx,		33	fuga, fugae, f.	*escape*
	gen. ferōcis	*fierce, ferocious*	12	fugiō, fugere, fūgī	*run away,*
13	fessus, fessa, fessum	*tired*			*flee (from)*
6	festīnō, festīnāre, festīnāvī	*hurry*		fugitīvus, fugitīvī, m.	*fugitive, runaway*
	fēstus, fēsta, fēstum	*festive, holiday*		fuī *see* sum	
	diēs fēstus, diēī fēstī, m.	*holiday*		fulgeō, fulgēre, fulsī	*shine, glitter*
	fībula, fībulae, f.	*brooch*	22	fundō, fundere, fūdī, fūsus	*pour*
14	fidēlis, fidēlis, fidēle	*faithful, loyal*	12	fundus, fundī, m.	*farm*
26	fidēs, fideī, f.	*loyalty, trustworthiness*		fūnis, fūnis, m.	*rope*
	fidem servāre	*keep a promise, keep*		fūnus, fūneris, n.	*funeral*
		faith	6	fūr, fūris, m.	*thief*
	fīgō, fīgere, fīxī, fīxus	*fix, fasten*		furcifer, furciferī, m.	*scoundrel, crook*
	figūra, figūrae, f.	*figure, shape*		furēns, furēns, furēns,	
1	fīlia, fīliae, f.	*daughter*		*gen.* furentis	*furious, in a rage*
1	fīlius, fīliī, m.	*son*		fūstis, fūstis, m.	*club, stick*
	factus sum	*I became*			
	fīxus *see* fīgō				
	flagrō, flagrāre, flagrāvī	*blaze*			**g**
12	flamma, flammae, f.	*flame*		garriō, garrīre, garrīvī	*chatter, gossip*
16	flōs, flōris, m.	*flower*		garum, garī, n.	*sauce*
24	flūmen, flūminis, n.	*river*	27	gaudeō, gaudēre	*be pleased, rejoice*
19	fluō, fluere, flūxī	*flow*	34	gaudium, gaudiī, n.	*joy*
21	fōns, fontis, m.	*fountain, spring*		gāza, gāzae, f.	*treasure*
	fōrma, fōrmae, f.	*beauty, shape*	28	gemitus, gemitūs, m.	*groan*
18	fortasse	*perhaps*		gemma, gemmae, f.	*jewel, gem*
19	forte	*by chance*	30	gēns, gentis, f.	*family, tribe*
6	fortis, fortis, forte	*brave, strong*		ubi gentium?	*where in the world?*
12	fortiter	*bravely*		genū, genūs, n.	*knee*
	fortitūdō, fortitūdinis, f.	*courage*	23	gerō, gerere, gessī, gestus	*wear*
	fortūna, fortūnae, f.	*fortune, luck*	26	bellum gerere	*wage war, campaign*
	fortūnātus, fortūnāta,			gladiātor, gladiātōris, m.	*gladiator*
	fortūnātum	*lucky*	8	gladius, gladiī, m.	*sword*
	forum, forī, n.	*forum, business center*		glōria, glōriae, f.	*glory*
	Forum Rōmānum	*the Roman Forum*		glōriāns, glōriāns, glōriāns,	
	fossa, fossae, f.	*ditch*		*gen.* glōriantis	*boasting, boastfully*
	fragor, fragōris, m.	*crash*		Graecia, Graeciae, f.	*Greece*
34	frangō, frangere, frēgī,			Graecus, Graeca, Graecum	*Greek*
	frāctus	*break*		grānum, grānī, n.	*grain*
				grātiae, grātiārum, f.pl.	*thanks*

19	grātiās agere	thank, give thanks
	grātīs	free
	grātulāns, grātulāns, grātulāns, *gen.* grātulantis	congratulating
	grātulātiō, grātulātiōnis, f.	congratulation
	grātulor, grātulārī, grātulātus sum	congratulate
21	gravis, gravis, grave	heavy, serious
17	graviter	heavily, soundly, seriously
	graviter dolēre	be extremely painful
	graviter ferre	take badly
	gustō, gustāre, gustāvī, gustātus	taste
	guttur, gutturis, n.	throat

h

4	habeō, habēre, habuī, habitus	have
	in animō habēre	have in mind, intend
	in memoriā habēre	keep in mind, remember
	prō certō habēre	know for certain
	prō hostibus habēre	consider as enemies
	sermōnem habēre	have a conversation, talk
10	habitō, habitāre, habitāvī	live
	hāc, hae, haec *see* hic	
	haereō, haerēre, haesī	stick, cling
	haesitō, haesitāre, haesitāvī	hesitate
	hanc *see* hic	
	haruspex, haruspicis, m.	soothsayer
	hās *see* hic	
19	hasta, hastae, f.	spear
34	haud	not
31	haudquāquam	not at all
	hauriō, haurīre, hausī, haustus	drain, drink up
	hercle!	by Hercules!
	hērēs, hērēdis, m.f.	heir
7	heri	yesterday
	heus!	hey!
8	hic, haec, hoc	this

33	hīc	here, in this place
	hiems, hiemis, f.	winter
	hilarē	cheerfully
	hinc	from here
	Hispānia, Hispāniae, f.	Spain
	hoc, hōc *see* hic	
5	hodiē	today
9	homō, hominis, m.	person, man
	homunculus, homunculī, m.	little man, pip-squeak
23	honor, honōris, m.	honor, official position
	honōrō, honōrāre, honōrāvī, honōrātus	honor
21	hōra, hōrae, f.	hour
	horreum, horreī, n.	barn, granary, warehouse
	hortātus *see* hortor	
34	hortor, hortārī, hortātus sum	encourage, urge
1	hortus, hortī, m.	garden
	hōrum *see* hic	
9	hospes, hospitis, m.	guest, host
22	hostis, hostis, m.f.	enemy
17	hūc	here, to this place
	hūc illūc	here and there, up and down
	huic, huius *see* hic	
	humilis, humilis, humile	low-born, of low class
	humus, humī, f.	ground
24	humī	on the ground
	humum	to the ground
	hunc *see* hic	

i

12	iaceō, iacēre, iacuī	lie, rest
23	iaciō, iacere, iēcī, iactus	throw
22	iactō, iactāre, iactāvī, iactātus	throw
12	iam	now, already
	iamdūdum	for a long time
3	iānua, iānuae, f.	door
	ībam *see* eō	
18	ibi	there
	id *see* is	
31	īdem, eadem, idem	the same

31	identidem	*repeatedly*	

31	identidem	*repeatedly*		imposuī, impositus	*impose, put into, put onto*
	iecur, iecoris, n.	*liver*		importō, importāre,	
	Ierosolyma, Ierosolymae, f.	*Jerusalem*		importāvī, importātus	*import*
12	igitur	*therefore, and so*		imprecātiō, imprecātiōnis, f.	*curse*
27	ignārus, ignāra, ignārum	*not knowing, unaware*		impudēns, impudēns,	
8	ignāvus, ignāva, ignāvum	*cowardly, lazy*		impudēns, *gen.* impudentis	*shameless*
	ignis, ignis, m.	*fire*		impulī *see* impellō	
	ignōrō, ignōrāre, ignōrāvī	*not know about*	1	in	*(1) (+ ACC) into, onto*
32	ignōscō, ignōscere,				*(2) (+ ABL) in, on*
	ignōvī (+ DAT)	*forgive*		inānis, inānis, ināne	*empty, meaningless*
	ignōtus, ignōta, ignōtum	*unknown*	29	incēdō, incēdere, incessī	*march, stride*
	iī *see* eō		27	incendō, incendere,	
9	ille, illa, illud	*that, he, she*		incendī, incēnsus	*burn, set fire to*
19	illūc	*there, to that place*		incēnsus, incēnsa, incēnsum	*inflamed, angered*
	hūc illūc	*here and there, up and down*		incertus, incerta, incertum	*uncertain*
				incidō, incidere, incidī	*fall*
	illūcēscō, illūcēscere, illūxī	*dawn, grow bright*	22	incipiō, incipere, incēpī,	
	imitātus, imitāta, imitātum	*having imitated*		inceptus	*begin*
	imitor, imitārī, imitātus			incitō, incitāre, incitāvī,	
	sum	*imitate, mime*		incitātus	*urge on, encourage*
	immineō, imminēre,			inclūsus, inclūsa, inclūsum	*shut up, imprisoned, trapped*
	imminuī (+ DAT)	*hang over*			
	immo	*or rather*		incurrō, incurrere, incurrī	*run onto, collide with, bump into*
	immortālis, immortālis,				
	immortāle	*immortal*		inde	*then*
	dī immortālēs!	*heavens above!*		indicium, indiciī, n.	*sign, evidence*
	immortālitās,			indignus, indigna, indignum	*unworthy, undeserved*
	immortālitātis, f.	*immortality*		induō, induere, induī,	
23	immōtus, immōta,			indūtus	*put on*
	immōtum	*still, motionless*		inest *see* īnsum	
	impatiēns, impatiēns,			īnfāns, īnfantis, m.	*baby, child*
	impatiēns, *gen.*		21	īnfēlīx, īnfēlīx, īnfēlīx,	
	impatientis	*impatient*		*gen.* īnfēlīcis	*unlucky*
15	impediō, impedīre,		20	īnferō, īnferre, intulī, inlātus	*bring in, bring on, bring against*
	impedīvī, impedītus	*delay, hinder*			
	impellō, impellere,			iniūriam īnferre	*do an injustice, bring injury*
	impulī, impulsus	*push, force*			
16	imperātor, imperātōris, m.	*emperor*		īnfestus, īnfesta, īnfestum	*hostile, dangerous*
	imperium, imperiī, n.	*empire*		īnfīgō, īnfīgere, īnfīxī,	
27	imperō, imperāre,			īnfīxus	*fasten onto*
	imperāvī (+ DAT)	*order, command*		īnflīgō, īnflīgere, īnflīxī,	
	impetus, impetūs, m.	*attack*		īnflīctus	*inflict*
	impetum facere	*charge, make an attack*		īnflō, īnflāre, īnflāvī	*blow*
	impōnō, impōnere,			īnfundō, īnfundere,	

	īnfūdī, īnfūsus	pour into	truth
	ingenium, ingeniī, n.	character	
7	ingēns, ingēns, ingēns,		6 intentē	intently
	gen. ingentis	huge	16 inter (+ ACC)	among, between
	ingravēscō, ingravēscere	grow worse	inter sē	among themselves, with each other
34	ingredior, ingredī,		24 intereā	meanwhile
	ingressus sum	enter	13 interficiō, interficere,	
22	ingressus, ingressa,		interfēcī, interfectus	kill
	ingressum	having entered	interrogō, interrogāre,	
	iniciō, inicere, iniēcī,		interrogāvī, interrogātus	question
	iniectus	throw in	interrumpō, interrumpere,	
	inimīcitia, inimīcitiae, f.	feud, dispute	interrūpī, interruptus	interrupt
	inimīcus, inimīcī, m.	enemy	2 intrō, intrāre, intrāvī	enter
30	iniūria, iniūriae, f.	injustice, injury	intulī see īnferō	
	iniūriam īnferre	do an injustice, bring injury	intus	inside
			10 inveniō, invenīre, invēnī,	
	inlātus see īnferō		inventus	find
	innītor, innītī, innīxus sum	lean, rest	invicem	in turn
	innīxus, innīxa, innīxum	leaning	11 invītō, invītāre, invītāvī,	
	innocēns, innocēns, innocēns,		invītātus	invite
	gen. innocentis	innocent	17 invītus, invīta, invītum	unwilling, reluctant
	inopia, inopiae, f.	poverty	iō!	hurrah!
4	inquit	says, said	iocus, iocī, m.	joke
	inquam	I said	Iovis see Iuppiter	
	īnsānia, īnsāniae, f.	insanity	14 ipse, ipsa, ipsum	himself, herself, itself
	īnsāniō, īnsānīre, īnsānīvī	be crazy, be insane	28 īra, īrae, f.	anger
	īnsānus, īnsāna, īnsānum	crazy, insane	3 īrātus, īrāta, īrātum	angry
	īnscrībō, īnscrībere,		īre see eō	
	īnscrīpsī, īnscrīptus	write, inscribe	irrumpō, irrumpere, irrūpī	burst in, burst into
27	īnsidiae, īnsidiārum, f.pl.	trap, ambush	is, ea, id	he, she, it
	īnsolēns, īnsolēns, īnsolēns,		14 iste, ista, istud	that
	gen. īnsolentis	rude, insolent	16 ita	in this way
	īnsolenter	rudely, insolently	13 ita vērō	yes
9	īnspiciō, īnspicere, īnspexī,		Ītalia, Ītaliae, f.	Italy
	īnspectus	look at, inspect, examine, search	17 itaque	and so
			19 iter, itineris, n.	journey, trip, progress
26	īnstruō, īnstruere, īnstrūxī,		9 iterum	again
	īnstrūctus	draw up, set up	21 iubeō, iubēre, iussī, iussus	order
17	īnsula, īnsulae, f.	island; apartment building	iussū Silvae	at Silva's order
			Iūdaeī, Iūdaeōrum, m.pl.	Jews
	īnsula Tiberīna	Tiber Island	Iūdaeus, Iūdaea, Iūdaeum	Jewish
	īnsum, inesse, īnfuī	be inside	4 iūdex, iūdicis, m.	judge
7	intellegō, intellegere,		iūdicō, iūdicāre, iūdicāvī,	
	intellēxī, intellēctus	understand	iūdicātus	judge
	rem intellegere	understand the		

	iugulum, iugulī, n.	throat	
	Iuppiter, Iovis, m.	Jupiter (god of the sky, greatest of Roman gods)	
	iussī see iubeō		
27	iussum, iussī, n.	order, instruction	
	iūstitia, iūstitiae, f.	justice	
	ēn iūstitia!	so this is justice!	
	iuvat, iuvāre	please	
	mē iuvat	it pleases me	
5	iuvenis, iuvenis, m.	young man	
	iuxtā (+ ACC)	next to	

1

L. = Lūcius

	labefaciō, labefacere, labefēcī, labefactus	weaken
	lābor, lābī, lāpsus sum	fall
32	labor, labōris, m.	work
1	labōrō, labōrāre, labōrāvī	work
	labrum, labrī, n.	lip
22	lacrima, lacrimae, f.	tear
	lacrimīs effūsīs	bursting into tears
7	lacrimō, lacrimāre, lacrimāvī	cry, weep
	lacus, lacūs, m.	lake
	lacus Asphaltītēs, lacūs Asphaltītae	the Dead Sea
	laedō, laedere, laesī, laesus	harm
	laetē	happily
2	laetus, laeta, laetum	happy
	lānx, lancis, f.	dish
	lāpsus see lābor	
	latebrae, latebrārum, f.pl.	hiding-place
25	lateō, latēre, latuī	lie hidden
	later, lateris, m.	brick
	Latīnī, Latīnōrum, m.pl.	the Latini (early tribe in Italy)
	latrō, latrōnis, m.	robber
	lātus, lāta, lātum	wide
2	laudō, laudāre, laudāvī, laudātus	praise
	lavō, lavāre, lāvī, lautus	wash

	lectīca, lectīcae, f.	sedan-chair, carrying-chair
15	lectus, lectī, m.	couch, bed
26	lēgātus, lēgātī, m.	commander (of a legion)
26	legiō, legiōnis, f.	legion
	lēgō, lēgāre, lēgāvī, lēgātus	bequeath
11	legō, legere, lēgī, lēctus	read
	lēniō, lēnīre, lēnīvī, lēnītus	soothe, calm down
	lēniter	gently
15	lentē	slowly
3	leō, leōnis, m.	lion
	lēx, lēgis, f.	law
18	libenter	gladly
10	liber, librī, m.	book
11	līberālis, līberālis, līberāle	generous
29	līberī, līberōrum, m.pl.	children
20	līberō, līberāre, līberāvī, līberātus	free, set free
32	lībertās, lībertātis, f.	freedom
6	lībertus, lībertī, m.	freedman, ex-slave
	līmen, līminis, n.	threshold, doorway
	lingua, linguae, f.	tongue
	littera, litterae, f.	letter
	līvidus, līvida, līvidum	lead-colored
19	locus, locī, m.	place
23	locūtus, locūta, locūtum	having spoken
	longē	far
	longē errāre	make a big mistake
	longurius, longuriī, m.	pole
	longus, longa, longum	long
	loquāx, loquāx, loquāx, gen. loquācis	talkative
34	loquor, loquī, locūtus sum	speak
	lūbricus, lūbrica, lūbricum	slippery
	lūcem see lūx	
	lūceō, lūcēre, lūxī	shine
	lucerna, lucernae, f.	lamp
	lūdō, lūdere, lūsī	play
33	lūdus, lūdī, m.	game
	lūgeō, lūgēre, lūxī	lament, mourn
20	lūna, lūnae, f.	moon
	lutum, lutī, n.	mud
18, 29	lūx, lūcis, f.	light, daylight

m

M. = Marcus

madidus, madida, madidum *soaked through, drenched*

magicus, magica, magicum *magic*

magis *see* magnopere

magister, magistrī, m. *master, foreman*

magistrātus, magistrātūs, m. *public official*

magnificē *splendidly, magnificently*

magnificus, magnifica, magnificum *splendid, magnificent*

30 magnopere *greatly*

    magis *more, rather*

24 maximē *very greatly, very much, most of all*

3 magnus, magna, magnum *big, large, great*

    maior, maior, maius, *gen.* maiōris *bigger, larger, greater*

17 maximus, maxima, maximum *very big, very large, very great, greatest*

    Pontifex Maximus *Chief Priest*

malignus, maligna, malignum *spiteful*

29 mālō, mālle, māluī *prefer*

    mālim *I would prefer*

28 malus, mala, malum *evil, bad*

    peior, peior, peius, *gen.* peiōris *worse*

20 pessimus, pessima, pessimum *very bad, worst*

23 mandātum, mandātī, n. *instruction, order*

28 mandō, mandāre, mandāvī, mandātus *order, entrust, hand over*

19 māne *in the morning*

9 maneō, manēre, mānsī *remain, stay*

27 manus, manūs, f. *hand; band*

    margō, marginis, m. *edge*

14 marītus, marītī, m. *husband*

    marmor, marmoris, n. *marble*

    Mārs, Mārtis, m. *Mars (god of war)*

    Masada, Masadae, f. *Masada (a fortress in Judea)*

    massa, massae, f. *block*

1 māter, mātris, f. *mother*

    mātrimōnium, mātrimōniī, n. *marriage*

    mātrōna, mātrōnae, f. *lady, married woman*

24 maximē *see* magnopere

17 maximus *see* magnus

    mē *see* ego

    medicāmentum, medicāmentī, n. *ointment, medicine, drug*

    medicus, medicī, m. *doctor*

9 medius, media, medium *middle*

16 melior *see* bonus

    melius est *see* bonus

    memor, memor, memor, *gen.* memoris *remembering, mindful of*

    memoria, memoriae, f. *memory*

    in memoriā habēre *keep in mind, remember*

    mendāx, mendāx, mendāx, *gen.* mendācis *lying, deceitful*

    mendīcus, mendīcī, m. *beggar*

    mēns, mentis, f. *mind*

32 mēnsa, mēnsae, f. *table*

    mēnsis, mēnsis, m. *month*

2 mercātor, mercātōris, m. *merchant*

    meritus, merita, meritum *well-deserved*

28 metus, metūs, m. *fear*

5 meus, mea, meum *my, mine*

    meī, meōrum, m.pl. *my family*

    mī Haterī *my dear Haterius*

    mī Quīnte *my dear Quintus*

    mihi *see* ego

18 mīles, mīlitis, m. *soldier*

    mīlitō, mīlitāre, mīlitāvī *be a soldier*

28 mīlle *a thousand*

28	mīlia	thousands
11	minimē	no; least, very little
22	minimus *see* parvus	
	minor *see* parvus	
	minor, minārī, minātus sum	threaten
12	mīrābilis, mīrābilis, mīrābile	marvelous, strange, wonderful
	mīrus, mīra, mīrum	extraordinary
	aliquid mīrī	something extraordinary
	misceō, miscēre, miscuī, mixtus	mix
15	miser, misera, miserum	miserable, wretched, sad
	ō mē miserum!	oh wretched me!
12	mittō, mittere, mīsī, missus	send
34	modo	just, now, only
	modo … modo	now … now
	nōn modo … sed etiam	not only … but also
23	modus, modī, m.	manner, way, kind
22	quō modō?	how? in what way?
	rēs huius modī	a thing of this kind
	molestus, molesta, molestum	troublesome
	molliō, mollīre, mollīvī, mollītus	soothe
	mollis, mollis, molle	soft, gentle
	mōmentum, mōmentī, n.	importance
22	moneō, monēre, monuī, monitus	warn, advise
12	mōns, montis, m.	mountain
	mora, morae, f.	delay
21	morbus, morbī, m.	illness
	moriēns, moriēns, moriēns, *gen.* morientis	dying
34	morior, morī, mortuus sum	die
	(eī) moriendum est	(he) must die
	moritūrus, moritūra, moritūrum	going to die
	moror, morārī, morātus sum	delay
20	mors, mortis, f.	death
	mortuus, mortua, mortuum	dead

7	mortuus *see* morior	
	mōs, mōris, m.	custom
	mōtus, mōtūs, m.	movement
33	moveō, movēre, mōvī, mōtus	move
9	mox	soon
	multitūdō, multitūdinis, f.	crowd
	multō	much
	multum	much
5	multus, multa, multum	much
5	multī	many
19	plūrimī, plūrimae, plūrima	very many
	plūrimus, plūrima, plūrimum	very much, most
	plūris est	is worth more
	plūs, plūris, n.	more
	plūs vīnī	more wine
	mūnītiō, mūnītiōnis, f.	defense, fortification
11	mūrus, mūrī, m.	wall
	mūs, mūris, m.f.	mouse
	mussitō, mussitāre, mussitāvī	murmur
	mūtātiō, mūtātiōnis, f.	posting station, way station

n

	nactus, nacta, nactum	having seized
18	nam	for
7	nārrō, nārrāre, nārrāvī, nārrātus	tell, relate
	rem nārrāre	tell the story
34	nāscor, nāscī, nātus sum	be born
	(diēs) nātālis, (diēī) nātālis, m.	birthday
	trīgintā annōs nātus	thirty years old
	nāsus, nāsī, m.	nose
	nātālis, nātālis, nātāle	natal
	nātū maximus	eldest
30	nātus, nāta, nātum	born
15	nauta, nautae, m.	sailor
16	nāvigō, nāvigāre, nāvigāvī	sail
3	nāvis, nāvis, f.	ship

31	nē	*that … not, so that … not*	
32	nē … quidem	*not even*	
32	nec … nec	*neither … nor*	
32	nec	*and not, nor*	
	utrum … necne	*whether … or not*	
14	necesse	*necessary*	
7	necō, necāre, necāvī, necātus	*kill*	
	neglegēns, neglegēns, neglegēns, *gen.* neglegentis	*careless*	
31	neglegō, neglegere, neglēxī, neglēctus	*neglect*	
17	negōtium, negōtiī, n.	*business*	
17	negōtium agere	*do business, work*	
18	nēmō (acc. nēminem)	*no one, nobody*	
	neque	*and not, nor*	
24	neque … neque	*neither … nor*	
25	nescio, nescīre, nescīvī	*not know*	
	niger, nigra, nigrum	*black*	
7	nihil	*nothing*	
	nihilōminus	*nevertheless*	
30	nimis	*too*	
23	nimium, nimiī, n.	*too much*	
33	nisi	*except, unless*	
30	nōbilis, nōbilis, nōbile	*noble, of noble birth*	
	nōbīs *see* nōs		
	nocēns, nocēns, nocēns, *gen.* nocentis	*guilty*	
27	noceō, nocēre, nocuī (+ DAT)	*hurt*	
	noctis *see* nox		
	noctū *see* nox		
13	nōlō, nōlle, nōluī	*not want, refuse*	
	nōlī, nōlīte	*do not, don't*	
25	nōmen, nōminis, n.	*name*	
3	nōn	*not*	
	nōndum	*not yet*	
16	nōnne?	*surely?*	
21	nōnnūllī, nōnnūllae, nōnnūlla	*some, several*	
	nōnus, nōna, nōnum	*ninth*	
10	nōs	*we, us*	
11	noster, nostra, nostrum	*our*	
26	nōtus, nōta, nōtum	*known, well-known, famous*	
20	novem	*nine*	
19	nōvī	*I know*	
13	novus, nova, novum	*new*	
22	nox, noctis, f.	*night*	
	noctū	*by night*	
13	nūllus, nūlla, nūllum	*not any, no*	
14	num? (1)	*surely … not?*	
26	num (2)	*whether*	
	numerō, numerāre, numerāvī, numerātus	*count*	
33	numerus, numerī, m.	*number*	
17	numquam	*never*	
11	nunc	*now*	
10	nūntiō, nūntiāre, nūntiāvī, nūntiātus	*announce*	
8	nūntius, nūntiī, m.	*messenger, message, news*	
21	nūper	*recently*	
	nusquam	*nowhere*	

O

	obdormiō, obdormīre, obdormīvī	*fall asleep*	
	obeō, obīre, obiī (+ DAT)	*meet, go to meet*	
	obēsus, obēsa, obēsum	*fat*	
	obiciō, obicere, obiēcī, obiectus	*present*	
	oblītus, oblīta, oblītum	*having forgotten*	
	obscūrus, obscūra, obscūrum	*dark, gloomy*	
	obstinātiō, obstinātiōnis, f.	*stubbornness, obstinacy*	
	obstinātus, obstināta, obstinātum	*stubborn*	
18	obstō, obstāre, obstitī (+ DAT)	*obstruct, block the way*	
	obstupefaciō, obstupefacere, obstupefēcī, obstupefactus	*amaze, stun*	
9	obtulī *see* offerō		
	obviam eō, obviam īre, obviam iī (+ DAT)	*meet, go to meet*	
	occāsiō, occāsiōnis, f.	*opportunity*	
28	occīdō, occīdere, occīdī, occīsus	*kill*	

occidō, occidere, occidī		set
occupātus, occupāta, occupātum		busy
occupō, occupāre, occupāvī, occupātus		seize, take over
occurrō, occurrere, occurrī (+ DAT)		meet
28	octōgintā	eighty
20	oculus, oculī, m.	eye
29	ōdī	I hate
	odiō sum, odiō esse	be hateful
9	offerō, offerre, obtulī, oblātus	offer
	oleum, oleī, n.	oil
6	ōlim	once, some time ago
	ōmen, ōminis, n.	omen
30	omnīnō	completely
7	omnis, omnis, omne	all
	omnia	all, everything
28	opēs, opum, f.pl.	money, wealth
	oportet, oportēre, oportuit	be right
	mē oportet	I must
21	oppidum, oppidī, n.	town
32	opprimō, opprimere, oppressī, oppressus	crush, overwhelm
24	oppugnō, oppugnāre, oppugnāvī, oppugnātus	attack
12	optimē see bene	
5	optimus see bonus	
	optiō, optiōnis, m.	optio
30	opus, operis, n.	work, construction
	ōrātiō, ōrātiōnis, f.	speech
	orbis, orbis, m.	globe
	orbis terrārum	world
	ōrdō, ōrdinis, m.	row, line
	orior, orīrī, ortus sum	rise
	ōrnāmentum, ōrnāmentī, n.	ornament, decoration
	ōrnātus, ōrnāta, ōrnātum	decorated, elaborately furnished
23	ōrnō, ōrnāre, ōrnāvī, ōrnātus	decorate
31	ōrō, ōrāre, ōrāvī	beg
	ortus see orior	
	ōs, ōris, n.	face

	ōsculum, ōsculī, n.	kiss
9	ostendō, ostendere, ostendī, ostentus	show
	ostentō, ostentāre, ostentāvī, ostentātus	show off, display
32	ōtiōsus, ōtiōsa, ōtiōsum	at leisure, with time off, idle, on vacation

p

12	paene	nearly, almost
	pallēscō, pallēscere, palluī	grow pale
	pallidus, pallida, pallidum	pale
	pallium, palliī, n.	cloak
	pantomīmus, pantomīmī, m.	pantomime actor, dancer
	parātus, parāta, parātum	ready, prepared
22	parcō, parcere, pepercī (+ DAT)	spare
	parēns, parentis, m.f.	parent
23	pāreō, pārēre, pāruī (+ DAT)	obey
7	parō, parāre, parāvī, parātus	prepare
18	pars, partis, f.	part
	extrēma pars	edge
	in prīmā parte	in the forefront
6	parvus, parva, parvum	small
	minor, minor, minus, gen. minōris	less, smaller
22	minimus, minima, minimum	very little, least
24	passus, passa, passum	having suffered
	pāstor, pāstōris, m.	shepherd
24	patefaciō, patefacere, patefēcī, patefactus	reveal
1	pater, patris, m.	father
	patera, paterae, f.	bowl
	patientia, patientiae, f.	patience
34	patior, patī, passus sum	suffer, endure
	patrōnus, patrōnī, m.	patron
17	paucī, paucae, pauca	few, a few
	paulīsper	for a short time
	paulō/paulum	a little
32	pauper, pauper, pauper,	

	gen. pauperis	*poor*	
	pauper, pauperis, m.	*a poor man*	
30	pavor, pavōris, m.	*panic*	
10	pāx, pācis, f.	*peace*	
4	pecūnia, pecūniae, f.	*money*	
	pedem *see* pēs		
	peior *see* malus		
	pendeō, pendēre, pependī	*hang*	
6	per (+ ACC)	*through, along*	
	percutiō, percutere, percussī, percussus	*strike*	
	perdomitus, perdomita, perdomitum	*conquered*	
16	pereō, perīre, periī	*die, perish*	
29	perficiō, perficere, perfēcī, perfectus	*finish*	
	perfidia, perfidiae, f.	*treachery*	
	perfidus, perfida, perfidum	*treacherous, untrustworthy*	
	perfodiō, perfodere, perfōdī, perfossus	*pick (teeth)*	
	perfuga, perfugae, m.	*deserter*	
	perīculōsus, perīculōsa, perīculōsum	*dangerous*	
19	perīculum, perīculī, n.	*danger*	
	periī *see* pereō		
	perītē	*skillfully*	
25	perītus, perīta, perītum	*skillful*	
	permōtus, permōta, permōtum	*alarmed, disturbed*	
	perpetuus, perpetua, perpetuum	*perpetual*	
	in perpetuum	*forever*	
	perrumpō, perrumpere, perrūpī, perruptus	*burst through, burst in*	
	persecūtus, persecūta, persecūtum	*having pursued*	
	persōna, persōnae, f.	*character*	
	persōnam agere	*play a part*	
	perstō, perstāre, perstitī	*persist*	
20	persuādeō, persuādēre, persuāsī (+ DAT)	*persuade*	
	perterreō, perterrēre,		

	perterruī, perterritus	*terrify*	
4	perterritus, perterrita, perterritum	*terrified*	
	perturbō, perturbāre, perturbāvī, perturbātus	*disturb, alarm*	
17	perveniō, pervenīre, pervēnī	*reach, arrive at*	
8	pēs, pedis, m.	*foot, paw*	
	pedem referre	*step back*	
	pessimē	*very badly*	
20	pessimus *see* malus		
	pestis, pestis, f.	*pest, rascal*	
	petauristārius, petauristāriī, m.	*acrobat*	
5, 18	petō, petere, petīvī, petītus	*head for, attack; seek, beg for, ask for*	
	philosopha, philosophae, f.	*(female) philosopher*	
	philosophia, philosophiae, f.	*philosophy*	
	philosophus, philosophī, m.	*philosopher*	
	pīpiō, pīpiāre, pīpiāvī	*chirp, peep*	
11	placet, placēre, placuit	*please, suit*	
5	plaudō, plaudere, plausī, plausus	*applaud, clap*	
	plaustrum, plaustrī, n.	*wagon, cart*	
	plausus, plausūs, m.	*applause*	
21	plēnus, plēna, plēnum	*full*	
	pluit, pluere, pluit	*rain*	
	plūrimus *see* multus		
21	plūs, plūris, n.	*more*	
	pōculum, pōculī, n.	*cup (often for wine)*	
25	poena, poenae, f.	*punishment*	
25	poenās dare	*pay the penalty, be punished*	
4	poēta, poētae, m.	*poet*	
	poliō, polīre, polīvī, polītus	*polish*	
	polliceor, pollicērī, pollicitus sum	*promise*	
	polyspaston, polyspastī, n.	*crane*	
	pompa, pompae, f.	*procession*	
	Pompēiānus, Pompēiāna, Pompēiānum	*Pompeian*	
16	pōnō, pōnere, posuī, positus	*put, place, put up*	
24	pōns, pontis, m.	*bridge*	
	poposcī *see* poscō		

29	populus, populī, m.	people	
	porrō	more, furthermore	
8	porta, portae, f.	gate	
	porticus, porticūs, f.	colonnade	
3	portō, portāre, portāvī, portātus	carry	
10	portus, portūs, m.	harbor	
19	poscō, poscere, poposcī	demand, ask for	
16	positus see pōnō		
	possideō, possidēre, possēdī, possessus	possess	
13	possum, posse, potuī	can, be able	
9	post (+ ACC)	after, behind	
18	posteā	afterwards	
	posterī, posterōrum, m.pl.	future generations, posterity	
	postīcum, postīcī, n.	back gate	
6	postquam	after, when	
	postrēmō	finally, lastly	
16	postrīdiē	(on) the next day	
8	postulō, postulāre, postulāvī, postulātus	demand	
16	posuī see pōnō		
	potēns, potēns, potēns, gen. potentis	powerful	
	potentia, potentiae, f.	power	
33	potestās, potestātis, f.	power	
	potius	rather	
	potuī see possum		
26	praebeō, praebēre, praebuī, praebitus	provide	
27	praeceps, praeceps, praeceps, gen. praecipitis	headlong, rash	
	praecipitō, praecipitāre, praecipitāvī	hurl	
	praecō, praecōnis, m.	herald, announcer	
	praeda, praedae, f.	booty, plunder, loot	
	praedīcō, praedīcere, praedīxī, praedictus	foretell, predict	
	praeficiō, praeficere, praefēcī, praefectus	put in charge	
27	praemium, praemiī, n.	prize, reward, profit	
	praeruptus, praerupta, praeruptum	sheer, steep	

	praesēns, praesēns, praesēns, gen. praesentis	present, ready	
	praesertim	especially	
	praestō, praestāre, praestitī	show, display	
	praesum, praeesse, praefuī (+ DAT)	be in charge of	
	praeter (+ ACC)	except	
	praetereā	besides	
	praetereō, praeterīre, praeteriī	pass by, go past	
	praetōriānus, praetōriānī, m.	praetorian (member of emperor's bodyguard)	
	praetōrius, praetōria, praetōrium	praetorian	
	ōrnāmenta praetōria	honorary praetorship, honorary rank of praetor	
	prāvus, prāva, prāvum	evil	
22	precātus, precāta, precātum	having prayed (to)	
	precēs, precum, f.pl.	prayers	
34	precor, precārī, precātus sum	pray (to)	
	prēnsō, prēnsāre, prēnsāvī, prēnsātus	take hold of, clutch	
	pretiōsus, pretiōsa, pretiōsum	expensive, precious	
	prīmō	at first	
	prīmum	first	
11	prīmus, prīma, prīmum	first	
	in prīmā parte	in the forefront	
	in prīmīs	in particular	
15	prīnceps, prīncipis, m.	chief, chieftain	
	prīncipia, prīncipiōrum, n.pl.	headquarters	
29	prius	earlier	
34	priusquam	before, until	
18	prō (+ ABL)	in front of, for, in return for	
	prō certō habēre	know for certain	
	probus, proba, probum	honest	
9	prōcēdō, prōcēdere, prōcessī	advance, proceed, step forward	
34	procul	far off	
	prōcumbō, prōcumbere, prōcubuī	fall down	

prōcūrātor, prōcūrātōris, m.	*manager*	
prōditor, prōditōris, m.f.	*traitor*	
prōdō, prōdere, prōdidī, prōditus	*betray*	
32	profectus, profecta, profectum	*having set out*
34	proficīscor, proficīscī, profectus sum	*set out*
34	prōgredior, prōgredī, prōgressus sum	*advance, step forward*
31	prōgressus, prōgressa, prōgressum	*having advanced, having stepped forward*
	prohibeō, prohibēre, prohibuī, prohibitus	*prevent*
11	prōmittō, prōmittere, prōmīsī, prōmissus	*promise*
	prōmoveō, prōmovēre, prōmōvī, prōmōtus	*promote*
	prōnūntiō, prōnūntiāre, prōnūntiāvī, prōnūntiātus	*proclaim, preach*
7	prope (+ ACC)	*near*
	prophēta, prophētae, m.	*prophet*
	prōpōnō, prōpōnere, prōposuī, prōpositus	*propose, put forward*
	prōsiliō, prōsilīre, prōsiluī	*leap forward, jump*
	prōspectus, prōspectūs, m.	*view*
	prōspiciō, prōspicere, prōspexī	*look out*
	prōvincia, prōvinciae, f.	*province*
27	proximus, proxima, proximum	*nearest, next to*
	prūdēns, prūdēns, prūdēns, *gen.* prūdentis	*shrewd, intelligent, sensible*
	prūdentia, prūdentiae, f.	*prudence, good sense, shrewdness*
	psittacus, psittacī, m.	*parrot*
	pūblicus, pūblica, pūblicum	*public*
5	puella, puellae, f.	*girl*
8	puer, puerī, m.	*boy*
	pugiō, pugiōnis, m.	*dagger*
11	pugna, pugnae, f.	*fight*
8	pugnō, pugnāre, pugnāvī	*fight*

9	pulcher, pulchra, pulchrum	*beautiful*
6	pulsō, pulsāre, pulsāvī, pulsātus	*hit, knock on, whack, punch*
	pūmiliō, pūmiliōnis, m.	*dwarf*
16	pūniō, pūnīre, pūnīvī, pūnītus	*punish*
	pūrgō, pūrgāre, pūrgāvī, pūrgātus	*clean*
	pūrus, pūra, pūrum	*pure, clean, spotless*
	pyra, pyrae, f.	*pyre*

q

	quā *see* quī	
20, 28	quadrāgintā	*forty*
	quae *see* quī	
	quaedam *see* quīdam	
4	quaerō, quaerere, quaesīvī, quaesītus	*search for, look for, inquire*
27	quālis, quālis, quāle tālis … quālis	*what sort of such … as*
10, 14	quam (1) quam celerrimē	*how as quickly as possible*
10	quam (2)	*than*
	quam (3) *see* quī	
14	quamquam	*although*
	quandō	*when*
22	quantus, quanta, quantum	*how big*
30	quārē?	*why?*
	quārtus, quārta, quārtum	*fourth*
34	quasi	*as if*
20, 28	quattuor	*four*
14	-que	*and*
	quendam *see* quīdam	
15	quī, quae, quod	*who, which, what*
33	quia	*because*
28	quicquam *see* quisquam	
	quid? *see* quis?	
	quid vīs? *see* quis?	
32	quīdam, quaedam, quoddam	*one, a certain*

	quidem	*indeed*
32	nē ... quidem	*not even*
	quiēs, quiētis, f.	*rest*
	quiēscō, quiēscere, quiēvī	*rest*
	quiētus, quiēta, quiētum	*quiet*
	quīngentī, quīngentae, quīngenta	*five hundred*
20, 28	quīnquāgintā	*fifty*
20, 28	quīnque	*five*
	quīntus, quīnta, quīntum	*fifth*
4	quis? quid?	*who? what?*
	quid vīs?	*what do you want?*
28	quisquam, quicquam/quidquam	*anyone, anything*
	quisque, quaeque, quidque	*each one*
	optimus quisque	*all the best people*
18	quō? (1)	*where? where to?*
	quō (2) *see* quī	
22	quō modō?	*how? in what way?*
6	quod (1)	*because*
	quod (2) *see* quī	
2	quoque	*also, too*
	quōs *see* quī	
26	quot?	*how many?*
	quotiēns	*whenever*

r

31	rapiō, rapere, rapuī, raptus	*seize, grab*
	raptim	*hastily, quickly*
	ratiō, ratiōnis, f.	*sum, addition*
	ratiōnēs, ratiōnum, f.pl.	*accounts*
	ratiōnēs subdūcere	*write up accounts*
	raucus, rauca, raucum	*harsh*
	rē *see* rēs	
	rebellō, rebellāre, rebellāvī	*rebel, revolt*
	rēbus *see* rēs	
17	recipiō, recipere, recēpī, receptus	*recover, take back*
	sē recipere	*recover*
	recitō, recitāre, recitāvī, recitātus	*recite, read out*

	recumbō, recumbere, recubuī	*lie down, recline*
18	recūsō, recūsāre, recūsāvī, recūsātus	*refuse*
4	reddō, reddere, reddidī, redditus	*give back, make*
	redēmptor, redēmptōris, m.	*contractor, builder*
15	redeō, redīre, rediī	*return, go back, come back*
	redeundum est vōbīs	*you must return*
	reditus, reditūs, m.	*return*
	redūcō, redūcere, redūxī, reductus	*lead back*
26	referō, referre, rettulī, relātus	*bring back, carry, deliver, tell, report*
	pedem referre	*step back*
33	reficiō, reficere, refēcī, refectus	*repair*
33	rēgīna, rēgīnae, f.	*queen*
	Regnensēs, Regnēnsium, m.pl.	*Regnenses (a British tribe)*
	rēgnō, rēgnāre, rēgnāvī	*reign*
26	rēgnum, rēgnī, n.	*kingdom*
34	regredior, regredī, regressus sum	*go back, return*
23	regressus, regressa, regressum	*having returned*
	relēgō, relēgāre, relēgāvī, relēgātus	*exile*
20	relinquō, relinquere, relīquī, relictus	*leave*
	reliquus, reliqua, reliquum	*remaining*
6	rem *see* rēs	
	remedium, remediī, n.	*cure*
	remittō, remittere, remīsī, remissus	*send back*
	repetō, repetere, repetīvī, repetītus	*claim*
	rēpō, rēpere, rēpsī	*crawl*
6	rēs, reī, f.	*thing, business, affair*
	rē vērā	*in fact, truly, really*
	rem administrāre	*manage the task*
	rem cōgitāre	*consider the problem*

	rem cōnficere	*finish the job*
	rem intellegere	*understand the truth*
	rem nārrāre	*tell the story*
	rem suscipere	*undertake the task*
32	rēs adversae	*misfortune*
	rēs contrāria	*the opposite*
	rēs huius modī	*a matter of this kind*
17	resistō, resistere, restitī (+ DAT)	*resist*
	respiciō, respicere, respexī	*look at, look upon*
3	respondeō, respondēre, respondī	*reply*
	respōnsum, respōnsī, n.	*answer*
	resurgō, resurgere, resurrēxī	*rise again*
	retineō, retinēre, retinuī, retentus	*keep, hold back*
	retrō	*back*
	rettulī *see* referō	
9	reveniō, revenīre, revēnī	*come back, return*
	revertor, revertī, reversus sum	*turn back, return*
	revocō, revocāre, revocāvī, revocātus	*recall, call back*
14	rēx, rēgis, m.	*king*
	rhētor, rhētoris, m.	*teacher*
3	rīdeō, rīdēre, rīsī	*laugh, smile*
	rīdiculus, rīdicula, rīdiculum	*ridiculous, silly*
	rīpa, rīpae, f.	*riverbank*
	rīsus, rīsūs, m.	*smile*
7	rogō, rogāre, rogāvī, rogātus	*ask*
	Rōma, Rōmae, f.	*Rome*
	Rōmae	*at Rome*
	Rōmānī, Rōmānōrum, m.pl.	*Romans*
	ēn Rōmānī!	*so these are the Romans!*
	Rōmānus, Rōmāna, Rōmānum	*Roman*
	rosa, rosae, f.	*rose*
	rumpō, rumpere, rūpī, ruptus	*break, split*
13	ruō, ruere, ruī	*rush*
	rūpēs, rūpis, f.	*rock, crag*
25	rūrsus	*again*

S

	saccārius, saccāriī, m.	*stevedore, dockworker*
21	sacer, sacra, sacrum	*sacred*
15	sacerdōs, sacerdōtis, m.	*priest*
	sacerdōtium, sacerdōtiī, n.	*priesthood*
	sacrificium, sacrificiī, n.	*offering, sacrifice*
	sacrificō, sacrificāre, sacrificāvī, sacrificātus	*sacrifice*
8	saepe	*often*
	saeviō, saevīre, saeviī	*be in a rage*
26	saevus, saeva, saevum	*savage, cruel*
	saltātrīx, saltātrīcis, f.	*dancing girl*
	saltō, saltāre, saltāvī	*dance*
29	salūs, salūtis, f.	*safety, health*
	salūtātiō, salūtātiōnis, f.	*the morning visit*
2	salūtō, salūtāre, salūtāvī, salūtātus	*greet*
3	salvē!	*hello!*
	sānē	*obviously*
8	sanguis, sanguinis, m.	*blood*
	sānō, sānāre, sānāvī, sānātus	*heal, cure, treat*
	sānus, sāna, sānum	*well, healthy*
21	sapiēns, sapiēns, sapiēns, *gen.* sapientis	*wise*
	sapientia, sapientiae, f.	*wisdom*
	sarcinae, sarcinārum, f.pl.	*bags, luggage*
4	satis	*enough*
30	saxum, saxī, n.	*rock*
	scaena, scaenae, f.	*stage, scene*
	scālae, scālārum, f.pl.	*ladders*
25	scelestus, scelesta, scelestum	*wicked*
29	scelus, sceleris, n.	*crime*
	scīlicet	*obviously*
31	scindō, scindere, scidī, scissus	*tear, tear up, cut up, cut open, carve*
23	sciō, scīre, scīvī	*know*
	scrība, scrībae, m.	*secretary*
6	scrībō, scrībere, scrīpsī, scrīptus	*write*
	sculpō, sculpere, sculpsī,	

	sculptus		sculpt, carve
	scurrīlis, scurrīlis, scurrīle		obscene, dirty
13	sē		himself, herself, themselves
	inter sē		among themselves, with each other
	sēcum		with him, with her, with them
	sēcum cōgitāre		consider to oneself
30	secō, secāre, secuī, sectus		cut
	sēcrētus, sēcrēta, sēcrētum		secret
	secundus, secunda, secundum		second
	secūris, secūris, f.		axe
32	secūtus, secūta, secūtum		having followed
4	sed		but
1	sedeō, sedēre, sēdī		sit
	sēdēs, sēdis, f.		seat
	sēditiō, sēditiōnis, f.		rebellion
	sēditiōnem facere		revolt
	sella, sellae, f.		chair
	sēmirutus, sēmiruta, sēmirutum		rickety
10	semper		always
11	senātor, senātōris, m.		senator
	senectus, senectūtis, f.		old age
5	senex, senis, m.		old man
	sententia, sententiae, f.		opinion
12	sentiō, sentīre, sēnsī, sēnsus		feel, notice
	sepeliō, sepelīre, sepelīvī, sepultus		bury
20, 28	septem		seven
	septimus, septima, septimum		seventh
28	septuāgintā		seventy
	sepulcrum, sepulcrī, n.		tomb
34	sequor, sequī, secūtus sum		follow
	sequēns, sequēns, sequēns, gen. sequentis		following
	serēnus, serēna, serēnum		calm, clear
	sermō, sermōnis, m.		conversation
	sermōnem habēre		have a conversation,

			talk
	serviō, servīre, servīvī		serve (as a slave)
	servitūs, servitūtis, f.		slavery
10	servō, servāre, servāvī, servātus		save, protect
	fidem servāre		keep a promise, keep faith
1	servus, servī, m.		slave
	sēstertius, sēstertiī, m.		sesterce (coin)
	sēstertium vīciēns		two million sesterces
	sevērus, sevēra, sevērum		severe, strict
20, 28	sex		six
26	sī		if
	sibi see sē		
28	sīc		thus, in this way
	siccō, siccāre, siccāvī, siccātus		dry
20	sīcut		like, as
	significō, significāre, significāvī, significātus		mean, indicate
	signō, signāre, signāvī, signātus		sign, seal
4	signum, signī, n.		seal, signal
	silentium, silentiī, n.		silence
	sileō, silēre, siluī		be silent
8	silva, silvae, f.		woods, forest
	simul		at the same time
16	simulac, simulatque		as soon as
34	sine (+ abl)		without
	situs, sita, situm		situated
30	sōl, sōlis, m.		sun
	sōlācium, sōlāciī, n.		comfort
18	soleō, solēre		be accustomed
11	sollicitus, sollicita, sollicitum		worried, anxious
	sōlum		only
	nōn sōlum … sed etiam		not only … but also
10	sōlus, sōla, sōlum		alone, lonely, only, on one's own
	solūtus, solūta, solūtum		relaxed
34	sonitus, sonitūs, m.		sound
	sordidus, sordida, sordidum		dirty
30	soror, sorōris, f.		sister

	sors, sortis, f.	lot
	sorte ductus	chosen by lot
	spargō, spargere, sparsī, sparsus	scatter
8	spectāculum, spectāculī, n.	show, spectacle
	spectātor, spectātōris, m.	spectator
5	spectō, spectāre, spectāvī, spectātus	look at, watch
29	spernō, spernere, sprēvī, sprētus	despise, reject
31	spērō, spērāre, spērāvī	hope, expect
28	spēs, speī, f.	hope
	spīna, spīnae, f.	thorn, toothpick; central platform of a race course
	splendidus, splendida, splendidum	splendid, impressive
	sportula, sportulae, f.	handout
	squālidus, squālida, squālidum	covered with dirt, filthy
	stābam see stō	
8	statim	at once
	statiō, statiōnis, f.	post
	statua, statuae, f.	statue
	statūra, statūrae, f.	height
	stēlla, stēllae, f.	star
	sternō, sternere, strāvī, strātus	lay low
	stilus, stilī, m.	pen, stick
5	stō, stāre, stetī	stand, lie at anchor
	Stōicus, Stōicī, m.	Stoic
	stola, stolae, f.	(long) dress
	strēnuē	hard, energetically
	strepitus, strepitūs, m.	noise, din
	studium, studiī, n.	enthusiasm, zeal
	stultitia, stultitiae, f.	stupidity, foolishness
11	stultus, stulta, stultum	stupid, foolish
25	suāvis, suāvis, suāve	sweet
	suāviter	sweetly
27	sub (+ abl or acc)	under, beneath
	subdūcō, subdūcere, subdūxī, subductus	draw up
	ratiōnēs subdūcere	draw up accounts, write up accounts

6	subitō	suddenly
	sublātus see tollō	
	subscrībō, subscrībere, subscrīpsī, subscrīptus	sign
	subterrāneus, subterrānea, subterrāneum	underground
32	subveniō, subvenīre, subvēnī (+ DAT)	help, come to help
	suffīgō, suffīgere, suffīxī, suffīxus	nail, fasten
	Sūlis, Sūlis, f.	Sulis
1	sum, esse, fuī	be
	estō!	be!
16	summus, summa, summum	highest, greatest, top
	sūmptuōsē	lavishly
	sūmptuōsus, sūmptuōsa, sūmptuōsum	expensive, lavish, costly
	superbē	arrogantly
	superbia, superbiae, f.	arrogance
31	superbus, superba, superbum	arrogant, proud
6	superō, superāre, superāvī, superātus	overcome, overpower
	superstes, superstitis, m.	survivor
3	surgō, surgere, surrēxī	get up, stand up, rise
	suscipiō, suscipere, suscēpī, susceptus	undertake, take on
	rem suscipere	undertake the task
28	suspicātus, suspicāta, suspicātum	having suspected
	suspīciō, suspīciōnis, f.	suspicion
	suspīciōsus, suspīciōsa, suspīciōsum	suspicious
34	suspicor, suspicārī, suspicātus sum	suspect
	suspīrium, suspīriī, n.	heartthrob
	sustulī see tollō	
	susurrō, susurrāre, susurrāvī	whisper, mumble
10	suus, sua, suum	his, her, their, his own
	suī, suōrum, m.pl.	his men, his family, their families

t

T. = Titus

3	taberna, tabernae, f.	store, shop, inn
	tabernārius, tabernāriī, m.	store-owner, storekeeper
	tablīnum, tablīnī, n.	study
	tabula, tabulae, f.	tablet, writing tablet
10	taceō, tacēre, tacuī	be silent, be quiet
	tacē!	shut up! be quiet!
7	tacitē	quietly, silently
27	tacitus, tacita, tacitum	quiet, silent, in silence
	taedet, taedēre, taeduit	be tiring
	mē taedet	I am tired, I am bored
23	tālis, tālis, tāle	such
	tālis … quālis	such … as
20	tam	so
7	tamen	however
	tamquam	as, like
12	tandem	at last
	tangō, tangere, tetigī, tāctus	touch
	tantum	only
27	tantus, tanta, tantum	so great, such a great
	tapēte, tapētis, n.	tapestry, wall hanging
	tardius	too late
	tardus, tarda, tardum	late
	taurus, taurī, m.	bull
	tē see tū	
	tēctum, tēctī, n.	ceiling, roof
	tēgula, tēgulae, f.	tile
	temperāns, temperāns, temperāns, gen. temperantis	temperate, self-controlled
	tempestās, tempestātis, f.	storm
12	templum, templī, n.	temple
20	temptō, temptāre, temptāvī, temptātus	try, put to the test
31	tempus, temporis, n.	time
	tenebrae, tenebrārum, f.pl.	darkness
15	teneō, tenēre, tenuī, tentus	hold, own
12, 20	tergum, tergī, n.	back
12	terra, terrae, f.	ground, land

	orbis terrārum	world
7	terreō, terrēre, terruī, territus	frighten
	terribilis, terribilis, terribile	terrible
	tertius, tertia, tertium	third
	testāmentum, testāmentī, n.	will
25	testis, testis, m.f.	witness
	theātrum, theātrī, n.	theater
	thermae, thermārum, f.pl.	baths
	Tiberis, Tiberis, m.	river Tiber
	tibi see tū	
	tībia, tībiae, f.	pipe
	tībiīs cantāre	play on the pipes
	tībīcen, tībīcinis, m.	pipe player
	tignum, tignī, n.	beam
12	timeō, timēre, timuī	be afraid, fear
	timidē	fearfully
	timidus, timida, timidum	fearful, frightened
30	timor, timōris, m.	fear
	tintinō, tintināre, tintināvī	ring
	titulus, titulī, m.	advertisement, slogan, inscription, label
	toga, togae, f.	toga
16	tollō, tollere, sustulī, sublātus	raise, lift up, hold up
	tormentum, tormentī, n.	torture
	torqueō, torquēre, torsī, tortus	torture, twist
19	tot	so many
8	tōtus, tōta, tōtum	whole
9	trādō, trādere, trādidī, trāditus	hand over
13	trahō, trahere, trāxī, tractus	drag
	tranquillē	peacefully
	trāns (+ acc)	across
24	trānseō, trānsīre, trānsiī	cross
	trānsfīgō, trānsfīgere, trānsfīxī, trānsfīxus	pierce, stab
	trānsiliō, trānsilīre, trānsiluī	jump through
	tremō, tremere, tremuī	tremble, shake
28	trēs, trēs, tria	three
	tribūnal, tribūnālis, n.	platform

	tribūnus, tribūnī, m.	*tribune*	
	trīciēns sēstertium	*three million sesterces*	
	triclīnium, triclīniī, n.	*dining room*	
20,28	trīgintā	*thirty*	
	tripodes, tripodum, m.pl.	*tripods*	
24	trīstis, trīstis, trīste	*sad*	
4	tū, tuī	*you (singular)*	
	tēcum	*with you (singular)*	
	tuba, tubae, f.	*trumpet*	
	tubicen, tubicinis, m.	*trumpeter*	
6	tum	*then*	
	tum dēmum	*then at last, only then*	
	tunica, tunicae, f.	*tunic*	
5	turba, turbae, f.	*crowd*	
22	tūtus, tūta, tūtum	*safe*	
	tūtius est	*it would be safer*	
6	tuus, tua, tuum	*your (singular), yours*	
	Tyrius, Tyria, Tyrium	*Tyrian (colored with dye from city of Tyre)*	

u

5, 14	ubi	*where, when*	
	ubi gentium?	*where in the world?*	
29	ubīque	*everywhere*	
	ulcīscor, ulcīscī, ultus sum	*take revenge on*	
	ūllus, ūlla, ūllum	*any*	
26	ultimus, ultima, ultimum	*furthest, last*	
	ultiō, ultiōnis, f.	*revenge*	
	ululō, ululāre, ululāvī	*howl*	
	umerus, umerī, m.	*shoulder*	
23	umquam	*ever*	
	ūnā cum (+ abl)	*together with*	
15	unda, undae, f.	*wave*	
21	unde	*from where*	
31	undique	*on all sides*	
12, 20, 28	ūnus, ūna, ūnum	*one*	
	urbānus, urbāna, urbānum	*fashionable, sophisticated*	
5	urbs, urbis, f.	*city*	
	Urbs, Urbis, f.	*Rome*	
	ursa, ursae, f.	*bear*	

	usquam	*anywhere*	
	usque ad (+ ACC)	*right up to*	
28	ut (+ INDIC)	*as*	
26	ut (+ SUBJUNCT)	*that, so that, in order that*	
	ūtilis, ūtilis, ūtile	*useful*	
33	utrum	*whether*	
	utrum … an	*whether … or*	
	utrum … necne	*whether … or not*	
10	uxor, uxōris, f.	*wife*	

v

	vacuus, vacua, vacuum	*empty*	
	vah!	*ugh!*	
7	valdē	*very much, very*	
11	valē	*good-bye, farewell*	
	valēdīcō, valēdīcere, valēdīxī	*say good-bye*	
	valtūdō, valētūdinis, f.	*health*	
	varius, varia, varium	*different*	
10	vehementer	*violently, loudly*	
31	vehō, vehere, vexī, vectus	*carry*	
34	vel	*or*	
	vel … vel	*either … or*	
	velim, vellem *see* volō		
	vēnālīcius, vēnālīciī, m.	*slave dealer*	
	vēnātiō, vēnātiōnis, f.	*hunt*	
6	vēndō, vēndere, vēndidī, vēnditus	*sell*	
	venēnātus, venēnāta, venēnātum	*poisoned*	
23	venēnum, venēnī, n.	*poison*	
	venia, veniae, f.	*mercy*	
5	veniō, venīre, vēnī	*come*	
	venter, ventris, m.	*stomach*	
28	ventus, ventī, m.	*wind*	
	Venus, Veneris, f.	*Venus (goddess of love); the highest throw at dice*	
	vēr, vēris, n.	*spring*	
	verber, verberis, n.	*blow*	
11	verberō, verberāre, verberāvī, verberātus	*strike, beat*	

22	verbum, verbī, n.	word	
	vereor, verērī, veritus sum	fear, be afraid	
	versus, versa, versum	having turned	
	versus, versūs, m.	verse, line of poetry	
16	vertō, vertere, vertī, versus	turn	
	sē vertere	turn around	
24	vērum, vērī, n.	truth	
33	vērus, vēra, vērum	true, real	
33	rē vērā	in fact, truly, really	
29	vester, vestra, vestrum	your (plural)	
34	vestīmenta, vestīmentōrum, n.pl.	clothes	
	vestrum see vōs		
	vetus, vetus, vetus, gen. veteris	old	
19	vexō, vexāre, vexāvī, vexātus	annoy	
	vī see vīs		
1	via, viae, f.	street, way	
	vīciēns sēstertium	two million sesterces	
	victī see vincō		
	victī, victōrum, m.pl.	the conquered	
	victima, victimae, f.	victim	
	victor, victōris, m.	victor, winner	
	victōria, victōriae, f.	victory	
	victus see vincō		
	vīcus, vīcī, m.	town, village, settlement	
3	videō, vidēre, vīdī, vīsus	see	
	videor, vidērī, vīsus sum	seem	
	vigilō, vigilāre, vigilāvī	stay awake	
20,28	vīgintī	twenty	
	vīlla, vīllae, f.	villa, (large) house	
31	vinciō, vincīre, vīnxī, vīnctus	bind, tie up	
15	vincō, vincere, vīcī, victus	conquer, win, be victorious	
3	vīnum, vīnī, n.	wine	
11	vir, virī, m.	man	
	vīrēs, vīrium, f.pl.	strength	
	virgō, virginis, f.	virgin	
	Virginēs Vestālēs	Vestal Virgins	
22	virtūs, virtūtis, f.	courage	
	vīs, f. (acc. vim)	force, violence	

13	vīs see volō		
	vīsitō, vīsitāre, vīsitāvī, vīsitātus	visit	
3	vīsus see videō		
13	vīta, vītae, f.	life	
	vītam agere	lead a life	
	vitium, vitiī, n.	sin	
22	vītō, vītāre, vītāvī, vītātus	avoid	
6	vituperō, vituperāre, vituperāvī, vituperātus	find fault with, tell off, curse	
19	vīvō, vīvere, vīxī	live, be alive	
29	vīvus, vīva, vīvum	alive, living	
19	vix	hardly, scarcely, with difficulty	
	vōbīs see vōs		
	vōcem see vōx		
4	vocō, vocāre, vocāvī, vocātus	call	
13	volō, velle, voluī	want	
	quid vīs?	what do you want?	
	velim	I would like	
31	volvō, volvere, volvī, volūtus	turn	
	in animō volvere	wonder, turn over in the mind	
10	vōs	you (plural)	
	vōbīscum	with you (plural)	
19	vōx, vōcis, f.	voice	
13	vulnerō, vulnerāre, vulnerāvī, vulnerātus	wound, injure	
20	vulnus, vulneris, n.	wound	
13	vult see volō		
31	vultus, vultūs, m.	expression, face	

Index of cultural topics

Aesculapius 196
Agricola 91, 100-104, 135, 138
amphitheater 115, 118, 138
Apollo 51, 215, 233
Appian Way 66, 68
Aquae Sulis (Bath) 1, 14-19, 29, 34-36, 39, 52-53, 139, 215
aqueducts 180, 187, 198
aquila 116, 120
aquilifer 83, 87, 116
arch of Titus 153, 159, 162, 178, 196, 236
archaeology 135-138
archers 87
arches 178, 180-181, 194, 198
architecture (see engineering)
Arval Brotherhood 52
astrology 217-218
augurs 51
Augustales 256-257
Augusti libertus 241, 256
Augustus 53, 148, 160-163, 180-181, 215, 225, 235, 256
auxiliaries 82, 87, 100, 138

barges 69, 178
barracks 115-118
basilica 115-116, 148, 160-161
baths 14-20, 115, 117-118, 148, 163, 180-81, 198
Boudica 53, 101

Caesar (Julius) 135, 160-163, 235
Caligula 100
Calleva (Silchester) 138-139
Campus Martius 196, 198, 236
Camulodunum (Colchester) 53, 139
Capitoline hill 160-162, 180, 187, 196, 201, 215, 236
castra (see legionary fortress)
cavalry 87, 100, 103
cella 16, 215
cement 178, 180
censors 200
centurion 83, 86-87, 100, 118
Ceres 51
chariot racing 187, 198, 232-234, 237
Chief Priest 49, 52-53
Christianity 217, 225
Cicero 253

Circus Maximus 187, 196, 198, 233-235, 237, 256
Claudius 53, 195, 225, 256-257
clients 199-201, 253-255
Cloaca Maxima 148, 196, 198, 202
Cogidubnus 18, 49
Colosseum (see Flavian amphitheater)
communication 66-69, 138-139
concrete 66, 178, 180-181
consuls 91, 148, 162, 250
cranes 167, 178-179, 181
curia (senate-house) 160-162, 201

defixiones (curse tablets) 21, 34-36, 135, 234
Deva (Chester) 15, 62, 84, 91, 96, 102, 105, 116, 118, 130, 139-142
Diana 51
Dido 234
Dionysus 215
divination 50-51
domes 180-181
Domitia 248
Domitian 86, 91, 103, 135, 160, 162-163, 178, 180-181, 196, 199, 201, 215, 233-235, 241, 248, 256, 258

Eboracum (York) 84, 119, 139
Eleazar ben Ya'ir 163
engineering 14, 17, 66, 82, 176, 178-182, 201
Epaphroditus 218, 239, 241, 256-257
Epictetus 218
equites 100, 200-201, 233, 253
Esquiline hill 196-197

feriae 219
Fishbourne 136-137, 139
Flavian amphitheater 180-181, 187, 196, 235, 238
Forum Romanum 159-162, 187, 196, 201, 215, 235
freedmen 218, 239, 241, 253-256
freedwomen 253-257

games 232-238
genius (protecting spirit) 53, 142
granaries (horrea) 107, 115, 117, 195

Hadrian's Wall 117, 119, 217
haruspex 18, 37, 50-51
Haterii 175, 178-180
Horace 68, 256

Imperial Post 68
inscriptions 84, 91, 135, 138, 140-142, 239, 241, 254-255,
          257
insulae 180, 197-198
Isis 215

Jerusalem 163, 178
Jews 163, 166, 225
Josephus 163, 236
Judaism 163, 217, 225
Judea 163, 225
Juno 51, 215
Jupiter 51, 116, 162, 180, 187, 215, 236
Juvenal 181, 197, 199, 256

lares and penates 50
legatus 87, 91, 100, 116
legionary fortress 115-119, 138-139
legionary soldier 71, 74, 82-88
legions 82, 87, 89, 101, 138, 140-141, 163, 253
lictor 250
Londinium (London) 139, 220

Maecenas 256
magic 34-36
manumission 239, 241, 253, 255-256
Mark Antony 162
Mars 34, 51-53, 100, 234
Martial 199
Masada 150, 163-165
Massilia (Marseilles) 100
Memor, L. Marcius 8, 16, 39, 50
mime 234
Minerva 16, 51, 53, 215
Mithraea 216-217
Mithras 215-216, 220
Mons Graupius 102, 139
munera 234-235
mystery religions 215-217

naumachiae 235
Neptune 16,
Nero 163, 180, 225, 241, 256
Nerva 160
numina (spirits) 49

omens 35, 51,
optio 86-87, 118, 141-142
Ostia 195

Palatine hill 148, 160-162, 181, 187, 196, 234, 256
Pallas 257
Pantheon 180-181
pantomimus 233, 236
Paris (actor) 233-234, 236, 248
patronage 199-201, 253-257
Petronius 256
plebs 201
Pliny 68, 254, 256-257
Pompey the Great 163, 235
Pontifex Maximus (see Chief Priest)
praetor 257
praetorium 115-117
praefectus castrorum 86-87, 115
principia 115-116
prison 115, 162
propraetor 100-101

quaestor 201, 218

religion 14, 19, 35, 49-54, 215-217
Remus 148
roads 57, 62, 66-68, 70, 138-139, 160
Rome (Roma) 53, 68, 143, 148, 180-181, 195-198,
          215-217, 225, 233-238, 253
Roman Republic 148, 199-201, 215, 233, 235
Roman state religion 51-52, 160
romanization 16, 53, 102
Romulus 148
Rostra 162, 196
Rufilla 52

sacellum 115-116
sacrifices 37-38, 49-51, 236
Salvius 52, 199, 250
Saturn 160-161, 218
Scotland 102-103
senate 100, 135, 148, 218
senators 100, 160, 200, 233, 253, 256
ships 69, 162, 183, 195
signifier 86-87
Silva (Flavius) 163-164
Silvanus 50
slaves 178, 196, 218, 241, 253-256
slingers 87
St Paul 225
Stoicism 218-219

Index of grammatical topics

Time chart

Date	Britain	Rome and Italy
BC *c.* 2500	Salisbury Plain inhabited	
c. 2200–1300	Stonehenge built	
c. 1900	Tin first used in Britain	
c. 1450	Wessex invaded from Europe	
c. 900	Celts move into Britain	
c. 750	Plow introduced into Britain	
post 500	Maiden Castle, Iron Age fort in Britain	Rome founded (traditional date) 753
		Kings expelled and Republic begins, 509
4th C	Hill forts used by Celts	*Duodecim Tabulae*, 450
c. 330–320	Pytheas, Greek, circumnavigates Britain	Gauls capture Rome, 390
c. 300	Druid lore increases in Britain	Rome controls Italy/Punic Wars, 300–200
		Hannibal crosses the Alps, 218
		Rome expands outside Italy, 200–100
c. 125	Gallo-Belgic coins introduced	Gracchi and agrarian reforms, 133–123
		Cicero, Roman orator (106–43)
55–54	Julius Caesar invades Britain	
		Julius Caesar assassinated, 44
		Augustus becomes emperor, 27
		Virgil, author of the *Aeneid*, 70–19
AD 30–41	Cunobelinas, ruler in S.E. (Roman ally)	Tiberius becomes emperor, 14
c. 51	Cartimandua, client queen of Brigantes	Nero emperor, 54–68
60	Boudica leads Iceni revolt	Great Fire at Rome/Christians blamed, 64
		Vespasian emperor, 69–79
c. 75	Fishbourne Palace begun	Colosseum begun, *c.* 72
78–84	Agricola governor in Britain	Titus emperor, 79–81
c. 80	Salvius arrives in Britain	Vesuvius erupts, 79
		Tacitus, historian, *c.* 56–117
		Domitian emperor, 81–96
		Trajan emperor, 98–117
		Hadrian emperor, 117–138
143–163	Antonine Wall in Scotland	Septimius Severus dies in Britain, 211
c. 208	St Alban martyred at Verulamium	Constantine tolerates Christianity, 313
from 367	Picts, Scots, Saxons raid	Bible translated into Latin, *c.* 385
410	Rome refuses Britain help against Saxons	Alaric the Goth sacks Rome, 410
		Last Roman emperor deposed, 476

World history	World culture	Date
Babylonian/Sumerian civilizations		BC c. 3000
Pharaohs in Egypt		c. 3000–332
Indo-European migrations, c. 2100	Maize cultivation, American SW	c. 2000
Hammurabi's Legal Code, c. 1750	Epic of Gilgamesh	post 2000
Minoan civilization at its height, c. 1500	Rig-Veda verses (Hinduism) collected	c. 1500
Israelite exodus from Egypt, c. 1250	Development of Hinduism	c. 1450
Israel and Judah split, c. 922	Phoenician alphabet adapted by Greeks	c. 1000–800
Kush/Meroe kingdom expands	*Iliad* and *Odyssey*	c. 800
	First Olympic Games	776
Solon, Athenian lawgiver, 594	Buddha	c. 563–483
	Confucius	551–479
	Golden Age of Greece	500–400
Persia invades Egypt and Greece, c. 525–400	Death of Socrates	399
Conquests of Alexander the Great		335–323
	Museum founded in Alexandria	290
Great Wall of China built		c. 221
Judas Maccabaeus regains Jerusalem	Feast of Hanukkah inaugurated	165
	Adena Serpent Mound, Ohio	2nd C
Julius Caesar in Gaul, 58–49	Canal locks exist in China	50
	Glassblowing begins in Sidon	post 50
Cleopatra commits suicide		30
Herod rebuilds the Temple, Jerusalem		c. 20
Roman boundary at Danube, 15	Birth of Jesus	c. 4
	Crucifixion of Jesus	AD c. 29
	St Peter in Rome	42–67
Britain becomes a Roman province, 43	St Paul's missionary journeys	45–67
	Camel introduced into the Sahara	1st C
Sack of Jerusalem and the Temple		70
Roman control extends to Scotland		77–85
	Paper invented in China	c. 100
		c. 56–117
	Construction at Teotihuacán begins	c. 100
Roman empire at its greatest extent		98–117
Hadrian's Wall in Britain		122–127
"High Kings" of Ireland		c. 200–1022
Byzantium renamed Constantinople, 330	Golden Age of Guptan civilization, India	c. 320–540
	Last ancient Olympic Games	393
Mayan civilization		c. 300–1200
Byzantine empire expands		518

Date	Britain	Rome and Italy
? 537	Death of King Arthur	Gregory the Great, pope, 590–604
9th–10th C	Saxon forts against the Vikings	Period of turmoil in Italy, 800–1100
c. 900	Alfred drives Danes from England	Republic of St Mark, Venice, 850
1189–1199	Richard the Lionheart	
12th C	Robin Hood legends circulated	
		Independent government in Rome, 1143–1455
1258	Salisbury Cathedral finished	Marco Polo travels to the East, 1271–1295
1346	Battle of Crécy, cannon first used	Dante, poet, 1265–1321
1348	Black Death begins	Renaissance begins in Italy, c. 1400
1485	Henry VII, first Tudor king	Botticelli, painter, 1445–1510
1509–1547	Henry VIII	Leonardo da Vinci, 1452–1519
		Titian, painter, 1489–1576
		Rebuilding of St Peter's begins, 1506
1518	Royal College of Physicians founded	Michelangelo starts Sistine Chapel ceiling, 1508
1536–1540	Dissolution of Monasteries	Rome sacked by German/Spanish troops, 1527
1558–1603	Elizabeth I	Spain controls much of Italy, 1530–1796
1577–1580	Drake circumnavigates the globe	
1588	Defeat of Spanish Armada	Fontana rediscovers Pompeii, 1594
1603	James I, first Stuart king	Galileo invents the telescope, 1610
1649	Charles I executed	Bernini, architect and sculptor, 1598–1680
1649–1659	Cromwellian Protectorate	
1660	Restoration of Charles II	
1675	Wren begins St Paul's Cathedral	
1760–1820	George III	
1789	Wilberforce moves to end slave trade	
1795–1821	John Keats, poet	Napoleon enters Italy, 1796
1796	Smallpox vaccination in England	
1798	Nelson defeats French at the Nile	Verdi, composer, 1813–1901
1833	Factory Act limits child labor in Britain	G. Leopardi, poet, dies, 1837
1837–1901	Victoria, queen	Mazzini, Garibaldi, Cavour, active 1846–1861
1844	Railways begin in Britain	Victor Emmanuel II, united Italy, 1861
1846–1849	Irish potato famine	Rome, Italy's capital, 1870
1859	Dickens' Tale of Two Cities	Marconi uses wireless telegraphy, 1896
1876	School attendance compulsory	
1903	Emily Pankhurst leads suffragettes	Mussolini controls Italy, 1922–1945
1940	Churchill Prime Minister	Italy a republic, 1946
1946	National Health Act	

World history	World culture	Date
	Birth of Muhammad	570
Charlemagne crowned, 800	Arabs adopt Indian numerals	*c.* 771
	1001 Nights collected in Iraq	ante 942
Vikings reach America, *c.* 1000	*Tale of Genji*, Japan	1010
Norman invasion of England, 1066	Ife-Benin art, Nigeria	1100–1600
First Crusade, 1096	Classic Pueblo Cliff dwellings	1050–1300
	Al-Idrisi, Arab geographer	1100–1166
Magna Carta, 1215	Arabs use black (gun) powder in a gun	1304
Genghis Khan, 1162–1227	Chaucer's *Canterbury Tales*	ante 1400
Mali empire expands, 1235		
Joan of Arc dies, 1431	Gutenberg Bible printed	1456
Inca empire expands, 1438	Building at Zimbabwe	*c.* 15th C–*c.* 1750
Turks capture Constantinople, 1453	Vasco da Gama sails to India	1497–1498
Moors driven from Spain, 1492		
Columbus arrives in America, 1492		
	Martin Luther writes *95 Theses*	1517
		1519–1522
Cortez conquers Mexico	Magellan names Pacific Ocean	1520
Mogul dynasty established	Copernicus publishes heliocentric theory	1543
French settlements in Canada, 1534	Shakespeare	1564–1616
Turks defeated, Battle of Lepanto, 1571	Muskets first used in Japan	*c.* 1580
Burmese empire at a peak	Cervantes publishes *Don Quixote*	1605
Continuing Dutch activity in the East	Taj Mahal begun	1632
Pilgrims land at Plymouth Rock, 1620	Palace of Versailles begun	1661
Manchu dynasty, China, 1644–1912	Newton discovers the Law of Gravity	1682
Peter the Great rules Russia, 1682–1725	J. S. Bach, composer	1685–1750
	Mozart, composer	1756–1791
Industrial Revolution begins, *c.* 1760	Quakers refuse to own slaves	1776
US Declaration of Independence	Washington, US President	1789
French Revolution begins	Bolivar continues struggle, S. America	1815
Napoleon defeated at Waterloo	S. B. Anthony, women's rights advocate	1820–1906
Mexico becomes a republic, 1824	Communist manifesto	1848
American Civil War, 1861–1865		1863
Lincoln's Emancipation Proclamation	French Impressionism begins	1867
Canada becomes a Dominion	Mahatma Gandhi	1869–1948
Serfdom abolished in Russia, 1861	Edison invents phonograph	1877
Cetewayo, king of the Zulus, 1872	First modern Olympic Games	1896
	Model T Ford constructed	1909
First World War, 1914–1918	Bohr theory of the atom	1913
Bolshevik Revolution in Russia, 1918	US Constitution gives women the vote	1920
		1939–1945
Second World War		
United Nations Charter		1945